Politics, Personality, and Nation Building:

Burma's Search for Identity

POLITICS, PERSONALITY,

AND NATION BUILDING:

BURMA'S SEARCH FOR IDENTITY

BY LUCIAN W. PYE

New Haven and London, Yale University Press

© 1962 by Massachusetts Institute of Technology.
Second printing, June 1963
Set in Times Roman type and
printed in the United States of America by
The Carl Purington Rollins Printing-Office
of the Yale University Press.

Library of Congress catalog card number: 62-8260

FOR MARY

who shared the quest and the journey

Foreword

The emerging nations of the underdeveloped world pose a challenge for the social sciences that their practitioners are only just beginning to recognize. The complexity of the forces interacting in rapidly evolving national societies has posed for these infant disciplines a number of problems of research methodology which must be faced if the issues involved are to be rendered intellectually manageable.

There is first the dilemma of precision versus realism in the design of the analytic model to be employed to represent the human system we are trying to comprehend. Precision and sharp clarity can be achieved only, as the economists have discovered, by sharply limiting the number of variables, defining them rigorously and preferably quantitatively, and postulating very explicit relations among them. But no such model can capture more than a tiny segment of the rich nexus of influences determining the pattern of contemporary events in a new nation. For some time to come we shall have to rely, for insights into what is happening in particular situations and why, on a more impressionistic and intuitive treatment than the strict cannons of scientific method would permit. On the other hand, if we are to make progress toward verifiable generalizations applicable to more than one case, the analysis must be based on at least a tentative model which can be used to compare instances. The appropriate blend of the historian's art and the social scientist's discipline is a hard one to come by, and can be achieved only by an analyst who has both a flair for rigorous model building and an intuitive talent for sensing the complex overtones of a total human situation.

A second related issue concerns the emphasis to be put on detailed case studies of particular countries on the one hand and wide-ranging surveys of particular functions as performed in a large number of countries on the other. Clearly both are needed. But the case study runs the risk of so emphasizing the unique features of a particular culture that common elements are overlooked, while the functional study tends, by isolating one function for examination, to underestimate the interaction among a wide variety of functions in a closely knit society. Again, there is a tendency for one type of person to want to spend his career learning all there is to know about Lower Slobovia while another becomes encyclopedic on all the possible varieties of parliamentary structures. The most hopeful solution is to find a man who can move back and forth between these two kinds of inquiry with a taste for both.

A third problem concerns how to achieve cross-fertilization between macrostudies and microstudies of a particular culture. The behavior of a nation can be looked upon as a function of its national history and culture, its institutions, and its resources. Certain of the social sciences, notably political science, economics, and history, have conventionally operated from the perspective of national aggregates. At a deeper level, however, the behavior of the aggregates is determined by the behavior and interaction of individuals and small groups whose actions and attitudes can be thoroughly understood only by the sort of painstaking observational and interviewing techniques that are the traditional tools of the psychologist and anthropologist. While the numbers of people who are influential in the emerging nations are a small fraction of their populations, they are too many to be individually analyzed, and generalization from a manageably small sample may seriously distort the national pattern. On the other hand, anyone who confines himself to the available aggregate information runs the risk of entirely overlooking critical influences and relationships. Here again the only answer is an eclectic one. Bridges between micro- and macro- can be built only by a scholar who is at home in both.

Finally there is the problem of statics versus dynamics. The emerging nations are by definition societies undergoing rapid transformation. But even the more modern tools of the social sciences have a strong static bias. They tend to focus attention more on states of affairs than on processes of evolution. Even in the cases in which social science models are emerging from a static into a dynamic phase of their own, the empirical observation of change presents serious problems to the investigator who has only a few months in which to do his field work. He cannot interview people ten years ago, nor can he wait ten years to see in which direction the variables he now observes are moving. He will find in most instances that the available historical materials were designed to answer very different questions from the ones he is asking, and that no data comparable to those he now collects exist for earlier periods. Faced with this dilemma, he must do the best he can, attempting to weave the incomplete historical materials available to him into a story that highlights the dimensions of the process of change which his new tools are designed to explore.

This study of contemporary Burmese politics shows us how dilemmas like this can be dealt with by a man who brings to it the wide range of talents necessary to the task. There is a general model of the political process here, but the Burmese case is not so rudely forced into the model that it is stripped of all the flavorful eccentricities that make it unique. It is a case study in a sense, and yet its main points are made in a way that leaves us hoping the author will tackle the job of testing them in other cultures. Extended interviews have been carried out with individual politicians and administrators, yet these are so skillfully placed in the context of the society of which these people are a part that the bridge between macro- and micro-analysis is an organic part of the narrative and not a piece of connective machinery imposed on it from outside. Finally what emerges from this account is a motion picture of a nation in transition rather than a snapshot of a moment in its history.

The Center for International Studies presents this volume in confidence that those interested in contemporary Burma will gain from it a deeper insight into that country's behavior; that those who concern themselves with the structure of the emerging science of comparative politics will find outlined here new and useful tools of their novel trade; and that those who, whether out of intellectual curiosity or pragmatic necessity, seek a more profound understanding of the transition from tradition to modernity will come away from a reading of this book feeling better able to comprehend many of the events taking place around them.

MAX F. MILLIKAN

Contents

V. POLITICAL ACCULTURATION AND REACTIONS TO CHANGES IN IDENTITY

VI. EPILOGUE

Preface

Research enterprises tend to generate a dynamic of their own which can rarely be foreseen in the planning. In the beginning, my intention was to carry out an investigation parallel to the study I had made of the personal and political meaning of communism for people in a transitional society who had been attracted to the Communist party.[1] That study made me acutely aware of many of the psychological problems which can haunt people who find their social and political worlds erratically changing. In order to comprehend better the process of political development, it seemed necessary to learn more about how people equally caught up in rapidly changing circumstances but who do not become Communists have come to understand the realm of politics and to perceive their own political identities.

How have those who would build democratic institutions in transitional societies arrived at their commitments, and how have their experiences affected their capacities to build such institutions? What in fact are the range of personal aspirations of people who are being introduced to the modern world, and what are the relationships between these aspirations and their expectations as to the probable consequences of political action? What are the dynamic relationships between such typical and apparently contradictory features of behavior in a newly-emerging country as the tendency toward ideological agitation and at the same time apathy toward substantive programs, between professed expectations and actual commitments to action, between ambitions for new forms and tenacious adherence to old practices?

Led on by such questions as these, I decided to explore the dynamics of a particular transitional system—that of Burma—by investigating the basic attitudes and orientations of various key groups in the society toward the political process. Once the interviewing began, it became increasingly evident that I must concern myself with a broader range of

---

1. *Guerrilla Communism in Malaya: Its Social and Political Meaning* (Princeton, Princeton University Press, 1956).

xiii

problems than those with which I had expected to deal. The more minutely and intimately I delved into the lives of my respondents, the more it became necessary to expand the study of the general historical and social setting of their life histories. Their personal lives reflected the experience of their entire society, and it was essential to know whether they reflected it accurately—whether the respondents were distorting the record, where they were magnifying and where they were telescoping, and where they had blind spots. Moreover, I soon realized that the life histories were also providing me with perspectives for understanding Burmese history.

Thus, in a sense, microanalysis and macroanalysis each reinforced the other, and what was discovered in the one level of analysis led to new appreciation of what had to be dealt with in the other. This is no more than to say that any form of political analysis, whether it be an adventure in political theory or a recommendation for public policy, must inevitably rest upon some set of assumptions and theories about human psychology on the one hand and a body of sociological knowledge and a philosophy of history on the other. For the political analyst, whether given to a contemplative, reflective approach or bent upon action and manipulation, must always deal with the interactions of individual choices and historical trends—with the relationships between the individual and the group, the statesman and the state, the lawmaker and the law. Any particular analysis may be based upon more or less sophisticated theories about the nature of either the individual or the collectivity, but the growth of our knowledge in political science depends upon a constant striving to incorporate more profound understanding of both levels of human life. Indeed, if we ever allow ourselves to become content with any particular and limited theories of either psychology or sociology—say, if we settle for a flat unidimensional, "common sense" view of human personality—then political theory will surely begin to stagnate.

In the interviews, as I traced the relationships between private experiences and public events, it became increasingly apparent that such dramatic and vivid phenomena of human existence as colonialism and the quest for national identity cannot possibly be described or fully comprehended by the limited language of politics. There was much more to the story than mere alien domination followed by a search for sovereignty. For colonialism and nationalism are only partial aspects of a far more profound historical process—the process of change, of acculturation and transformation in which both whole societies and individual personalities are forced to take new forms. A shorthand label for this complex process could be the diffusion of the world culture: a culture which represents the essence of much of the culture of the West, its place of origin, but which no longer has clear geographic boundaries; a culture composed of such basic concepts and practices as the secular state and the industrialized organization of human activities, the reliance upon rational and conscious choice and a faith in impartial justice, and the acceptance of the virtue of merit and of rewards according to skill.

In exploring the political aspects of this diffusion of the world culture, I was led to focus on the problems of building a modern nation-state and increasingly to center research on the single question: Why should transitional societies have such great difficulties in creating an effective modern state system?

Many of the problems of transitional societies are manifest and objective: shortage of capital, absence of trained personnel, inadequate social and educational facilities, excessive population in relation to land, and grossly imperfect means for mobilizing both human and material resources. However, beneath this manifest level there seems to be a level of psychological problems involving attitudes and sentiments which create equal if not more serious difficulties. At this level a vicious circle somehow seems to develop in transitional societies: fears of failure in the adventure of nation building create deep anxieties, which tend to inhibit effective action; thus imagined problems become real and fears of failure become the realities of failure; and these failures further heighten anxieties. The dynamics of such psychological inhibitions to effective action, particularly in relation to the politics of modernization, can permeate and restrain the entire process of nation building.

Public policy and social science theory are both urgently needed in the quest for a better understanding of these subtle but tenacious obstacles in the modernization process. When the colonial period was coming to a close at the end of World War II, it was generally felt that the newly emerging countries could look with optimism to the future. Although the objective problems might be immense in particular cases, the enthusiasm and the will of newly independent peoples were assumed to be unlimited. The shocking fact has been that in the last decade the new countries of Asia have had more difficulties with the psychological than with the objective economic problems basic to nation building. The trend has been toward stagnation, toward a readiness to rely upon authoritarian methods, to accept military rule. Now the African states are beginning their new adventures, and attention is again fixed on the conspicuous and manifest economic and social problems. But again it is not unlikely, that their experiences will prove to be much the same as the Asian ones and that in time it will become more apparent that they too are crucially affected by deep psychological conflicts.

The problems of nation building thus seem to reside in that complex of attitudes and practices which we may call the political culture and which reflects both the historical evolution of the society and the psychological reactions to social change of the society's political actors. In transitional societies the mixture of sentiments and modes of calculation governing the flow of decisions and actions and providing the substance of the political culture is determined in part by the universal qualities of the modernization process and in part by the essence of the particular culture. This distinction between general processes and particular experiences, and the differing possible relationships between the two, points to the conflicting demands on the attention of the social scientist. He must show equal appreciation of both the universal aspects of the nation-building process and the subtle realities of the particular context.

These considerations suggest that up to a point it is important and useful to deal with the common and widespread problems of nation building on a general basis. In Part I we shall be following such an approach. However, when it becomes appropriate to probe the dynamics of the political culture and to relate psychological patterns and profound sentiments, there is a compelling need to turn to the richness of the particular social setting and of individual life experiences. In this study we shall first confront the general experiences of Burmese society and then personal experiences of individual members. In order to emphasize the fact that a political culture is shaped by both the history of the society and the life histories of its individuals we have interposed our general characterization of the Burmese political culture between the historical and the individual psychological analyses.

Although we shall be relying heavily upon Burmese experiences, this is not in the conventional sense a case study of political developments in Burma. We have had to focus on the relationship of political culture to nation building, and we have turned to Burmese materials to illuminate this relationship and to provide us with a more sensitive basis for appreciating the general problems of political development throughout the underdeveloped world.

A word of caution is in order here regarding generalizations we shall be making when we construct a model of the transitional political system and when we characterize the essence of a particular political culture. Readers sometimes misunderstand the nature and purpose of such models and generalized discussions and assume that the author is suggesting that each proposition advanced represents a completely unique quality found only in that particular type of system or that individual culture. This confusion may even lead readers to believe that the author is trying to suggest that in, say, transitional or non-Western political systems, or in the particular culture he is describing, behavior is grossly different from that found in Western systems. No such meaning is intended. Indeed, many separate elements of transitional systems exactly resemble those found in the more stable modern systems. Certainly, when we are describing particular features of Burmese behavior, no reader should conclude that the same practices do not exist elsewhere; more often than not they do. Above all, no one should conclude that the exact opposite practices are to be found elsewhere. We know of no political process which is the polar opposite of the Burmese one. On the contrary, the nature of human personality and human society being what they are, there is remarkably little tolerance for differences, particularly with respect to the isolated elements of the total system and culture. The important consideration is that the accumulated effects of these elements constitute our general model of a total political culture which is significantly different. That is, the individual parts of a transitional system may not be particularly distinctive, nor even the key aspects of a political culture, but the way in which the different parts or aspects are combined does produce significant differences.

In examining the emotional reactions and conflicting sentiments of transitional people, we are, of course, only treating one side of one of the most complex and psychologically involved relationships known to history. On the other side are all the intense and equally contradictory feelings and attitudes of Westerners toward the underdeveloped areas. As yet the West is still unable to conduct its relations with the new countries according to the customary considerations and calculations which are normally assumed to govern international relations. All the illogical reactions of race and class, of paternalism and pity, of pride and prejudice combine in various ways to blur the Westerners' image of transitional peoples. At the one extreme there are those in the West who idealize and romanticize the efforts of the new countries. At the other extreme are those who contemplate with horror the end of an old order and the "descent of barbarians upon the small corner of the civilized world."

We are fully aware that the complexity of Western feelings runs far deeper than the sentiments that can be articulated in the realm of politics. In some respects the fantasies of the West about the transitional peoples spring from some of the deepest anxieties of the human personality: the concepts of "control" and "frustrations" that lie behind the image of "explosive peoples" caught in a "revolution of rising expectations" seem to be readily related to the deep emotions that surround the mechanisms of control in the personality.

It is hoped that by frankly and openly recognizing the complexity of reactions and emotions on both sides of the process of cultural diffusion we can make possible more honest and more effective relationships. If relations between the industrial countries and the underdeveloped regions are to improve in the postcolonial epoch, and if there is to be a joint effort to apply knowledge to conquer misery, then those on both sides must learn to face reality honestly.

We realize that parts of this study may be disturbing to transitional peoples just as a study of Western emotions might be disturbing to many Westerners. All cultures value the privacy of deep human feelings, and such privacy should be violated only for truly important reasons. The justification for repeating and interpreting what others have told us in confidence about their lives is the hope that by stimulating a broader discussion of some of these matters it will help both Westerners and transitional peoples to see reality more clearly. It is with considerable regret that we accept the inevitable and recognize that the reporting of social research can hurt precisely the people it would help. Instead of being able to repay, as we wish we could, the kindness and cooperation of our Burmese respondents, we are disturbed to think that we may be causing them some discomfort and displeasure. We do hope that they may realize that the true friends of Burma are not those who would dwell just on pleasant matters but those who would help in facing the truth even when it is painful.

We regret also the need for anonymity and the fact that we cannot even acknowledge by name those who so graciously assisted us in making this study possible. In a culture in which it is normal to distrust the foreign observer, they were willing to cooperate in our attempt to probe beneath the surface.

This work has been heavily colored by two related research enterprises on the politics of transitional countries. First, my thinking reflects in more ways than could possibly be documented my involvement in the work of the Committee on Comparative Politics of the Social Science Research Council under the imaginative leadership of Gabriel A. Almond. The conferences, the research planning, and the actual studies of the committee have all influenced the development of this study; and those acquainted with the language and the theoretical point of view that have emerged from the committee's work will be quick to recognize that this work really represents an attempt to explore the consequences of the basic "functions" of "political socialization" and "recruitment" in the development of a political process.

The second powerful intellectual influence on this study has been my involvement with the members of the Center for International Studies at the Massachusetts Institute of Technology on various projects relating to political development, and particularly the collective endeavor which led to *The Emerging Nations: Their Growth and U.S. Policy*.[2] That association has left its stamp on this study in many ways, but most especially by sharpening my awareness that the problems of the underdeveloped regions represent a profound historical and dynamic process unique to our age, a process which must somehow rest upon and reflect in a systematic fashion the multidimensional character of human life.

A large number of people provided generous assistance in facilitating my field work in Burma and in offering advice from their deep understanding of Burmese culture. In particular, I am happy to acknowledge my indebtedness to Professor William C. Johnstone and Dr. William C. Hamilton, and to James Dalton, J. S. Furnivall, Haldor Hanson, Arthur Hummel, Hazel Hitson, Dr. Kyaw Thet, Dr. Sein Tu, Herbert Spivack, David Steinberg, U Tun Myaing, U Tin Maung Yin, Daw Mya Sein, Professor William Paw, Frank Trager, and Daphne Whittam. Others who read the manuscript in whole or in part and contributed valuable criticisms and suggestions are Gabriel A. Almond, Charles T. Cross, Everett Hagen, Harold Isaacs, Robert Lane, Dr. Maung Maung, James Mosel, Guy J. Pauker, Ithiel Pool, and Myron Weiner.

I owe a warm and extremely personal debt of gratitude to Richard W. Hatch for his thoughtful and sensitive editing which transformed my manuscript into a book. Donald L. M. Blackmer served as a friendly but firm adviser, critic, and editor throughout this research effort; and my indebtedness to him, both personal and professional, extends beyond all measurement for the generous ways he gave without hesitation of his time, his care, and his creative imagination.

Alice Preston, Audrey Mathews, Sarah Warren, and Dagmar Bothwell with great accuracy and speed deciphered my script and typed the various drafts.

I greatly appreciate the support of the Carnegie Corporation in financing the field work for this study, and, in expressing my indebtedness, I

2. Max F. Millikan and Donald L. M. Blackmer, eds. (Boston, Little, Brown, 1961).

want also to absolve that corporation of any responsibilities for any of the statements made in this study. Administratively my work was greatly facilitated by Arthur Singer's skillful and thoughtful assistance.

With the help of all of these it is manifest that all the errors and failings are my own doing.

LUCIAN W. PYE

Cambridge, Mass.
June 1961

PART I

The Problem of Nation Building

CHAPTER 1

The Human Dimension of Nation Building

This is an era of nation building. Since the end of World War II, half a billion people have become citizens of newly independent countries, and nearly a billion more are citizens of old countries striving to become modern nations. In the new countries alone, over 30 million people are employed in administering the business of government according to their visions of a modern state, and another 100 million depend upon government and politics, both civil and military, for their livelihood. In both the new countries and the changing old countries the great objective is to achieve the impressive elements of organization that characterize the modern nation-state; and their almost universal problem is that they have the form but not the substance of nationhood.

This is also a time of faith in the miraculous powers of politics. The belief has been rampant that all aspects of life will be different with a change in sovereignty, with the elevation of new leaders to old offices, with the manipulation of new slogans and the worship of new symbols. Works of civilization which in other times were assumed to follow only from the patient application of skill and diligence and the acceptance of sustained effort are now thought to be conceived by the potency of political acts. In the new countries, where politics unlimited is sovereign and where it is believed all problems can be solved by its methods, other activities tend to lose their charm and their worth. Thus rationalization in politics has never been greater; never have more people been able to play the game with greater self-assurance that in doing so they are performing a public service. Older nations have been built upon the myth that if each seeks his interests, the interests of all will be served; new countries are trying to be built upon the myth that if each strives to get ahead in government and politics, the public good will be served.

3

This is also a time of personal insecurity, for millions must make frightening adjustments in their personal perspectives on life. Never has the extent of basic social change touched the lives of so many, shaking the intellectual, moral, and emotional foundations of their individual worlds. In addition to suffering the pain and discomfort of being torn from the old and the known, they are confronted with the most basic of human issues, that of individual integrity and personal identity. For the old is, above all, that which both friend and foe must use without hesitation or qualification to define the uniqueness of the self, of the "we" which is the essence of identity in the human community; and the new is seen by friend and foe alike as the essence of that which is unmistakably the foreign, the West, the "they." The logic of tragedy underlies the psychological travail of millions as they seek to adjust to the new, because the "they" of the new once conquered or dominated or belittled the "we" of the old.

Most disturbing of all, the "they," the West, with insensitivity and un-fathomable motives, has zealously offered self-sacrificing assistance to make the "we" more like the "they." The insensitivity of the helping "they," whether appearing in the guise of the earlier champions of the "white man's burden" or of the latter-day ideologues of economic development, comes from the blinding effects of their possessing a correct historical perspective. To them, since change is inevitable, it can only be temporarily painful; it cannot be appreciated as being psychologically intolerable. The motives of the "they" are beyond comprehension—and hence are disturbing—for even the decision makers of the West cannot tell what mixture of self-interest and self-sacrifice, of hard calculation and human charity, have inspired their acts. American policy makers, for example, need to reassure themselves repeatedly that foreign aid is only an expression of enlightened self-interest and not an act of charity for less fortunate peoples, but they become irate whenever the recipients of such aid tell them that this is precisely the way it is.

The quest for nationhood, the awe of politics, and the widespread ambivalences of personal identity are clearly related phenomena, but it is not clear by what logic they are related. At the least, a circuitous pattern is present: the search for individual identity hinges on the existence of a national identity, and the latter calls for a coherent and consensus-bound political process; but people cannot fundamentally respect their political spokesmen when they are not sure that they can respect themselves, and so back to the issue of personal integrity and identity. A dilemma is framed: the need for self-identity produces the need for a nation-state, and the need for reassurance of individual worth produces the need for a politics of status—and yet such a politics is inconsistent with the requirements of nation building.

There is, of course, a psychological dimension to politics in all societies; but in transitional countries the political process often has to bear to an inordinate degree the stresses and strains of people responding to personal needs and seeking solutions to intensely private problems. People who are caught up in all the uncertainties of social change may turn to political action to gain an element of individual security, to re-establish links with their fellow human beings, and to find a sense of personal identity. Both the drama and the mechanisms of politics can attract people engrossed, either consciously or unconsciously, in all manner of personal concerns which cannot in any way find their solutions in the enactment of any particular public policies. Politics can give legitimacy to feelings of aggression and hostility, and a cloak of virtue to sordid motives. Politics can also provide the excitement of creativity and the sense of comradeship to people who have long felt themselves suppressed and isolated.

People who come to politics out of such motivations will not be satisfied with the realization of any particular goals of public policy; for them the meaning of politics is to be found in the drama of participation, in the excitement of controversy and the security of association, and above all in the reassurance of being superior to others. For such people, one alternative of public policy can be quite as satisfying as another. There is thus no rational way for relating private needs and public programs.

Here both the source and the consequence of political instability meet to produce a destructive spiral. Few societies appear to have greater need for the rational application of administrative programs than those in search of nationhood; yet it is those very societies in which the psychic needs of the people are often opposed to the routinized nature of administration. The need to utilize the forms and spirit of politics to solve private problems compromises the extent to which politics can solve general social problems. And yet until these community problems are resolved and the society modernized, there will be a continuing demand to use politics for its psychologically therapeutic powers.

More fundamentally, it is a tragedy of the transitional society that the processes of change create profound insecurities in its people which cause them to feel a deep need to be bound to others, to escape the sense of individual isolation. These psychological needs tend in turn to cause political leaders, whether conservatives, reformers, or revolutionaries, to delude themselves into believing that their feelings and opinions must be those of the people as a whole. For in an atmosphere of personal insecurity it is especially difficult for anyone to admit that he might stand alone or be in a minority; thus there arises a compelling need to insist upon conformity at precisely the moment when even the rudiments of genuine consensus are lacking, and so leaders and governments easily believe that they represent the true genius of their people. But in the absence of any genuine mobilization of public opinion, self-doubts linger on, and in an insidious fashion, leaders begin to clutch at the apparent certainties of authoritarian methods.

The Need for a Doctrine of Democratic Development

The problems of transitional societies—the interwoven political, social, and personal frustrations, the urge to press forward clouded by uncertainty, the lack of consensus or national coherence—possess the elements of a great historical drama, and the task of nation building in the new countries is widely recognized as one of the critical issues of the times. It is, therefore, extraordinary that there has not been a plethora of theories, doctrines, and prescriptions offered up for guiding the transitional societies to the goal of modern nationhood. The leaders of the new countries have been provided with glowing expositions of the virtues of democratic values and the glories of republican institutions. They can obtain extensive advice on limited technical matters of applied administration which are of varying degrees of relevance for their particular situations. But they are not offered any systematic guide to the nature of national development which can provide a sound basis for judging progress and for determining priorities for action. We seem to have neither the theoretical nor the applied knowledge to provide the basis of strategies for nation building.

The leaders of the new countries are constantly being reminded that they have not realized their objectives, but they are not being told how they might realize them. By stressing democratic ideals rather than the methods of democratic nation building, we tend inevitably to spotlight the gap between reality and aspiration in the transitional societies. The anxieties that already plague the leaders and the reflective citizens of unstable countries are further aroused, and many are left wondering whether they do in fact have the ability to create democracies. Our suggestions that they need not, indeed should not, necessarily conform to our methods but should follow practices more in tune with their own traditions can be very easily, and in fact usually are, interpreted as a slur on their capacity to realize our standards.

The lack of doctrine prevents us from providing helpful interpretations about the significance of various trends and tendencies common to transitional societies. Is the emergence of army rule a sign of antidemocratic tendencies? Or is it a process that can be readily expected at particular stages of national development? Must the central government try to obliterate all traditional communal differences, or can the unfettered organization and representation of conflicting interests produce ultimately a stronger sense of national unity? Should the new governments strive to maintain the same levels of administrative efficiency as the former colonial authorities did, or is it possible that, because administrative efficiency was the prime justification for the legitimacy of the colonial rule and because the new governments have other claims of legitimacy, this is no longer as crucial a problem? The questions mount, and we are not sure what trends are dangerous and what are only temporary phases with little significance.

The lack of doctrine has paralyzed constructive criticism and permitted the political dialogue in the new countries to become mired down in cant. Without the reassurance of meaningful standards of appraisal for evaluating behavior, people will feel incapable of exposing politics to the benefits of rigorous tests of judgments. Whenever people feel inhibited in discussing the realities of politics and seek to rationalize the need for optimistic fictions, the danger increases that even common varieties of political skulduggery will become immune to attack. Foreigners and men of good will can then innocently protect the work of rogues while those who are inside become cynical about the judgment of those who would wish well of such societies. For example, in the absence of a doctrine for democratic development, little can be done to oppose the perverse notion that somehow democracy can be equated with inefficiency, incompetence, and administrative slovenliness, while totalitarian methods are equated with efficiency, intelligence, and steadfastness of purpose. Leaders of new countries have been able to rationalize all manner of human failings as manifestations of their commitment to the democratic approach and thus claim virtues for their follies.

Unquestionably the development of doctrines on nation building has been inhibited primarily by the belief that political development is a natural and even automatic phenomenon which cannot be rationally planned or directed. Faith in democracy is frequently confused with an unreasoned expectation of the inevitable emergence of democratic practices and institutions. Therefore, as Americans, we believed we had a complete policy in our anticolonial tradition, for we assumed once a people had independence, they would inevitably and spontaneously move toward democracy. This romantic and anti-intellectual view of national development has tended to deter us from hard, rational analysis of the problem of nation building, and has possibly made us attach inordinate importance to emotional and irrational considerations.

The lack of adequate theories of national development has meant that our thinking about the problems of the new countries has been peculiarly vulnerable to mood and sentiment, both those of our own making and those of the ambivalent transitional peoples. The mixture of excitement and anxiety which heralds the gaining of independence first colored our popular thinking about the new countries. As with all births, hope and excitement have accompanied the emergence of the new nations. For the world, the drama has been in beholding new entities asserting themselves and striving for identity. For the peoples of the new countries of Asia, Africa, and the Middle East, there has been the deeper elation of finding themselves suddenly in a new world with new status. Indeed, change and innovation are never quite so exciting as when they involve a new life for an entire people. Imaginations are stirred in many directions.

The spirit of the new countries has not been unambiguously creative and positive; it has harbored elements of fear and the sense of possible failure and hopelessness. With time it has often become increasingly a peculiar mixture of elation and anxiety, of hope and frustration, of aspiration and apathy. In a decade of great cyclical changes in the dominant mood of popular discussions of the prospects for the underdeveloped countries, there has been a secular trend from optimism to pessimism, from an expectation of democratic performance to an acceptance of authoritarian ways. These changes in mood have not been guided by knowledge. They have followed in large part from a failure to define a rational approach to the question of national development.

For the citizens of the former colonial countries, the lack of theories and doctrines of democratic development is especially serious and disturbing. Their problem is acutely personal, for they desperately need respectable and widely accepted explanations of their current backwardness and convincing reassurances that progress and dignity are possible for them.

During the time of their subjugation, they could identify a single cause for all their misfortunes: colonialism. This ready explanation of their poverty and weakness contained the comforting suggestion that all evil was related to a foreign "they" and that the self was blameless. Thus it carried the implicit message of their salvation: once the exploiters had been eliminated, then all could spontaneously arise to realize the better life they had so long been forcibly denied. Those who subscribed to such neo-Marxist views had the same expectations as the Western liberals: both believed that progress and national development would follow naturally and automatically upon the removal of the artificial restraints of colonial domination.

Events of the last decade have demonstrated the pathetic inadequacy of such theories. The European powers, instead of experiencing a setback on losing their colonies, have shown an almost indecent propensity to prosper. The new countries, on the other hand, instead of feeling a burden lifted from their economies, have found it almost impossible to obtain from within their own meager economies the wherewithal to support even the level of public services they were accustomed to during the colonial era.[1] Yet many of their thinkers and leaders continue to cling to the neo-Marxist interpretations even when they can no longer enthusiastically believe them, for the only plausible alternative to the exploitation theory is that there may be something inherently inferior about them and their peoples. Many of the leaders are acutely aware that the dreams and ambitions they have for their countries, which are often called unrealistic, are really nothing more than the commonplaces of life in other countries. When the goal is to do what others are already doing, the haunting fears of failure are related not to the disappointments of broken dreams but to disturbing doubts about the worth of the self.

The seeds of such doubts were, of course, planted by the mechanics of colonialism, which inescapably cast one people in the role of superior and the other in the role of inferior. Moreover, the master peoples usually drove the point home with permanent effect by employing either consciously or unconsciously all the thousand and one techniques and tricks by which most elites throughout time have sought to demonstrate their natural rights of mastership and to unnerve and demoralize the common people. When it is remembered that in Europe the bourgeoisie, in spite of all its material successes, is still unsure of itself before the aristocracy, it becomes hard to imagine when the sting of colonialism will lose its psychologically paralyzing effects on those it treated with either contempt or indifference. The colonialists' casual but ceaseless stress on class, on style, on form, and above all their inflexible self-assurance, even when dead wrong, has left whole generations of aspiring leaders with incipient doubts as to their own ability to rule. The victims of such experiences may

1. Current research is only now exploring many of the "hidden" costs which the metropole powers bore under colonialism. A partial listing of some of these costs is to be found in Eugene V. Rostow, *Planning For Freedom* (New Haven, Yale University Press, 1959).

either be frozen by their anxieties and fail to perform as competently as they should, or they may be driven to compulsively denying reality, to proclaiming false achievements, and to insisting that all admire them in their Emperor's new clothes.

For all these reasons the need for realistic guides to the problems of nation building has been increasing. Although practical political doctrines are generally independent of systematic knowledge, the enormity of the problems of nation building seems to make the development of practical guides for action dependent on the expansion of knowledge about the mysteries of social, economic, and political change. The immediate problems of nation building are clearly a part of profound historical developments in which the spirit of traditional communities must give way to the ethos of modern forms for organizing human life, and their comprehension calls for a multidimensional and multidisciplinary approach.[2]

The World Culture and Nation Building

Although nation building is essentially a domestic process, it comes about in response to international forces. Indeed, the concept of the nation-state and the standards of modern state behavior have little meaning except within the context of a world-wide nation-state system. Societies throughout history have generated change, and cultures have mingled; the distinctive character of social change in the new countries of today is that it is occurring largely in response to the diffusion of what we may call a world culture based upon modern science and technology, modern practices of organization, and modern standards of governmental performance. It is helpful to think of all of these elements of the modern world as representing a culture, for from the point of view of the society as a whole or of the individual personality they are related to each other in much the same coherent fashion as the elements of a culture are felt to be. The concept of culture is also helpful in that it suggests that there may be an inner logic to the process of change and that the act of becoming a part of the modern world is in essence a process of acculturation.

It is customary to speak of the Western impact on the rest of the world, and to talk of peoples in Asia and Africa becoming Westernized. The fact that much of the modern world culture originated in the West is his-

---

2. For a discussion and demonstration of the value of such an approach to the problems of modernization, see Max F. Millikan and Donald L. M. Blackmer, eds., *The Emerging Nations: Their Growth and U.S. Policy* (Boston, Little, Brown, 1961).

torically undeniable, and it continues to be powerfully significant in coloring the feeling of the non-Western world toward the West; but by now the
diffusion has reached a point, and the culture has achieved such a dynamics of its own, that the culture can no longer be claimed entirely by
the West. It is also customary to speak of the process as one of modernization. But there are some elements of the culture, particularly from a political point of view, which have long and honored histories and do not belong entirely to our age. The diffusion of this world culture has been going
on over the last two centuries, and to a large extent through the institution
of colonialism.[3] The pace of the diffusion, however, has been greatly
accelerated during recent decades. Although the world culture of modernization touches on all phases of human life, it is based upon the nation-
state as the critical unit of human social organization. Implicit in it are
certain fundamental standards for government which are the prerequisites
of statehood.

This means that the process of nation building in the new countries is
neither autonomous in its dynamics nor free to select at random its goals.
The impact of the modern world on traditional societies has been a pressure in set directions. And this has become increasingly the situation as
the gap in technology has widened between the participants in the world
culture and the more tradition-bound peoples. When the West first came
in contact with Asia, each could learn something of value from the other.
Taoism and Confucianism, for example, had great attraction to Voltaire,
the French physiocrats, and the early exponents of the doctrine of laissez
faire; the Chinese practice of recruiting a civil service by competitive ex-
aminations was earnestly studied by both British and Americans who were
still relying upon bureaucracies of family and favoritism; and in a multitude of other ways Europe was enriched by its associations with the East.
Now, however, the flow of respected learning is almost entirely in one
direction, and there is an embarrassingly artificial quality in all the Western protests that the underdeveloped areas have much to offer in ex-
change. There has thus been a decline in the reciprocal character of relations between the more technologically advanced countries and the pre-
industrial societies; any sense of mutual interest seems to be increasingly
limited to an effort to make the latter more like the former.

3. For thoughtful evaluations of the profound nature of colonialism and its
capacity to spread the concepts of the modern nation and modern government,
see Rupert Emerson, *From Empire to Nation* (Cambridge, Mass., Harvard University Press, 1960); and John Plamenatz, *Alien Rule and Self-Government* (London,
Longmans, Green, 1960).

This disturbing trend makes it apparent that there are two processes at work simultaneously, and that, although a growing awareness of the world culture has brought changes to traditional societies, the force of technological advance in the industrial world has accelerated at an even faster rate so that the gap in technology has widened. At one time Asia was separated from the West by little more than the steam engine and the joint-stock company. Now the gap is so great that the main thrusts of advancing technology have little immediate relevance for countries just beginning to enter the state of constant innovation. There was a time when the introduction of the most advanced forms of technology into an Asian or African society could be expected to produce with only minor adaptations significant increases in efficiency. It was possible under such conditions to think of progress as moving along a direct path from the traditional to the modern, and all advances could be considered as accumulative and accepted in nearly random order. At present, however, the effort to introduce the most advanced forms of technology can lead to inefficiencies, to highly irrational uses of resources, and to setbacks to national development. This is only to say that progress now increasingly involves choices which can be acutely painful because they usually involve conflicts between pride and efficiency, between dignity and rationality, between adopting the most modern or accepting the merely appropriate.

A further complication is that, since the diffusion of the world culture can weaken and destroy the structure of traditional societies but cannot so easily reconstitute a more modernized society, the consequence of the international impact has more often been chaos and tension rather than a new order. It seems that the destruction of old relationships is proceeding at an increasingly faster rate than the pace of social reconstruction, and thus another widening gap seems to exist.

When the European powers first reached out to intervene in the lives of traditional societies and to set in motion the process of change, they invariably relied upon the persisting grip of the ancient indigenous traditions to maintain the basic fabric of the society. Colonial rule brought radical changes in the formal organization of government, and it set loose swelling waves of change; but colonial rule was only possible as long as the traditional order was able to give structure and form to the society. The handful of Europeans who governed most of Asia and Africa could do their job because the peoples they ruled were still governed throughout the cycle of their lives by traditional systems. Habit, custom, and village relationships gave discipline and order to the lives of most of the people, and the colonial rulers had to treat only with elite relationships at the top of the societies.

However, as the Western impact continued to weaken the old order, the inescapable consequence was a rise in the need for the formal, legal system of government and administration to provide the basis of social order. The eroding of the one system placed greater demands upon the other, and soon it became only a matter of time before the costs of trying to give political order and shape to the disarrayed transitional societies became prohibitive for the colonial powers. The transfer of sovereignty has thus often meant a transfer of the costs of and the responsibilities for putting together again an effective social system.

By weakening the cohesion of societies while simultaneously suggesting the unlimited potentialities of coherent political systems, the diffusion of the world culture has created the cruel but fundamental problem of the underdeveloped areas of today. On the one hand, the idea has been spread throughout the world that all people should belong to a nation-state, that the nation-state is the most appropriate and natural unit of political life and should provide the basis for a sense of collective identity. On the other hand, the very process that has communicated this idea has also threatened the capacities of people to act effectively in all phases of their political and social life. The acculturation process calls for the creation of all the numerous forms of organization necessary to support the social, political, and economic activities associated with modern life; but at the same time the experience of acculturation taxes the abilities of people to create and maintain modern organizations.

Thus at the heart of the problem of nation building is the question of how the diffusion of the world culture can be facilitated while its disruptive consequences are minimized. Historically the emergence of new nation-states has always been accompanied by more or less serious disruptions of the international system. Generally there were disruptions which followed from new nations asserting the power and realities of their new sovereignties, but the international system can also be strained by the weaknesses of new states, by the legal recognition of new sovereignties involving peoples who lack many of the classic attributes of sovereign communities. Whether it is the relationship of the United Nations to the Congo or the industrial nations to India's third five-year plan, the problem of nation building must inevitably place demands upon the international system. Thus whether the problem is viewed from the perspective of the individual country trying to develop its modern forms or that of the international system seeking to maintain its stability, nation building at this time is intimately bound up with the diffusion of the modern culture.

In order to gain a fuller appreciation of the problems of nation building, it is helpful to begin with a general view of the character of politics common to transitional societies.

CHAPTER 2

The Nature of Transitional Politics:
An Analytical Model[1]

Compared with either traditional or modern industrial societies, the transitional societies represent a far greater diversity, for differences in their traditions are compounded by differences in the degree, intensity, and form with which they have been affected by the diffusion of the world culture. Nevertheless, the political processes of most of them seem to show a striking number of shared characteristics, accounted for, it would seem, by their common experience of breaking down traditional forms and attempting to introduce institutions and practices which originated in the now industrialized areas. As Daniel Lerner has noted, the process of modernization has a distinctive quality of its own, and the elements that make it up "do not occur in haphazard and unrelated fashion" but go together regularly because "in some historical sense they had to go together." [2]

It should therefore be possible to outline in gross terms some of the main characteristics of what might be called the transitional or non-Western political process. Since these characteristics not only represent the reactions to profound processes of social change but also define the context and the parameters for all continuing efforts at national development, such an analytical model can serve as an approach in introducing the problems of nation building.

1. This chapter, in somewhat different form, first appeared as "The Non-Western Political Process" in *Journal of Politics, 20* (August 1958), 468–86.
2. Daniel Lerner, *The Passing of Traditional Society* (Glencoe, Ill., Free Press, 1958), p. 438.

Our model, thus conceived, follows.[3]

1. *The political sphere is not sharply differentiated from the spheres of social and personal relations.* Among the most powerful influences of the traditional order in any society in transition is the survival of a pattern of political relationships largely determined by the pattern of social and personal relations, with the inevitable result that the political struggle tends to revolve around issues of prestige, influence, and even of personalities, and not primarily around questions of alternative courses of policy action.

The elite who dominate the national politics of most non-Western countries generally represent a remarkably homogeneous group in terms of educational experience and social background. Indeed, the path by which individuals are recruited into their political roles, where not dependent upon ascriptive considerations, is essentially an acculturation process. It is those who have become urbanized, have received the appropriate forms of education, and have demonstrated skill in establishing the necessary personal relations who are admitted to the ranks of the elite. Thus there is in most transitional societies a distinctive elite culture which, although its criteria of performance are based largely on nonpolitical considerations, is the test for effectiveness in national politics.

At the village level it is even more difficult to distinguish a distinct political sphere. The social status of the individual and his personal ties largely determine his political behavior and the range of his influence, a condition which places severe limits on the effectiveness of any who come from the outside to perform a political role, be it that of an administrative agent of the national government or of a representative of a national party. Indeed, the success of such agents generally depends more on the manner in which they relate themselves to the social structure of the community than on the substance of their political views.

Thus the fundamental framework of non-Western politics is a communal one, and all political behavior is strongly colored by considerations

3. The picture of the "transitional" political process contained in this chapter is strongly influenced by George McT. Kahin, Guy J. Pauker, and Lucian W. Pye, "Comparative Politics in Non-Western Countries," *American Political Science Review, 49* (December 1955), 1022–41; Gabriel A. Almond, "Comparative Political Systems," *Journal of Politics, 18* (August 1956), 391–409, reprinted in *Political Behavior: A Reader in Theory and Research,* ed. by Heinz Eulau, Samuel J. Eldersveld, and Morris Janowitz (Glencoe, Ill., Free Press, 1956); Dankwart A. Rustow, "New Horizons for Comparative Politics," *World Politics, 9* (July 1957), 530–49, and also his *Politics and Westernization in the Near East* (Princeton, Center of International Studies, 1956).

of communal identification.[4] In the more conspicuous cases the larger communal groupings follow ethnic or religious lines. But behind these divisions lie the smaller but often more tightly knit social groupings, which range from the powerful community of Westernized leaders to the social structure of each individual village.

This essentially communal framework of politics makes it extremely difficult for ideas to command influence in themselves. The response to any advocate of a particular point of view tends to be attuned more to his social position than to the content of his views. Under these conditions it is inappropriate to conceive of an open market place where political ideas can freely compete for support on their own merits. Political discussion tends rather to assume the form of either intracommunal debate or the attempt of one group to justify its position toward another.

The communal framework also sharply limits freedom in altering political allegiances. Any change in political identification generally requires a change in one's social and personal relationships; conversely, any change in social relations tends to result in a change in political identification. The fortunate village youth who receives a modern education tends to move to the city, establish himself in a new subsociety, and become associated with a political group that may in no way reflect the political views of his original community. Even among the national politicians in the city, shifts in political ties are generally accompanied by changes in social and personal associations.

2. *Political parties tend to take on a world view and represent a way of life.* The lack of a clearly differentiated political sphere means that political parties tend to be clearly oriented not to a distinct political arena but to some aspect of the communal framework of politics. In reflecting the communal base of politics they tend to represent total ways of life; attempts to organize parties in terms of particular political principles or limited policy objectives generally result either in failure or in the adoption of a broad ethic which soon obscures the initial objective. Usually political parties represent some subsociety or simply the personality of a particularly influential individual.

Even secular parties devoted to achieving national sovereignty have tended to develop their own unique world views. Indeed, successful parties tend to become social movements. The indigenous basis for political parties is usually regional, ethnic, or religious groupings, all of which stress considerations not usually emphasized in Western secular politics.

4. Even Communist parties reflect this tendency; see Selig S. Harrison, "Caste and the Andhra Communists," *American Political Science Review, 1* (June 1956).

When a party is merely the personal projection of an individual leader, it is usually not just his explicitly political views but all facets of his personality which are significant in determining the character of the movement.

Nationalist movements in particular have tended to represent total ways of life, and even after independence the tendency remains strong, because such parties are inclined to feel they have a mission to change all aspects of life within their society, even conceiving of themselves as a prototype of what their entire country will become in time. Members of such movements frequently believe that their attitudes and views on all subjects will become the commonly shared attitudes and views of the entire population.

3. *There is a prevalence of cliques.* The lack of a distinct political sphere and the tendency for political parties to have world views together provide a framework within which the most structured units of political influence tend to be personal cliques. Thus, although general considerations of social status determine the broad outlines of power and influence, the particular pattern of political relationships at any time is largely determined by decisions made at the personal level. This is the case because the social structure in non-Western societies is characterized by functionally diffuse relationships; individuals and groups do not have sharply defined and highly specific functions and thus do not represent specific interests that distinguish them from other groupings. There is no clearly structured setting that can provide a focus for the more refined pattern of day-to-day political activities. Hence, in arriving at their expectations about the probable behavior of others, those involved in the political process must rely heavily upon judgments about personality and the particular relations of the various actors to each other. It follows that the pattern of personal associations provides one of the firmest guides for understanding and acting within the political process, and that personal cliques are likely to become the key units of political decision making in most non-Western societies.

Western observers often see the phenomenon of cliques as symptomatic of immoral and deviously motivated behavior. This may actually be the case. Considerations of motive alone, however, cannot explain either the prevalence of cliques in non-Western societies or their functions. For the fact that cliques are based on personal relations does not mean that there are no significant differences among them in their values and policy objectives. Since the members of a given clique are likely to have a common orientation toward politics, if their views were fully articulated they might constitute a distinct ideology significantly different from those of other factions.

In order to understand the workings of the political process in most non-Western countries it is necessary to analyze the character of inter-clique reactions. To ignore the importance of cliques would be comparable to ignoring the role of interest groups and elections in analyzing the behavior of American congressmen.

4. *The character of political loyalty gives political leaders a high degree of freedom in determining policies.*[5] The communal framework of politics and the tendency for political parties to have world views inspire a political loyalty which is governed more by a sense of identification with a concrete group than by identification with its professed policy goals. The expectation is that the leaders will seek to maximize all the interests of all the members of the group and not just seek to advance particular policies.

As long as the leaders appear to be working in the interests of the group as a whole, they usually do not have to be concerned that the loyalties of the members will be tested by current decisions. Under such conditions it is possible for leadership to become firmly institutionalized within the group without having to make any strong commitments to a specific set of principles or to a given political strategy.

Problems relating to the loyalty of the membership can generally be handled more effectively by decisions about intragroup relations than by decisions about the goals or external policies of the group. As long as harmonious relations exist within the group, it is generally possible for the leaders to make drastic changes in strategy. Indeed, it is not uncommon for the membership to feel that matters relating to external policy should be left solely to the leadership, and it may not disturb them that such decisions reflect mainly the idiosyncrasies of their leaders.

5. *Opposition parties and aspiring elites tend to appear as revolutionary movements.* Since the current leadership in non-Western countries generally conceives of itself as seeking to effect changes in all aspects of life, and since all political associations tend to have world views, any new group aspiring to national leadership seems to present a revolutionary threat. The fact that the ruling party in most non-Western countries identifies itself with an effort to bring about total change in the society makes it difficult to limit the sphere of political controversy. Isolated and specific

5. For excellent studies of this characteristic, see Myron Weiner, *Party Politics in India* (Princeton, Princeton University Press, 1957); and Keith Callard, *Pakistan: A Political Study* (New York, Macmillan, 1957).

questions tend to be transformed into fundamental questions about the destiny of the society.

In addition, the broad and diffuse interests of the ruling elites make it easy for them to maintain that they represent the interest of the entire nation. Those in opposition seeking power are thus often placed in the position of appearing to be, at best, obstructionists of progress or, at worst, enemies of the country. Competition is not between parties that represent different functional interests or between groups that claim greater administrative skills; rather, the struggle takes on some of the qualities of a conflict between differing ways of life.

This situation helps to explain the failure of responsible opposition parties to develop in most non-Western countries. For example, the Congress party in India has been able to identify itself with the destiny of the entire country to such a degree that the opposition parties find it difficult to avoid appearing either as enemies of India's progress or as groups seeking precisely the same objective as the Congress party. Since the frustration of opposition groups encourages them to turn to extremist measures, they may in fact come to be revolutionary movements.

6. *There is little or no integration among the participants due to the lack of a unified communications system.* In most non-Western societies political activities are not part of any single general process; rather there are several distinct and nearly unrelated political processes. The most conspicuous division is that between the dominant national politics of the more urban elements and the more traditional village level of politics. Those who participate in the political life of the village are not an integral part of the national politics, and they can act without regard to developments at the national level. Possibly even more significant, all the various village groups have their own separate and autonomous political processes.

This situation is a product of the communication system common to non-Western societies, where the mass media generally reach only elements of the urban population and those who participate in the national political process, and the vast majority of the people still communicate by traditional word-of-mouth means.[6] Even when the media of mass communication do reach the village through readers of newspapers or owners of radios, there is almost no "feedback" from the village level, and there-

6. A more detailed elaboration of such a communications system is contained in the author's "Communication Patterns and the Problems of Representative Government in Non-Western Societies," *Public Opinion Quarterly, 20* (Spring 1956), 249–57.

fore no reflection of the views of the vast majority of the population. Indeed, the Westerner often has less difficulty than the majority of the indigenous population in understanding the intellectual and moral standards reflected in the media of mass communication, for the media are controlled by the more Westernized elements who may be consciously seeking to relate them to the standards of the international systems of communication rather than to the local scene.

The lack of a unified communication system and the fact that there is no common political process limit the types of political issues that can arise. For example, although the non-Western societies are essentially agrarian and their industrial development is just beginning, their peoples have not been concerned with one of the issues basic to the history of Western politics: the clash between industry and agriculture, between town and countryside. The chief reason for this is that the rural elements are without a basis for mobilizing their combined strength and effectively advancing their demands on the government. It is possible that in time the rural masses, discovering that they have much in common, will find ways to mobilize their interests and so exert their full potential influence on the nation's political life. Such a development would drastically alter the national political character. In the meantime, however, the fragmented political process means that in fundamentally agrarian countries politics will continue to be more urbanized than it usually is in the industrial West. In many transitional societies one city alone dominates the politics of an entire country.

7. *New elements are recruited to political roles at a high rate.*[7] Two typical developments have caused a constant increase in the number of participants and the types of organizations involved in the political process. One is the extraordinary rise in the urban population, which has greatly increased the number of people who have some understanding about and interest in politics at the national level. A basic feature of the acculturation process which creates the subsociety of the elite is the development of attitudes common to urban life. The aspiring elites who demand to be heard generally represent a distinct stratum of urban dwellers who have been excluded from direct participation in national politics but whose existence affects the behavior of the current elite.

The other development is the more gradual reaching out of the mass media to the countryside, which stimulates a broadening awareness that, although participation in the nation's political life is formally open to all, the rural elements actually have little access to the means of influence. In

7. Kahin, Pauker, and Pye, p. 1024.

some places political parties, in seeking to reach the less urbanized elements, have opened up new channels for communicating with the powerful at the nation's center which may or may not be more effective than the old channels of the civil administration. In any case, the existence of multiple channels of contact with the national government tends to increase the number of people anxious to participate in national decision making.[8]

8. *There are sharp differences in the political orientation of the generations.* The process of social change in most non-Western societies results in a lack of continuity in the circumstances under which people are recruited to politics. Those who took part in the revolutionary movement against a colonial ruler are not necessarily regarded as indispensable leaders by succeeding generations; but their revolutionary role is still put forward as sufficient reason for their continued elite status. As a result, in some countries, as in Indonesia and Burma, and possibly in more acute form in most of Africa,[9] those who were not involved in the revolution feel that they are being arbitrarily excluded from the inner circle of national politics.

This problem is aggravated in societies where the population is rapidly growing because of a high birth rate. In Singapore, Malaya, and Burma, for example, over half the population is under voting age, and the median age in most non-Western countries is in the low twenties. There is thus a constant pressure from the younger generation, whose demands for political influence conflict with the claims of current leaders who consider themselves still young with many more years of active life ahead. In addition, in most of the newly independent countries the initial tendency was for cabinet ministers and high officials to be in their thirties and forties, a condition which has colored the career expectations of the youth of succeeding generations, who now face frustration if they cannot achieve comparable status at the same age.

This telescoping of the generations has sharpened the clash of views so that intellectually there is an abnormal gap in political orientations, creating a potential for extreme changes in policy should the aspiring elites gain power. Ideas and symbols deeply felt by the current leaders may have little meaning for a generation which has not experienced colonial rule.

9. *Little consensus exists as to the legitimate ends and means of polit-*

8. For an excellent discussion of this process, see Howard Wriggins, *Ceylon: The Dilemmas of a New Nation* (Princeton, Princeton University Press, 1960).

9. Cf. James S. Coleman, "The Politics of Sub-Saharan Africa," in *The Politics of the Developing Areas,* ed. by Gabriel A. Almond and James S. Coleman (Princeton, Princeton University Press, 1960).

ical action. The fundamental fact that transitional societies are engrossed in a process of discontinuous social change precludes the possibility of a widely shared agreement as to the appropriate ends and means of political activities. At one extreme in such societies are people who have so fully assimilated Western culture that their political attitudes and concepts differ little from those common in the West. At the other extreme are the village peasants who have been little touched by Western influences. Living in different worlds, the two can hardly be expected to display a common approach toward political action.

The profound social changes in the transitional process tend to compound uncertainty, depriving people of that sense of shared expectation which is the first prerequisite of representative government. The possible and the plausible, the likely and the impossible are so readily confused that both elation and resignation are repeatedly hitched to faulty predictions. Thus in the political realm, where conscious choice and rational strategies should vie in promoting alternative human values, it becomes difficult to discern what choices are possible and what are the truly held values of the people. The resulting drift is away from realism and toward either crudely emotional appeals or toward gentle ideals that offer respectability in Western circles but are irrelevant to the domestic scene.

Some people still adhere to traditional views and conceive of politics as primarily providing opportunities for realizing status, prestige, and honor. Such views are sustained by constant demonstrations that the masses in transitional societies still derive a sense of well-being from identifying with the grandeur and glory of their national leaders. There are others, taking their cues from the colonial period, who equate government with the security of office and the dignity of clerks in the civil service. For them government is above all the ritualization of routine where procedure takes precedence over all other considerations. Still others came to their appreciation of politics out of the excitement of independence movements; they continue to expect politics to be the drama of group emotions and to despise those who would give in to the humdrum calculation of relative costs and risks. For them the politician should remain the free and unfettered soul who can stand above tedious consideration of public policies. There are also those who look to politics and government to change their society and who feel that their dreams of a new world are shared by all. Some so grossly underestimate what must be done before the fruits of modernization can be realized that their ambitions incite little sustained effort and they are quick to declare themselves frustrated. Others who accept the need to deal first with the prerequisites of development may learn that all their energies can be absorbed in distasteful enterprises without visibly advancing the ends they seek. Thus the lack of a common, elementary orientation to the goals and the means of political action reduces the effectiveness of all.

Since such diversity in orientations makes it almost impossible to identify genuine social interests, the basic function of representative politics of sensitively aggregating the diverse values of a people and translating them into public policies cannot be readily realized. Without stable groups having limited interests, the processes by which power is accumulated and directed tend to be less responsive to social needs and more responsive to personal, individual desires.

This situation has direct effects on leadership. It reinforces the tendency for the personalities of the leaders to figure more prominently and for the idiosyncrasies of their followers to be more crucial in shaping developments than the functional needs of social and economic groupings throughout society. Moreover, although the national leadership may appear to represent a widely shared consensus about politics, more often than not this apparent national agreement reflects only the distinct qualities of the elite subsociety. The mass of the population cannot fully appreciate the values and concepts that underlie the judgments of the elite and guide its behavior.

Lastly, since most of the groupings within the political process represent total ways of life, few are concerned with limited and specific interests. Their functionally diffuse character tends to force each group to develop its own ends and means of political action, and the relationship of means to ends tends to be more organic than rational and functional. Indeed, in the gross behavior of the groups it is difficult to distinguish their primary goals from their operational measures. Consequently, the political actors in non-Western societies tend to demonstrate quite conspicuously the often forgotten fact that people generally show greater imagination and ingenuity in discovering goals to match existing means than in expanding their capabilities in order to reach distant goals; and it is difficult to distinguish within the general political discourse of the society a distinction between discussions of desired objectives and analyses of appropriate means of political action.

10. *The intensity and prevalence of political discussion bear little relationship to political decision making.* Western observers are impressed with what they feel is a paradoxical situation in most non-Western countries. The masses seem to be apathetic toward political action, and yet, considering the crude systems of communication, they are remarkably

well informed about political events. Peasants and villagers often engage in prolonged discussions on matters related to the political world outside their immediate lives, but they rarely seem prepared to translate the information they receive into action that might influence the course of national politics.

This is a survival of the traditional pattern of behavior. In most traditional societies an important function of the elite was to provide entertainment and material for discussion for the common people, but the people did not discuss the activities of the elite in any expectation that discussion should lead to action. Now the contemporary world of elite politics has simply replaced the drama of court life and royal officialdom.

A second explanation is that one of the important factors in determining social status and prestige within the village or local community is often a command of information about the wider world; knowledge of developments in the sphere of national and even international politics has a value in itself. But skill in discussing political matters again does not raise any expectation of actual participation in the world of politics.

There is also the fact that the common people of non-Western societies often seek to keep informed about political developments only in order to be able to adapt their lives to any major changes. The experience of former drastic changes has led them to seek advance warning of any developments which might again affect their lives; but it has not necessarily encouraged them to believe that their actions might influence such developments.

11. *Roles are highly interchangeable.*[10] It seems that in non-Western societies most politically relevant roles are not clearly differentiated but have a functionally diffuse rather than a functionally specific character. For example, the civil bureaucracy is not usually limited to the role of a politically neutral instrument of public administration but may assume some of the functions of a political party or act as an interest group. Sometimes armies act as governments.[11] Even within bureaucracies and governments individuals may be formally called upon to perform several roles.

A shortage of competent personnel encourages such behavior either

10. See Almond, "Comparative Political Systems," p. 402.
11. On the role of armies in transitional societies, see the forthcoming study sponsored by the RAND Corporation; Dankwart A. Rustow, "The Army and the Founding of the Turkish Republic," *World Politics, 11* (July 1959), 513–52; and Daniel Lerner and Richard D. Robinson, "Swords and Ploughshares: The Turkish Army as a Modernizing Force," *World Politics, 13* (October 1960), 19–44.

because one group may feel that the other is not performing its role in an effective manner or because the few skilled administrators are forced to take on concurrent assignments. However, the more fundamental reason for this phenomenon is that in societies just emerging from traditional status it is not generally expected that any particular group or organization will limit itself to performing a clearly specified function. Under these conditions there usually are not sharply defined divisions of labor in any sphere of life. All groups tend to have considerable freedom in trying to maximize their influence.

12. *There are relatively few explicitly organized interest groups with functionally specific roles.*[12] Although there are often large numbers of informal associations in non-Western countries, such groups tend to adopt diffuse orientations that cover all phases of life in much the same manner as the political parties and cliques. It is the rare association that represents a limited and functionally specific interest. Organizations which in name and formal structure are modeled after Western interest groups, such as trade unions and chambers of commerce, generally do not have a clearly defined focus.

Groups such as trade unions and peasant associations which in form would appear to represent a specific interest are often in fact agents of the government or of a dominant party or movement. Their function is primarily to mobilize the support of a segment of the population for the purposes of the dominant group, and not primarily to represent the interests of their constituency. Where the associations are autonomous, the tendency is for them not to apply pressure openly on the government in order to influence the formation of public policy but to act as protective associations, shielding their members from the consequences of governmental decisions and the political power of others.

The role of the protective association was generally a well-developed one in traditional societies and in countries under colonial rule. Under such authoritarian conditions, since informal associations could have little hope of affecting the formal lawmaking process, they focused on the law-enforcing process. Since they were likely to be more successful if they worked quietly and informally to establish preferential relations with the enforcing agents of the government, each association generally preferred to operate separately in order to gain special favors. The strategy of uniting in coalitions and alliances to present the appearance of making a popular demand on the government, as is common in an

12. For discussions of the problems of interest articulation throughout the non-Western world, see Almond and Coleman.

open democratic political process composed of pressure groups, would have only weakened the position of all as it would have represented a direct challenge to the existing governmental elite.

The fact that this approach to political activity was a common characteristic of traditional societies and still so widely survives as a feature of the politics of societies in transition suggests the following general hypothesis:

> Whenever the formally constituted lawmakers are more distant from and more inaccessible to the general public than the law-enforcing agencies, the political process of the society will be characterized by a high degree of latency, and interests will be represented by informally organized groups seeking diffuse but particularistically defined goals which will neither be broadly articulated nor claimed to be in the general interest.

The corollary of this hypothesis would, of course, read:

> Whenever the formally constituted lawmakers are less distant from and more accessible to the general public than the law-enforcing agencies, the political process of the society will be open and manifest, and interests will be represented by explicitly organized groups seeking functionally specific but universalistically defined goals which will be broadly articulated and claimed to be in the general interest.

13. *The national leadership must appeal to an undifferentiated public.* The lack of explicitly organized interest groups and the fact that not all participants are continuously represented in the political process deprive the national leadership of any readily available means for calculating the distribution of attitudes and values throughout the society. The national politician cannot easily determine the relative power of those in favor of a particular measure and those opposed; he cannot readily estimate the amount of effort needed to gain the support of the doubtful elements.

It is usually only within the circle of the elite or within the administrative structure that the national leaders can distinguish specific points of view and the relative backing that each commands. They have few guides as to how the public may be divided over particular issues. Thus, in seeking popular support, they cannot direct their appeal to the interests of particular groups. Unable to identify or intelligently discriminate among the various interests latent in the public, they are inclined to resort to broad generalized statements rather than to adopt specific positions on concrete issues; and whether the question is one of national or of merely local import, they must appear to be striving to mobilize the entire population.

The inability to speak to a differentiated public encourages a strong propensity toward skillful and highly emotional forms of political articulation. Forced to reach for the broadest possible appeals, the individual leader tends to concentrate heavily on nationalistic sentiments and to present himself as a representative of the nation as a whole rather than of particular interests within the society. This is one of the reasons why some leaders of non-Western countries are often seen paradoxically both as extreme nationalists and as men out of touch with the masses.

14. *Leaders are encouraged to adopt more clearly defined positions on international issues than on domestic issues.* Confronted with an undifferentiated public, leaders often find the international political process more clearly structured than the domestic political scene. Consequently, they can make more refined calculations as to the advantages in taking a definite position in world politics than they can in domestic politics. This situation not only encourages the leaders of some non-Western countries to seek a role in world politics that is out of proportion to their nation's power, but it also allows them to concentrate more on international than on domestic affairs. It should also be noted that in adopting a supranational role, the current leaders of non-Western countries can heighten the impression that their domestic opposition is an enemy of the national interest.

15. *The affective or expressive aspect of politics tends to override the problem-solving or public-policy aspect.* Traditional societies generally develop to a very high order the affective and expressive aspect of politics. Pomp and ceremony are basic features of their politics, and the ruling elite are generally expected to lead more interesting and exciting lives than those not involved in politics. In contrast, traditional societies do not usually emphasize politics as a means for solving social problems, questions of policy being largely limited to providing certain minimum social and economic functions and maintaining the way of life of the elite.

Although in transitional societies there is generally a somewhat greater awareness of the potentialities of politics as a means of rationally solving social problems than there is in traditional systems, the expressive aspects of politics usually continue to occupy a central place in determining the character of political behavior. The peculiar Western assumption that issues of public policy are the most important aspect of politics, and practically the only legitimate concern of those with power, is not fully accepted in non-Western politics. Indeed, in most non-Western societies the general assumption is not that those with power are committed to searching out and solving problems, but rather that they are the fortunate participants in an exciting and emotionally satisfying drama.

In part, the stress on the affective or expressive aspect of politics is related to the fact that, as we have already noted, questions of personal loyalties and identification are recognized as providing the basic issues of politics and the bond between leader and follower is generally an emotional one. In fact, in many non-Western societies it is considered highly improper and even immoral for people to make loyalty contingent upon their leaders' ability to solve problems of public policy.

There is also the fact that where the problem of national integration is of central importance, the national leaders often feel that they must emphasize the symbols and sentiments of national unity since substantive problems of policy may divide the people. It should be noted that the governmental power base of many non-Western leaders encourages them to employ symbols and slogans customarily associated with administrative policy in their efforts to strengthen national unity. The Western observer may assume that statements employing such symbols represent policy intentions when in fact their function is to create national loyalty and to condition the public to think more in policy terms.

16. *Charismatic leaders tend to prevail.*[13] Max Weber, in highlighting the characteristics of charismatic authority, specifically related the emergence of charismatic personalities to situations in which the hold of tradition has been weakened. By implication, he suggested that societies experiencing cultural change provide an ideal setting for such leaders, since a society in which there is confusion over values is more susceptible to a leader who conveys a sense of mission and appears to be God-sent.

The problem of political communication further reinforces the position of the charismatic leader. Since the population does not share the leadership's modes of reason or standards of judgment, it is difficult to communicate subtle points of view. Communication of emotions is not confronted with such barriers, especially if it is related to considerations of human character and personality. All groups within the population can feel confident of their ability to judge the worth of a man for what he is even though they cannot understand his mode of reasoning.

As long as a society has difficulties in communication, the charismatic leader possesses great advantage over his opponents, even though they

13. Kahin, Pauker, and Pye, p. 1025.

may have greater ability in rational planning. However, the very lack of precision in the image that a charismatic leader casts, especially in relation to policy, does make it possible for opposition to develop as long as it does not directly challenge the leader's charisma. Various groups with different programs can claim that they are in fact seeking the same objectives as those of the leader. For example, in both Indonesia and Burma the Communists have been able to make headway by simply claiming that they are not directly opposed to the goals of Sukarno and U Nu.

Charisma is likely to wear thin. A critical question in most non-Western societies that now have charismatic leaders is whether such leadership will become institutionalized in the form of rational-legal practices before this happens. This was the pattern in Turkey under Kemal Ataturk. Or will the passing of the charismatic leader be followed by confusion and chaos and possibly the rise of new charismatic leaders? The critical factor seems to be whether or not the leader encourages the development of functionally specific groups within the society that can genuinely represent particular interests.

17. *The political process operates largely without benefit of political "brokers."* In most non-Western societies there seems to be no institutionalized role for, first, clarifying and delimiting the distribution of demands and interests within the population, and, next, engaging in the bargaining operation necessary to accommodate and maximize the satisfaction of those demands and interests in a fashion consistent with the requirements of public policy and administration. In other words, there are no political "brokers."

In the Western view, the political broker is a prerequisite for a smoothly operating system of representative government. It is through his activities that, on the one hand, the problems of public policy and administration can be best explained to the masses in a way that is clearly related to their various specific interests and, on the other hand, that the diverse demands of the population can be articulated to the national leaders. This role in the West is performed by the influential members of the competing political parties and interest groups.

What is needed in most non-Western countries in order to have stable representative institutions are people who can perform the role that local party leaders performed in introducing the various immigrant communities into American public life. Those party leaders, in their fashion, were able to provide channels through which the immigrant communities felt they could learn where their interests lay in national politics and through which the national leaders could discover the social concerns of the new citizens.

In most non-Western societies, the role of the political broker has been partially filled by those who perform a mediator's role, which consists largely of transmitting views of the elite to the masses. Such mediators are people sufficiently acculturated to the elite society to understand its views but who still have contacts with the more traditional masses. In performing their role, they engage essentially in a public relations operation for the elite, and only to a marginal degree do they communicate to the elite the views of the public. They do not find it essential to identify and articulate the values of their public. Since their influence depends upon their relations with the national leadership, they have not generally sought to develop an autonomous basis of power or to identify themselves with particular segments of the population as must the political broker. As a consequence, they have not acted in a fashion that would stimulate the emergence of functionally specific interest groups.

CHAPTER 3

Analytical Approaches to Nation Building

In the preceding chapters we have outlined the problem of nation building
in the context, first, of contemporary history and then of the form of
political process characteristic of transitional societies in general. It is
now appropriate to try to isolate the basic nature of the problem of
nation building by turning to the theories of the social sciences. In
surveying the contributions of the social theorists and in examining
the theories of social and personal change, we shall be seeking intellectual
tools for analyzing the process of nation building.

Two points should be made at the beginning of a discussion of theories
about nation building. First, although all of the social sciences have a
great deal to offer that is relevant in one way or another to the complex
workings of society, there has been precious little explicit theorizing
about the processes of nation building. Even where there has been a
genuinely multidisciplinary approach, our current state of knowledge has
provided only some of the elements of a fully coherent theory of nation
building.

Second, the time dimension of nation building is always so long that
theories about the process cannot be readily tested empirically for the
accuracy of their predictions; hence it is peculiarly easy for people to
delude themselves into believing that they have found the truth. It seems
that whenever social scientists concern themselves with long-range problems that cannot be consistently or rigorously tested—for example, with
theories of economic development or of the consequences of child-rearing
methods—there is always considerable danger that they will find it difficult to wait patiently for the test of history and will feel compelled
to urge their theories on others through argumentation. It is thus not

strange that theories of economic history like Marx's are readily made into ideologies, and that hypotheses about child rearing provoke emotional and dogmatic assertions.

We would note here, then, that modesty and skepticism are called for in treating all theories about profound social change and the nation-building process.

The Tradition of Dichotomous Schemes

Our warning is not intended to minimize the extraordinary contributions that social thinkers throughout the ages have made to our understanding of modernization and nation building. It is possible, and a usual practice, to find a beginning in the insight and reasoning of Aristotle; one recalls specifically his typology of various states and societies and, even more significant, his search for explanations as to how societies passed from one form to another.

For our purposes it is important to begin only with that powerful tradition of Western social philosophy in which it is assumed that all societies can be classified according to a dichotomous scheme and in which all significant social and cultural changes are seen as related to the movement of a society from the one category to the other. There have, of course, been a host of labels for the two categories, each emphasizing different elements of the typologies: traditional and rational, rural and urban, agricultural and industrial, primitive and civilized, static and dynamic, sacred and secular, folk and urban, *societa* and *civitas, Gemeinschaft* and *Gesellschaft,* communal and associational, traditional and modern.

At the very dawn of the industrial revolution some social thinkers recognized the fundamental changes taking place in their societies. In articulating the changes of their time, they provided us with the concepts, and even with many of the terms, that still dominate our thinking about the processes of social, economic, and political development. Thus began a tradition of analysis which has lasted to this day.

What these social theorists have done is to create composite pictures of all traditional societies on the one hand and of all modern societies on the other; then they have selected from among the thousand and one differences between the two those key characteristics which they feel are the most significant in explaining the gross differences between them.

As early as 1861 Sir Henry Maine identified the two types of societies and postulated that all progress involved a movement from the "status" to the "contract" type.[1] Maine noted that a status society was characterized largely by the assignment of individual rights and duties on the basis of familial and kinship considerations, and that the tone of such societies was set by the awareness of individuals of the special and particular bonds that each had with each other. On the other hand, a contract society was based upon territorial ties, and individuals were bound to each other by secular, contractual relationships based upon specific considerations but enforced by the acceptance of a universally defined standard of ethics. In arguing that the development of societies involved the transition from tradition-bound, status-oriented relationships to rationally calculated and contractually negotiated relationships, Maine summed up the essential elements of what is a century later still the dominant social science view of the question.

Taking Maine's thesis as a point of departure, Ferdinand Toennies in 1887 made a further advance in his *Gemeinschaft und Gesellschaft* [2] by noting that human relations in the *Gemeinschaft* (community) form of association were highly affective, emphasizing the nonrational, emotional dimensions of the "natural will" of man which have their clearest expressions in the intimate feelings of kinship, comradeship, and neighborliness, while relations in the *Gesellschaft* (society) form of association were affectively neutral and emphasized the rational capacities of man by which he is able, first, to isolate and distinguish his goals of action, and then to employ, impersonally and deliberately, contractual arrangements as a part of strategies for optimizing his values. Thus Toennies stressed the distinction between the affective, emotion-based communal society in which everyone had a sense of belonging and the affectively neutral relationships of the modern society in which each individual builds his relations with others out of the ends-means calculations which guide his quest for his individual goals.

With both Maine and Toennies there was an acceptance of progress, but not without a note of nostalgia for the comfortable relationships of traditional societies and some anxiety over the prospects of a chillingly impersonal and ruthlessly calculating modern society. It is therefore noteworthy that Emile Durkheim, the father of modern sociology, in advancing his dichotomous scheme in 1893, not only stressed the virtues of the advanced form of social relationships but also employed odd and

1. Henry Maine, *Ancient Law: Its Connection with the Early History of Society, and Its Relation to Modern Ideas* (London, Lardon J. Murray, 1861).

2. Ferdinand Toennies, *Gemeinschaft und Gesellschaft* (1887); trans. by Charles P. Loomis, *Fundamental Concepts of Sociology* (New York, American Book Co., 1940).

seemingly reversed labels for his two categories of social solidarity.[3] He characterized the traditional order as having a "mechanical" form of solidarity which was based on the sharing of common attitudes and sentiment and in which legal authority had to be "repressive." In contrast "organic solidarity" was the basis of the advanced society, with its highly specialized division of labor in which interests and sentiments differed but were mutually complementary and hence legal authority was "restitutive." Instead of the class struggle of Marx, Durkheim saw the diversity of the modern plural society as providing the individual with unlimited opportunities for self-development and the expression of individual genius. A central contribution of Durkheim to any theory of nation building was the proposition that a national consensus built on merely a common set of shared values would always be more fragile and more open to authoritarian rule than one built on the need to aggregate the diverse but intensely real interests of all the elements of a society. Durkheim thus pointed to the fundamental importance of social roles and their relationships in the development of the modern and more complex society, and to the fact that the differentiation of roles increases rather than decreases the solidarity of a society.

It remained for Max Weber, however, to bring together the strands in the tradition of dichotomous schemes of social development.[4] In addition to elaborating, with great erudition and profound historical insight, the distinctive qualities of the traditional and the rational-legal forms of authority, Weber also identified the charismatic form of authority with its emphasis upon the affectual type of social action. In doing so, he brought to light a transitional form of society and pointed out the qualities of social action that tend to predominate when traditional forms are weakened. It would be hard to overemphasize Weber's contribution in developing his typologies of authority and social action. But probably an even greater contribution was his suggestion that there is an inner

3. Emile Durkheim, *De la Division du travail social* (1893); trans. by George Simpson, *The Division of Labor in Society* (Glencoe, Ill., Free Press, 1949).

4. A useful introduction to Weber's thinking on the problems of social change is to be found in Reinhard Bendix, *Max Weber: An Intellectual Portrait* (New York, Doubleday, 1960). The most pertinent parts of Weber's writing for the problems of nation building are to be found in translation in *The Theory of Social and Economic Organization*, trans. by A. M. Henderson and Talcott Parsons (New York, Oxford University Press, 1947; Glencoe, Ill., Free Press, 1957); *From Max Weber: Essays in Sociology*, trans., by Hans Gerth and C. Wright Mills (New York, Oxford University Press, 1946); *The Protestant Ethic and the Spirit of Capitalism*, trans. by Talcott Parsons (New York, Scribner, 1930; paperbound, 1958).

coherence to all societies in the form of a systematic relationship among the social, economic, legal, and political forms of behavior on the one hand and the nonrational spirit or ethos of the society, as best expressed in its religion, on the other. His successes in relating the rise of the rationalistic institutions of capitalism to the ascetic character of Calvinism led him to explore the relationship of the main religions of the East to the secular institutions they fostered. Through such endeavors Weber cleared the scene for a systematic analysis of the relationships between objective social forms and the subjective, psychological meaning of behavior. The social, economic, and political realms were seen as no more than different aspects of basic human acts, all conditioned and given coherence by the psychological make-up of man. Weber thus set the stage for relating questions of social structure to the profound psychological insights of Freud.

Using the central concepts of Max Weber as a point of departure, Talcott Parsons has brought about a higher degree of precision by relating the types of social action to the theory of role relationships and by identifying certain key "pattern variables." [5] In brief, Parsons noted that in the traditional society status rested upon *ascriptive* considerations while in the modern society *achievement* standards predominate, that in the traditional system role relationships tended to be functionally *diffuse* in the sense that all aspects of behavior may be considered relevant to any relationship, while in the modern system relationships tend to be functionally *specific* in the sense that they are limited only to the essential considerations relevant for maintaining the effectiveness of the system. Also, in the traditional system the normative basis of relationships was *particularistic* considerations and not the *universalistic* ones of the modern society. Others have followed Parson's lead and have sought either to make the key distinctions more logically rigorous or to construct conceptual models of political systems based upon them.[6] Parsons, however, must be personally credited with significantly advancing the discussion of the differences between traditional and modern social orders, and his

5. Talcott Parsons and Edward A. Shils, *Toward A General Theory of Action* (Cambridge, Mass., Harvard University Press, 1951); Talcott Parsons, *The Social System* (Glencoe, Ill., Free Press, 1951).

6. See, for example, the work of Marion J. Levy, *The Structure of Society* (Princeton, Princeton University Press, 1952); Francis X. Sutton, "Social Theory and Comparative Politics," Social Science Research Council's Committee of Comparative Politics; and Fred W. Riggs, "Agraria and Industria: Toward a Typology of Comparative Administration," in *Toward a Comparative Study of Public Administration,* ed. by W. J. Siffin (Bloomington, Indiana University Press, 1957), pp. 23–116; Robert N. Bellah, *Tokugawa Religion* (Glencoe, Ill., Free Press, 1957).

pattern variables have been widely accepted by contemporary social
scientists as illuminating the crucial differences between the two.

Limitations of the Dichotomous Scheme, and Development as the Fusion of Old and New

Parsons himself has been one of the first to note that the heightened
precision with which we can now distinguish between behavior in the
two types of societies has also brought to light some very serious limitations in the dichotomous scheme approach. The first is that such an
approach leaves highly ambiguous the nature and characteristics of transitional societies, the societies about which we are most concerned. The
increasingly clear picture we have of the two extreme types, the traditional
and the modern, has not clarified the processes of change that must take
place for a society to move from the one category to the other. It leaves
us with only the general impression that there should be a quantitative
decline in traditional forms of behavior and a corresponding increase in
behavior consistent with the modern pattern. There is not only the danger
of a tautology here but also the obvious fact that the process of social
change is infinitely more complex than this approach implies and that it
makes considerable difference precisely what changes occur and in what
order.[7]

A second and more serious limitation has been exposed by Gabriel
A. Almond in his observation that all political systems are mixed ones
in the sense that traditional patterns always exist and are of functional
significance in even the most advanced modern system.[8] Almond cites
in particular the recent research of Elihu Katz and Paul F. Lazarsfeld
demonstrating the crucial importance of face-to-face patterns of communications in shaping American opinion.[9] Other studies have shown
that personal associations and acquaintances continue to play an essential
function in all phases of American political behavior.[10] And, of course,

7. For a criticism of the static nature of this form of social analysis, see W. W.
Rostow, "Toward a General Theory of Action," *World Politics,* 5 (July 1953),
530–54.
8. Gabriel A. Almond, "A Functional Approach to Comparative Politics," in
The Politics of the Developing Areas, ed. by Almond and Coleman, pp. 20–25.
9. Paul F. Lazarsfeld, Bernard Berelson, and Hazel Gaudet, *The People's
Choice* (New York, Columbia University Press, 1944 and 1948); Elihu Katz and
Paul F. Lazarsfeld, *Personal Influence: The Part Played by People in the Flow
of Mass Communications* (Glencoe, Ill., Free Press, 1955); Elihu Katz, "The
Two-Step Flow of Communication: An Up-To-Date Report on an Hypothesis,"
Public Opinion Quarterly, 21 (Spring 1957).
10. See, for example, various contributions in *American Voting Behavior,* ed.
by Eugene Burdick and Arthur J. Brodbeck (Glencoe, Ill., Free Press, 1959);

the very essence of modern man, either in his occupational setting in the organization or in his social life in "suburbia," has been the value he has attached to functionally diffuse and highly particularistic relationships.[11] From these studies it would seem that the image of industrial or modern society held by the social theorist has been overly influenced by patterns common to a relatively modest level of technological development, such as existed in the West during the first decades of this century, and by an exaggerated vision of the ruthlessly impersonal future society of science fiction.

With respect to political development, it is apparent that we cannot think simply in terms of a quantitative decline in traditional role characteristics and a rise in modern ones. We must consider instead what mixture, or rather fusion, of traditional and modern patterns will lead to national development. In a sense, we can picture modern patterns of behavior as providing the superstructure of the advanced society, and thus conclude that the effective operation of the society depends upon whether the traditional patterns of behavior tend to reinforce and give greater substance and clarity to the modern superstructure pattern of relationships or whether they tend to undermine and disrupt the superstructure.

Development as the Creation of Effective Organizations

These considerations suggest that it may be fruitful to think of the problems of development and modernization as rooted in the need to create more effective, more adaptive, more complex, and more rationalized organizations. The story of the diffusion of the world culture has been one of countless efforts to establish modern organizational forms in traditional, status-oriented societies. Viewed in these terms, the apparently diverse activities of, say, the Western businessman and the Western educator, the colonial administrator and the missionary, and the activities of the leaders of nationalist movements and the officials of new governments have a common element. For all of them in their separate and often mutually antagonistic ways have been endeavoring to build highly differentiated and formally structured organizations in tradition-bound societies, and thus all of their efforts represent the very essence of social

---

forthcoming research of Ithiel de Sola Pool on communications in acquaintanceship networks.

11. See such studies as Robert C. Wood, *Surburbia: Its People and Its Politics* (Boston, Houghton Mifflin, 1959); William Whyte, *The Organization Man* (New York, Simon Schuster, 1956); David Reisman, *The Lonely Crowd* (New Haven, Yale University Press, 1950).

change in transitional societies. Nation building itself involves more than just the establishment of that most complex of modern organizations, the machinery of state; it also entails the creation of a host of organizations within the society. In the political sphere these would range from organizations capable of articulating the various interests of the society to those capable of aggregating these interests in the form of public policies which can become in turn the directives for guiding the organization of the state. In the economic sphere, modernization involves the formation of a multitude of other types of organizations: firms and factories, systems of communication and transportation, and above all the sensitive market. Socially, modernization entails the development of an array of organizations that can provide the individual with the necessary range of choices for association, so that whenever he steps beyond the family he can find opportunities to test his talents and to find his full identity as a social and a psychological being.

Once we conceive of the problem of political development and modernization as essentially the creation of adaptive and purposeful organizations, we are in a position to benefit from the insights of the theorists of social organization. Indeed, when we turn to the works of such thinkers it appears that they too, at an early stage, employed an essentially dichotomous scheme in which efficiency was attributed to patterns of behavior resembling those we have labeled as modern. Thus the early students of organization tended to employ the analogy of a smoothly functioning machine with interchangeable parts in picturing the ideal, efficient human organization, a point of view which was possibly carried to its extreme by Frederick W. Taylor and his successors in the scientific management movement.[12] In this approach, as with that of some social theorists who thought they were following the lead of Max Weber, efficiency was related to having clearly defined roles, or offices, based upon universalistic norms, functionally specific relationships, and rigid adherence to achievement considerations.

The entire modern trend of research on the organization has moved in almost a diametrically opposite direction in that it places far less importance on the legal or formal definition of roles and more on the positive components of functionally diffuse and even particularistic relationships. For example, Chester I. Barnard convincingly demonstrated that the efficiency and effectiveness of an organization depends less upon its formal, legal (modern) structure of relationships than it does upon

12. Frederick W. Taylor, *The Principles of Scientific Management* (New York, Harper, 1911).

the informal, personalized (traditional) forms of relationships.[13] Others have come to see organizations not just as pyramidings of posts or offices but as complex social processes, as systems of communication, and as the sensitive workings of decision-making processes.[14]

It now appears that the modern, formal superstructure of relationships can give an organization strength only if supported by the powerful emotional forces arising from particularistic loyalties and by the cohesive powers of the endlessly complex but functionally diffuse sentiments that human beings can provoke in each other. For example, Samuel A. Stouffer and his associates in their monumental study of the most complex and modern military machine known to history, the United States Army, learned that the behavior of the American soldier was determined less by his attachments to abstract values and universalistic standards than by the fundamental importance he attached to his face-to-face relationships and his particularistic loyalties to his immediate group.[15] Consistent with these findings has been the fact that when Americans were called upon to modernize and rebuild the South Korean and the Chinese Nationalist armies, they found that much of their attention had to be concentrated on strengthening face-to-face relationships and reducing reliance upon the formal procedures. It was learned that in many South Korean units the men's associations with each other were limited almost entirely to their formal military relationships and that there was little sense of group identity; most soldiers did not even know the names of their fellows.

Similarly, the bureaucracies of many transitional societies prove to be weak and ineffectual because they must depend to an exaggerated degree on formal, legalistic, and functionally specific relationships which are not reinforced by informal patterns of association and communication. Paradoxically, some of these bureaucracies come the closest to relying only upon what have been called the modern forms of relationships, while it is more common in advanced societies to find officials

13. Chester I. Barnard, *The Functions of the Executive* (Cambridge, Mass., Harvard University Press, 1938).

14. See, for example, Herbert A. Simon, *Administrative Behavior: A Study of Decision-making Processes in Administrative Organization* (New York, Macmillan, 1947); James A. Marsh and Herbert A. Simon, *Organizations* (New York, John Wiley, 1958). Karl W. Deutsch has played a leading role in assimilating these newer concepts to the study of nationalism; see his *Nationalism and Social Communication* (Cambridge, Mass., and New York, Technology Press of Massachusetts Institute of Technology and John Wiley, 1953).

15. Samuel A. Stouffer et al., *The American Soldier,* 4 vols. (Princeton, Princeton University Press, 1949).

cutting red tape, pushing aside formalistic procedures, exploiting personal and private associations, and generally getting on with the job despite bureaucratic obstacles. Again, if we trace the early steps in economic growth, we can find repeated evidence that the venture capital necessary for most forms of innovational developments has been more responsive to traditional, personal, and particularistic considerations than to universalistic standards. Similarly, the studies of industrial enterprises in different cultures demonstrate that high productivity is not so rigidly associated with the absence of traditional patterns of association as some social theorists have suggested. Studies of Japanese industrial practices suggest that it is precisely the reliance on supposedly traditional forms of behavior which explains their increasing efficiencies.[16]

We have gone into some detail to suggest the importance of the informal, highly personal, and what are customarily considered to be traditional forms of behavior in order to counter the idea that development is merely the strengthening of the more formal, more legalistic, and more narrowly functionally relevant patterns of behavior. The development of effective organizations depends fundamentally upon the capacity of individuals to associate with each other. This capacity calls into question a wide range of basic human values and the ability of individuals to make commitments—commitments as to the goals and purposes of group action, the means and spirit of associational relationships, the appropriate limits of such associations and the integrity of the self; in short, commitments as to one's fundamental identity both as a member of human societies (and subsocieties) and as an individual.

Once it is recognized that political and social development involves more than just the form of relationships defined in terms of their functional relevance for an organization, then the problems become largely those of understanding the human personality and understanding how in a particular setting the typical experience of personal development may either foster or inhibit the human potential and talents basic to all forms of effective group action.

It was precisely this range of problems which led Max Weber, in his search to explain Europe's economic development, to look to the basic ethos or values of people as primarily expressed in their religions. He was concerned with the set of values, the pattern of expectations, the cognitive forms, the content of memories, and the emotional responses that people tend to develop and share in any society. This is how Weber

16. James C. Abegglen, *The Japanese Factory: Aspects of Its Social Organization* (Glencoe, Ill., Free Press, 1958).

was able to set the stage for relating sociological situations with psychological forms. Since he wrote, great advances have been made in understanding the dynamics of personality development, but as yet we only clumsily relate these insights to our understanding of how objective social orders develop.

POLITICAL CHANGE AND PERSONAL IDENTITY

In reaching the tentative conclusion that the heart of the problem of nation building lies in the interrelationships among personality, culture, and the polity, we must be aware of the dangers at this point of accepting an unduly static form of analysis or of attaching excessive importance to factors of change significant only in relatively stable societies. This is a danger because most of the work on the broader implications of personality for social and political systems has been on the side of explaining continuity and the methods by which a people transmit their basic cultural values and preserve their institutions.

The main concern of the cultural anthropologists, for example, has been to bring to light the coherence of separate cultures and the symmetrical relationships between modal personality types and general cultural patterns. The results of such studies have been of great help in giving us an explanation in theory for many of the restraints that may inhibit the process of nation building. Unfortunately, the spirit of cultural relativism as known in anthropology has also provided the basis for an essentially static view of cultures. The strength of the approach has been in highlighting cultural difference; this has been useful in countering tendencies of ethnocentrism and helping Westerners to avoid the sin of pride, but it has been of pitifully little help to people in transitional societies who are desperately anxious to bring their countries into the modern world as effective nation states.

A similar orientation has also limited the usefulness of much of Western political thought. A cardinal assumption running throughout Western theory and as strong today as it was with the classical thinkers is that natural and presumably self-evident connections exist between state and society which dictate that the shape and form of any polity are only a reflection of the basic characteristics of the society at large. According to this view each society or culture, according to its peculiar genius, produces its distinctive political institutions, and these institutions continue thereafter to take their life from the dynamic forces which are in contention throughout the society. Although governmental actions in response to these pressures can, in turn, affect the development of the society, the dynamic element is usually assumed to lie permanently within the society. Thus the relationship between state and society is seen as an equilibrium system in which the social processes generate political processes which become the "inputs" and make demands on the governmental processes, which constitute the "outputs." [17]

This approach, however, unfortunately has peculiarly little relevance for understanding contemporary problems of nation building both because in most transitional societies the formal structures of government were arbitrarily introduced from abroad, and because the forces within the society are so poorly organized that they have little direct effect upon government. Indeed, the initiative for change more often than not comes from those in command of the arbitrarily introduced structures, and instead of the government responding to pressures from the society, the process is in many respects essentially reversed.[18] The gradual diffusion of a world culture has touched and transformed the realm of politics in all societies, and the whole range of modern political roles— from the civil servant on the planning board to the administrator in the district, from the cabinet minister and leader of political parties to the local party organizer—have appeared in transitional societies not through response to the internal needs of the society itself, but in response to supranational and foreign concepts of the appropriate standards of modern governmental and political behavior.

Significantly, among the contemporary social sciences this bias toward a static view seems to decline almost in direct proportion to the extent to which personality factors are minimized and an essentially rationalistic view of behavior accepted. Economists seeking to explain how continuing self-sustained growth comes about have taken the lead in constructing more dynamic theories and in breaking down the more relativistic view. By establishing arbitrary but useful indices and by stressing the significance of per capita income, economists have been able to rank countries according to their relative degree of development and to distinguish between "developing" and still stationary countries. This acceptance of an almost unilinear concept of progress has given an awakening shock to

17. The elaboration of this circular pattern is found in most of the literature on American interest groups and pressure groups; see especially V. O. Key, Jr., *Politics, Parties, and Pressure Groups* (New York, Knopf, 1958); David Truman, *The Governmental Process* (New York, Knopf, 1951); Avery Leiserson, *Parties and Politics* (New York, Knopf, 1958); David Easton, *The Political System* (New York, Knopf, 1953).

18. See James S. Coleman, "The Political System of the Developing Areas," in *The Politics of the Developing Areas,* ed. by Almond and Coleman.

other social scientists who considered themselves too sophisticated to use such an old-fashioned idea as social progress.

At the same time, however, the economists have become increasingly aware that they have tended toward a much too easy view of the prospects and possibilities for rapid change and development. More specifically, many economists have felt it necessary to attach prime significance to noneconomic factors in explaining the problems of economic growth, and thus they have been attracted to personality and cultural considerations.[19] In doing so these economists are becoming increasingly sensitive to complexities of the developmental process, and as a result they may find themselves pulled toward the more static outlook of those who have probed more deeply into the implications of personality and cultural variables.

These observations about our current state of knowledge point to the paradox that, although most approaches to problems of social change suggest the central importance of personality factors, efforts to deal with the relationship between personality and society tend to emphasize the basis of continuity and essentially static considerations. In order to avoid the excessively static bias of, say, classical anthropology while not going to the other extreme of, say, traditional economics in which change is seen as no more complex than rational choice, it will be helpful to elucidate the details of the relationships between personality and social change. This can usefully be done by first analyzing the various phases of the political socialization process and then noting the significance for social change of the different types of cultural values and attitudes produced by the socialization process. The theme running throughout such an analysis must be the quest of individuals to achieve appropriate political and social identities in their changing worlds.

The Stages of Socialization

It is helpful to picture the individual passing through three processes which condition his approach to political choice and action.

First, there is the basic socialization process through which the child is inducted into his particular culture and trained to become a member of his society. At the manifest level, this process involves learning the attitudes and values, the techniques and skills, the patterns of role relation-

19. For a pioneering systematic study of the total complex of factors underlying the phenomenon of economic development and which emphasizes in particular psychosocial considerations, see Everett E. Hagen's forthcoming study, "How Economic Growth Begins: A Study in the Theory of Social Change."

ships, the common knowledge, and all the other aspects of the particular society and culture within which the individual must find his adult position. At the latent level, there are all the experiences that shape the unconscious and determine the dynamics of the basic personality structure. Out of this socialization process the individual finds his identity as a member of society and achieves coherence as an effective person with a central perspective and direction and with a capacity to preserve his integrity and his essential characteristics. It can be assumed that, fundamental to this process of realizing one's identity, there exist some systematic relationships among the individual's constitutional givens, his effective psychological defense mechanisms, his successful sublimations, and the specific information he has stored in his memory, his developing cognitive processes, and the consistency with which circumstance has required him to assume particular roles. It can also be assumed that persons experiencing much the same process of socialization will develop roughly similar personalities which constitute the essence of their sense of common cultural identity.[20]

After the basic socialization process comes political socialization, through which the individual develops his awareness of his political world and gains his appreciation, judgment, and understanding of political events. Just as he was first socialized to his general culture, so now he is socialized to his political culture and realizes his political identity.[21] Political socialization also has its manifest and latent dimensions, but by this stage in the individual's growth new developments tend to be governed more by perception and cognition and conscious learning.[22]

Lastly, there is the process of political recruitment, when the individual goes beyond the passive role of citizen and observer to become an active

20. The concept of "basic personality structure" was first formulated in Abram Kardiner and Ralph Linton, *The Individual and His Society* (New York, Columbia University Press, 1939). The relationship of the socialization process to the formation of "national character" has been systematically explored in Abram Kardiner, *The Psychological Frontiers of Society* (New York, Columbia University Press, 1945); Margaret Mead, "The Study of National Character," in *The Policy Sciences: Recent Development in Scope and Method,* ed. by Daniel Lerner and Harold Lasswell (Stanford, Stanford University Press, 1951); Otto Klineberg, "A Science of National Character," *Journal of Social Psychology, 19* (1944), 147–62; Ralph Linton, *The Cultural Background of Personality* (New York, Appleton-Century, 1945); David M. Potter, *People of Plenty: Economic Abundance and the American Character* (Chicago, University of Chicago Press, 1959).

21. Gabriel A. Almond first formulated the concept of "political culture" in his "Comparative Political Systems," *Journal of Politics, 18* (1956).

22. For an excellent discussion of research in this field, see Herbert H. Hyman *Political Socialization: A Study in the Psychology of Political Behavior* (Glencoe, Ill., Free Press, 1959).

participant and to assume a dynamic and recognized role in the political process. He now gains a deeper and more esoteric understanding of politics, and he achieves a more clearly defined and more institutionalized identity. As a party politician or administrative official, as a minister or a judge, he must take on the qualities and spirit of his role and thus in a sense adapt to a further subculture.

In a stable and dynamically developing society there is a high degree of continuity in these three processes, each reinforcing the other, and thus there is a sense of coherence throughout the society. Standards of citizenship are foreshadowed in the early socialization experience, and the character of the eventual political roles is consistent with the norms of general social behavior. Even in the most stable societies, however, the match is never perfect. Some element of strain always exists, for learning to become a good citizen does not fully prepare for the command of power and the assertion of influence. And, of course, profound conflicts can arise for the individual between what he is consciously taught and how his subconscious personality is molded. It is these stresses and strains that provide much of the dynamic force for evolutionary political change, while at the same time the basic coherence among the processes gives a degree of order to the society and polity so that action can be purposeful and effective.

The situation in transitional societies is dramatically different. By definition, the three processes lack coherence. Basic socialization may still conform closely to traditional practices, in which case the child will not be appropriately trained for the kind of adult world he must eventually join. Even the children of the most modernized families are likely still to be trained mainly by either servants or grandparents who communicate standards appropriate only to a world of the past. Even more serious, the socialization process itself may be disjointed and convey a spirit of uncertainty. Theory can suggest the possible range of problems affecting the outlook and emotional stability of individuals exposed to such circumstances, but in the main this is a task for empirical investigation. The problem of finding an identity is so intimately associated with the particular context of individual experiences that the essence of the process is lost when viewed in abstract and general terms.

The process of political socialization is even more difficult whenever the process of cultural diffusion has left a confused and indistinct political arena. The uneven and unpredictable pace of social change confronts people with the fundamental dilemma of either attempting to adapt their behavior to a transitory political realm of the present, or of striving to adjust to a political world which still does not exist except in the domain of their hopes. People who were politically socialized under the aegis of a colonial regime may become timid and ineffectual souls once their world of orderly administration and rationally planned development has been shattered. Those inducted into politics through the enthusiasms of nationalist movements may similarly have their self-confidence eaten away by a shameful sense of incompetence when the test becomes that of management in the postindependence society.

The lack of stability and of consistency of direction in the basic socialization process reduces the prospects of the individual's finding a firm and reassuring sense of identity. The failure to resolve this basic identity crisis means in turn that the individual may seem to be peculiarly shallow, lacking in substance and commitment. For example, observers have often noted that the men who worked with colonial administrators, while perhaps appearing to be competent and even sincerely devoted to helping their people, were generally disturbingly weak and incomplete men. No matter what their behavior, they seemed to provoke suspicions of personal opportunism. Nationalist leaders often seemed to convey the sense of being more genuinely complete people; yet after independence many of them have also appeared to be hollow men, distressingly opportunistic and even cynical.

The question even arises as to whether the process of acculturation invariably produces this weakening of personality, this drift toward ineffectualness, among men who would deal with power and who seek to create new authorities.

Circumstances surrounding the political socialization process in transitional societies generally make it peculiarly difficult for people to achieve compatible but still differentiated personal and political identities. In such situations it is extraordinarily easy for people to treat personal complaints as political causes, to confuse private ambitions with ideals, and to see the spread of their personal authority as a growth in national unity and power. The confused nature of the political socialization process and the fact that this process is so enmeshed with the acculturation process cause a blurring in the boundaries between the private and public spheres. Since change is called for in both the objective realm of social institutions and the subjective realm of the individual personality, changes in the one can, indeed, be readily confused with changes in the other.

With respect to the third process, that of recruitment to active political roles, we have already outlined the main difficulties in characterizing the political process common to transitional societies. At this point we need only note that the problem is not just that the new political roles relevant to the operations of a modern state are imperfectly defined but also, and of more significance, that since the individual roles have generally been established at different times and even in isolated circumstances, their relation to each other becomes a further source of tension and confusion. For example, administrators were recruited to colonial civil services and trained to their tasks at a time when politicians were either nonexistent or relatively insignificant. On the other hand, politician classes have been trained in nationalist movements and have at best only a contempt for civil administrators. Thus both administrators and politicians tend to have little appreciation of the necessary bases for effective working relationships with each other. Since each class can picture its role as representing almost the entirety of the political process, people are still being mainly recruited into both classes in terms of a way of life and status considerations, not in terms of fulfilling particular and limited functions in the political process. Hence the general tendency of each group is to usurp all political functions and to resist the sharing of power and authority.

The Three Categories of Cultural Values and Attitudes

For our purposes of relating the socialization process to the political culture in order to clarify fundamental problems of nation building, it is helpful to distinguish three classes of cultural values and attitudes which are the consequences of the socialization process. These distinctions shed light on the ways in which the personality factor can be seen as either facilitating or inhibiting social change. The confusing of these different aspects of the socialization process can often explain the excessively optimistic or pessimistic expectations of Western observers about how fast a people can change their attitudes and values. It is important to recognize that some forms of cultural values and attitudes may be readily changed in response to changes in the environment, while other types, inculcated at a very early stage of the socialization process, constitute inherent elements of the personality and are nearly impervious to change. To exaggerate the extent to which apparent changes in cultural attitudes are possible because of evidence of changes in one of the categories would be just as wrong as to believe that all attitudes are permanently fixed because some are inflexibly a part of the personality.

Technical skills and competencies. The first category includes the skills, knowledge, techniques, and ideas which the members of a society are explicitly taught and which make it possible for them to maintain the existing level of the arts and sciences. The values and attitudes so instilled by the socialization process vary, of course, according to the general level of technology of the society. For many transitional societies one of the most obvious difficulties is the failure of the socialization process to produce enough people with adequate or appropriate skills to manage more modern forms of social, economic, and political life. The shortage of skilled personnel, ranging from administrators and technicians to doctors, engineers, teachers, and the like, poses serious obstacles to political development in most underdeveloped countries; but these problems are so self-evident there is no need for us to elaborate further about them. The need for more and varied forms of education in almost all transitional societies is a clear-cut problem which can be dealt with by appropriate public policies. Since the process of training is largely a conscious and rational one, it is possible to expect quick and significant changes from generation to generation; people in transitional societies are quite as capable as those in modern ones of learning technical skills.

The more rationalistic approaches to nation building tend to treat the problem of cultural attitudes and values almost entirely as a matter of formal education and the learning of skills—hence the tendency of those who follow such approaches to grossly oversimplify the problem of change and to interpret the difficulties mainly as the need for greater resources for the imparting of appropriate skills. Only those with a very shallow view of human behavior would expect significant changes to follow from improvements in this field alone.

Motivational goals. A second category of values and attitudes relates to the types of goals and behavior which the socialization process teaches as appropriate and legitimate objectives of personal motivations. These values and attitudes are associated with the deeper and more subtle relationships between basic personality formation and the conscious process of learning about the patterns of cultural values. The capacity to be strongly motivated and the ability to channel and focus human energies are clearly functions of personality development in which the early years of childhood are crucial. The goals or objectives toward which the individual feels he can or should direct his energies are learned at much later periods. Presumably it should be much easier for a people to learn new directions for expressing their motivations than to change their basic capacity to be motivated, since the first is associated with the conscious process of learning while the latter is governed by larger unconscious processes.

With respect to the problems of nation building and social development, the prime need is to direct human motivations from old forms of activity to newer ones. To achieve sustained economic development in most transitional societies, it will be necessary for people to become motivated more by secular activities relating to material development and less by, say, religious or ascetic concerns.

To explore the problems of development thus requires the examination of, first, whether the socialization process in the particular society instills a high degree of motivation in the basic personality type, and, second, what forms of activities are sanctioned as appropriate goals.[23] It is also necessary to examine how changes in sanctioned goals may affect the intensity of motivations and the capacity of people to strive for their professed goals.

Most discussions of the personality factor in the development process focus on this problem of motivation and goals. The conflict between traditional and modern values and the uncertainty about what people "really" want are seen as crucial obstacles to modernization. This is particularly common in studies of economic development which attach high importance to the entrepreneurial role, for it is assumed that economic development will follow if only the key decision makers are truly driven to the single-minded pursuit of economic activities. The premise of such approaches is that people usually get what they want, and that a society will not get economic growth unless there is a group within it which in a very profound psychological sense "wants" economic growth and is prepared to pay the costs.[24]

There is no questioning the extent to which the acculturation process in transitional societies twists and warps people's motivations and their capacities to strive effectively for any goals which they are able to articulate. Clearly this is a more complex and a more fundamental problem than that of rationally learning skills. The psychological problems of nation building, however, involve more than motivations. Indeed, there seem to be some cases in which people "want"—both in the superficial, articulate sense and in the deep, burning psychological sense—to have a modern state far, far too intensely to be able to have one. For in this domain,

23. David C. McClelland has developed the theory that there is a basic need for achievement in human life but that societies differ in the extent to which this need for achievement is strongly or weakly instilled into the personality. McClelland has also found a positive correlation between the level of need for achievement of a people and the state of their economic development. See his forthcoming book *The Achieving Society*.

24. Everett Hagen's forthcoming study, "How Economic Growth Begins," presents a theory about the psychocultural determinants of those motivations and attitudes essential for effective performance in the economic sphere.

possibly more than in most human spheres, exaggerated desires tend to be self-defeating. What is still missing is dependent upon a third category of values and attitudes which come out of the socialization process.

Associational sentiments and values affecting collective action. This third level of beliefs and attitudes consists of the feelings and calculations that determine the capacity of people to relate themselves to each other so as to facilitate collective action. It is this human potentiality for collective enterprise, for creating associations and corporate organizations, which makes possible all higher forms of civilization. The socialization process can either succeed or fail in inculcating the sentiments which make possible the more complex forms of social organization.[25]

As we have noted, the ultimate test of development is the capacity of a people to establish and maintain large, complex, but flexible organizational forms. This is not a capacity that can be readily learned. Indeed, as we suggested, complex and effectively operating organizations are impossible if excessive reliance has to be made on *the formal, explicit patterns* of relationships and channels of communication. The members of the organizational community must in their own ways and without explicit controls work out their relationships with each other so that their actions will contribute to the effectiveness of the organization. Another way of making this point is to note that complex organizational forms are not possible in a society if the organizations must bear all the costs of training people to collective action, and that the more the socialization process assumes the "costs" of this form of training, the more effective and complex can be the organizations in the society and the higher will be most forms of the civilization.

We shall be examining the specific associational sentiments that are most important in determining the prospects of nation building, but it should be said here that these do not involve simply feelings about cooperation and desires to reduce tensions and seek harmony in interpersonal relations. We have in mind much deeper sentiments which make it possible for effective organizational life to flourish even among people who do not particularly like each other and who may express considerable hostility and aggression toward each other. Indeed, most cultures—such as most of those of Southeast Asia—which place a high value upon,

25. An excellent study that analyzes the problem of associational sentiments as we are concerned with them and that deals explicitly with the problem of how the socialization process can produce people incapable of creating effective organizations who must thus remain economically underdeveloped is Edward C. Banfield, *The Moral Basis of a Backward Society* (Glencoe, Ill., Free Press, 1958).

or rather instill considerable anxiety about, "cooperation" may become
mechanisms for preventing organizational innovations and social development.

In any case, our concern is with the development of politics, and hence
with the management of conflict not with its denial. The real problem in
political development is therefore the extent to which the socialization
process of a people provides them with the necessary associational sentiments so that they can have considerable conflict without destroying the
stability of the system. When these sentiments are lacking, a polity cannot
even endure moderate levels of controversy. In short, it is associational
sentiments which make it possible for organizations to endure, and even
thrive upon, many forms of controversy.

The Crisis of Identity and the Issues of Predictability and Trust

The socialization process thus provides a link between personality and
political change. From the perspective of the individual's experience the
particular combination of these three dimensions of the socialization
process forms the basis of his personal sense of identity, while from the
larger perspective of the society as a whole the three levels provide the
essentials of the political culture. This is to say that the ways in which
skills, motivations, and the capacity to relate to others are combined in
the person's life history are crucial in determining his own self-image,
and that in the composite picture of the society the general distribution
of shared skills, motivations, and associational sentiments are crucial in
defining the spirit of politics.

Reasoning along these lines, we are now led to the conclusion that the
concept of ego identity, particularly as developed by Erik H. Erikson, can
serve as a powerful intellectual tool for understanding the process of nation building in transitional societies.[26] We can hypothesize that the strug-

26. It would be impossible to document fully the extent to which many key
parts of this study are dependent upon the insights and theories of Erik H. Erikson.
For the historian and political scientist the most pertinent of Erikson's works are
Childhood and Society (New York, Norton, 1950); *Young Man Luther: A Study
in Psychoanalysis and History* (New York, Norton, 1958); "Ego Development and
Historical Change," in *The Psychoanalytical Study of the Child, 2* (New York,
International University Press, 1946); "Growth and Crises in the 'Healthy Personality'," in *Personality in Nature, Society, and Culture,* ed. by Clyde K. Kluck-
hohn and Henry A. Murray (New York, Knopf, 1953); "The Problems of Ego
Identity," *Journal of the American Psychoanalytic Association, 4* (January 1956),
56–121; and "The First Psychoanalyst," *Yale Review* (Autumn 1956).

A discussion of Erikson's theories and their relevance for political analysis is
to be found in my "Personal Identity and Political Ideology," in *Political Decision-
Makers,* ed. by Dwaine Marvick (Glencoe, Ill., Free Press, 1960).

gles of large numbers of people in any society to realize their own basic sense of identity will inevitably be reflected in the spirit of the society's political life, and thus, more specifically, that those conscious and sub-conscious elements most crucial in determining the individual's identity crises must have their counterparts in the shared sentiments of the polity.[27] We must assume that in transitional societies in which the so-cialization process fails to give people a clear sense of identity there will be related uncertainty in the political culture of the people.

Although many citizens in transitional societies may be disturbed by the consequences of cultural diffusion and the need to adjust to the changing times, it is those intimately associated with power and politics who are the most disturbed over their own sense of identity. In part this is because their access to power leaves them peculiarly sensitive to the possibilities of advantage and disadvantage, being superior or inferior, honored or shamed, effective or ineffective. In part it is because they are the most deeply touched by the acculturation process, and they may have experienced moments of insight into the real meaning of being a modern man in a modern country, and forever after been left disturbed by the knowledge that on the matters that really count they have been rational-izing rather than describing the realities of their society. Their ambiv-alences have undermined their sense of judgment, of property, of tastes; their self-confidence has been sapped to the point where these men are consciously anxious about their own worth and unsure of their own identities.

More specifically, the breaking up of a traditional order, as Daniel Lerner has shown in his researches on the Middle East, affects the basic personality of a people by making them more psychically mobile and giving them, in Lerner's phrase, a greater sense of "empathy." [28] Tradi-tional man finds it hard to picture himself in the shoes of others, and hence

27. Erikson sees the link between personality and polity largely in terms of the relationship between the identity crisis of the great leader and the ideology he produces which can in turn help an entire people resolve its quest for identity. This suggests that the specific range of problems most fundamental to the indi-vidual's identity crisis must also find their place in any political ideology which receives a wide acceptance and is truly meaningful to a people.

This relationship between identity and ideology is somewhat similar to the concept of "sentiments" both personal and collective developed by Alexander H. Leighton in *My Name Is Legion: Foundations for a Theory of Man in Relation to Culture* (New York, Basic Books, 1959). Because of the suggestive value of Leighton's concept of "sentiments" we have chosen to label the most subtle dimen-sion of the socialization process that which produces "associational sentiments."

28. Lerner, *The Passing of Traditional Society.*

his aspirations are limited. Transitional man has broader horizons, and he can imagine much.

In our effort to understand the process of nation building, a crucial question now emerges: does the manner in which people attain this greater sense of empathy leave them more or less capable of working effectively with each other? In some situations the expanded perspective, when supported by a socialization process which has instilled strong associational sentiments, will make it possible for people to perform with greater effectiveness in organization roles. Under these conditions the ability of people to understand the feelings of others can produce constructive results in the development of new organizational forms and activities.

On the other hand, when the increased perspective is not reinforced by the necessary associational sentiments, the result can only be increased tensions and ineffectual organizations. Unfortunately, in most transitional societies which have been dislocated by the impact of the world culture, when people begin to put themselves mentally into the roles of others, they seem to "learn" that others have hidden hostile feelings toward them. Suddenly feelings of aggression which were once channeled and controlled by traditional patterns tend to be released in diffuse and unpredictable directions. We can hypothesize that with the increase in insecurity which change produces in most transitional societies, there must be a quantitative increase in the degree of aggression and hostility within the society.[29] There is at this stage a multiplier effect in the sense that once people can put themselves into the minds of others and if they tend to find in others the feeling of aggression which they are trying to control within themselves, they can quickly compound the amount of aggression which seems to exist within the society. Thus their sensitivity for the feelings of others can bring about a form of paralysis; and once people sense their own ineffectualness they may in fact become weak and impotent in their actions. Thus their fears are apparently confirmed.

Reduced to its basic essentials, the problem would seem to stem from two related issues, both crucial elements in effective associational sentiments.

First, there is the problem of certainty or predictability: people in transitional societies can take almost nothing for granted; they are plagued on all sides by uncertainty and every kind of unpredictable be-

29. For similar hypotheses, see Leonard W. Doob, *Becoming More Civilized: A Psychological Exploration* (New Haven, Yale University Press, 1960).

havior. In their erratically changing world, every relationship rests upon uncertain foundations and may seem to contain an unlimited potential for good or evil. People are not sure what they should get from any relationship, and so they are never sure whether they are getting what they should. The concepts of friend and foe become blurred. Above all else, the individual cannot be sure about the actions of others because he cannot be sure about himself.

Second, there is the related problem of a lack of trust in human relationships. The problem is broader and deeper than just the prevalence of distrust among individuals. It colors people's feelings about their relationship to their surrounding world, to the unfolding of events, and it affects their time perspective. The feeling of basic distrust leaves people unsure of their control over their world and hence fearful that the world is either against them or indifferent to them. Distrusting others, they must distrust their own capacity to influence others, and hence they have feelings of impotence. Unsure about the meaning of events, they are prone to distrust time, to believe that dreaming is dangerous and that nothing good is likely to come out of the future. Without a sense of basic trust and faith, political promises and even the most glowing plans for future development are likely to arouse suspicions on the part of the public. When basic trust is replaced with cynicism, a people will suspect that behind the screen of political promises their leaders are really "out to get everything for themselves."

At this point we have gone as far as we profitably can in dealing with the problem of nation building in general terms. We must now turn to an examination of the nuances and subtleties of a particular political culture to see how the socialization process can effect both negatively and positively the development of a coherent polity. Only in the context of particular life experiences and national histories can we hope to uncover the complex and ambivalent ways in which psychological reactions to social change can so affect the political culture as to impede collective action.

The theoretical considerations we have developed in this chapter not only provide the bases for ordering our empirical analysis but also point to the most crucial issues in determining the course of nation building. We are now particularly interested in how the primary socialization process and the secondary acculturation process can interact in the development of the personality so as to affect what we have called the associational sentiments or values. Broadly speaking, we are now putting to ourselves the question: how do different forms of social change affect the capacity of a people to work together in supporting modern organization processes?

PART II

The Traditional Order and the Varieties of Change

CHAPTER 4

Introducing Burma

The selection of Burma for an intensive study of the problems of nation building is suggested by many criteria. The country offers a remarkably clear picture of all the major experiences common to traditional societies responding to the demands of the modern world. Historically the Burmese monarchy was a relatively well-established system which incorporated the principal features of most traditional imperial systems. The initial contacts between the West and Burma brought into peculiarly sharp focus the clash between Western concepts of international relations and the views of a relatively isolated Asian society. Indeed, British relations with the Burmese monarchy were in all essential respects similar to the better known efforts of the British to establish formal relations with the Chinese monarchy.

The second stage in the Burmese experience with the modern world, that of colonial rule, was also unambiguous and assumed the classic form of imperial domination. The British destroyed the traditional structure of political authority and, on defeating the Burmese monarchy, had to establish a system of direct rule. The modern Burmese state was thus formed out of the structure of administrative authority introduced by the British with far fewer concessions to previous practices than were necessary where the colonial power relied upon indirect rule. The Burmese response to the Western impact was also apparently clear-cut and uncomplicated. The economic changes under British rule were conspicuous and well recorded, and hence readily accessible for analysis. So too were many of the social changes. Politically it would seem that the Burmese experience represents the classic response of nationalism, anticolonialism, anti-Westernism, and anticapitalism. Finally, Burma, on re-entering the family of nations as an independent country under the guidance of a nationalist movement dedicated to socialistic goals and the creation of a modern society, would again seem to be typical of many newly emergent countries.

Aside from its history, Burma is also a peculiarly inviting country for detailed study because it is small enough in population and size to be easily treated as a complete entity while still complex enough to have nearly all the problems common to the new nations. The country has a dual economy, a plural society, a host of minority peoples and ethnic divisions, a Westernized elite and a peasant mass, expanding urban centers and relatively static village units, a shortage of skilled personnel but an overabundance of university students.

There are, however, some other problems which many underdeveloped countries have but which Burma is fortunately spared, a circumstance that makes the country even more interesting as a case study of the problems of nation building. Burma is not overpopulated, there being adequate land to produce even a surplus of foodstuffs. It has mineral reserves in the form of oil, lead, tin, tungsten, and silver and, in the Irrawaddy River, a natural and economical system of transportation. Indeed, in terms of objective considerations, it would be difficult to find any serious reasons for Burma's not being able to develop its economy rapidly. It does not have the staggering problems of India or some of the Middle Eastern lands. The fact that there are so few objective handicaps to economic development in Burma suggests the extreme importance of nonobjective considerations in determining economic development in transitional societies. The fact that Burmese production, fifteen years after World War II, has just been restored to prewar levels suggests that the obstacles to its development may fall largely in the realm of political relations, psychological attitudes, and cultural values.[1] Thus an examination of the difficulties the Burmese have been experiencing should draw attention to the subjective obstacles to development which presumably are also at work beneath the surface in other underdeveloped countries.

There is no way to tell how typical Burma is of most underdeveloped countries. It is significant, however, that in a ranking based upon eleven indices of economic development Burma stood as the 26th out of 46

1. On objective grounds alone it is impossible to explain the difficulties the Burmese have had in rebuilding their economy. Although Burma was the scene of considerable fighting during the war, the country did not have a large capital plant that would have to be replaced. Thus an economist writing shortly after the war predicted that the country would be able to restore its economy to its prewar levels of production in a matter of months, and indeed this was nearly accomplished during the few months of British administration after the Japanese surrender and before independence. See J. Russell Andrus, *Burmese Economic Life* (Stanford, Stanford University Press, 1947), p. 344.

countries.[2] In a revised and updated compilation of the same data, Burma emerged as the 21st country out of 40.[3] Aside from certain striking exceptions, Burma belongs to a middle category of countries in most aspects of social and economic development. She has fewer radios in proportion to her population than most of her neighbors, but she claims a higher literacy rate. Her per capita national product is one of the lowest in all Asia, but she is on a par with most of the new African countries. Burma has fewer telephones than any other country in the world except Ethiopia, but about the same percentage of Burmese live in cities of over 100,000 people—5.2 per cent—as Nigerians, Ghanaians, and Pakistanis.

In size Burma is the second largest country of Southeast Asia, with an area about equal to that of Texas. The Burmese population of slightly over twenty million is about the same as that of Thailand and Iran, and slightly less than that of Vietnam or the Philippines. Constitutionally Burma, like many of the new countries, has a federal system, but in practice the government, again like most new ones, follows highly centralized procedures and opposes most forms of local autonomy. Also like most former colonial lands, the Burmese have a parliamentary system, a government by cabinet, and a president whose duties are primarily ceremonial. Burma has proportionately more lawyers than any other country of Southeast Asia except for the Philippines, but somewhat fewer than is common for Middle Eastern countries.

Thus, although Burma could not any more than any other country be classed as a typical underdeveloped land, it is striking how many qualities she shares with most such countries. Although this might be difficult to measure, it is not unlikely that the Burmese self-image is of a typical "Afro-Asian" country. In fact, however, the country is probably more isolated from the mainstream of modern cosmopolitan life than most new countries. It is definitely one of the new countries which at the moment is not experiencing substantial economic growth.

Finally it must be noted that in selecting Burma for intensive study, the author was responding to a strong personal attraction to the land and an idiosyncratic curiosity about many aspects of Burmese culture, both political and nonpolitical. We also suspected, when planning the project in the fall of 1957, that Burma might be entering its time of crisis as a newly independent country. By the next spring when field work was

2. James S. Coleman, "The Political Systems of the Developing Areas," in *The Politics of the Developing Areas,* ed. by Almond and Coleman, Table 4, p. 542.

3. Granville Sewell, "Data on Certain Underdeveloped Countries," Center for International Studies, Massachusetts Institute of Technology, 1961 (unpublished manuscript).

started, the dominant nationalist party which had ruled the country since independence had split into two strenuously contending factions, and, in the midst of interviewing, the Burmese army assumed authority, establishing a Caretaker government. So the situation was peculiarly advantageous for the interviewer; people were anxious to talk politics, to express their concerns with the fate of their land.

The field work in Burma consisted primarily of long, focused, but open-ended interviews with significant actors in the Burmese political process. Although the state of politics was discussed with numerous people, our study of attitudes is based primarily upon 34 interviews with administrative officials, 27 interviews with politicians, and 18 interviews with observers and critics of the political scene such as journalists, educators, and businessmen. Of the administrators, slightly over half were high echelon officials who began their professional careers before the war, nearly a quarter first became politically active during the Japanese occupation, and the remainder were younger men whose total experience with government was limited to the postindependence years. The group of politicians interviewed were somewhat more homogeneous: only four had significant political experiences outside of and before the nationalist movement which led to the formation of the AFPFL,[4] and nearly half of the remainder got their start in politics after the war.

The interviews tended to follow the pattern of a long discussion of the contemporary Burmese political scene followed by discussion of how events had arrived at the current state. Only after these preliminaries were the conversations turned to more explicitly autobiographical matters; these generally took the form of chronological accounts in which the respondent described his early years, how he had first become interested in politics and subsequently became involved in particular roles and learned his profession. All the interviews represented acts of courtesy on the part of the respondents, who were busy men with pressing concerns. The length, and naturally the depth, of the interviews varied greatly from individual to individual.

Before turning to the interview material, we must first gain an understanding of the Burmese political culture by examining the past and observing how the system has developed over time. Such a survey is necessary in order to distinguish between long established patterns of behavior and those of recent origin. The common expectation is that explorations

4. The letters AFPFL originally stood for the Anti-Fascist Peoples' Freedom League, but the words have long since lost their meaning while the letters continue to convey emotions and meaning.

into a tradition-bound past should provide sharply contrasting comparisons with the present state of affairs. In practice, more often than not it turns out that, in spite of the fundamental significance of change in transitional societies, most such societies continue for generations to bear greater over-all resemblance to their basic traditional forms than to the modern world of their aspirations. Basic patterns continue behind new labels, and new symbols and slogans are often related to old practices without disturbing the essentials. The dynamics of this process of more apparent than substantive change are much like those which compel a young generation to believe that its discoveries are revolutionary, calling for new terminologies, when in fact it is only coming across what the older generation has known and accepted, perhaps even as self-evident, for a long time. Embedded in the process of cultural change there must be a principle of economy of change at work, its effect being that a society will permit its members to dissipate freely their energies in proclaiming new titles for old forms so long as little of substance is changed.

This situation is well illustrated by the prevalent notion that most newly independent countries are inclined toward some form of socialism and that this represents a radical departure from their old practices. It is commonly held, for example, that such countries are anxious to follow a socialist pattern because they need the state's direction of the economy to force the pace of development, and that they distrust private business because they associate capitalism with their period of colonial exploitation. Presumably nationalist leaders learned their socialism from exposure to the European Left during their struggles for independence, from attending the London School of Economics and listening to Harold Laski, and from reading books from the Left Wing Book Club. Viewed in these terms it becomes a bit difficult to explain the failures of such converts to respect all the humane values of European socialism once they gained power.

The truth of the matter is that in traditional societies of any degree of political sophistication government has always tended to dominate all spheres of social and economic life. The values that could be respectably sought in the society—whether honor, prestige, power, or wealth, fame, or respectability—were all to be found by looking to a life in "government," which by definition generally encompassed the entire elite of the society. The ambitious only had one direction in which to turn, one avenue of possible advance—toward the domain of officialdom; and those who succeeded were trained to suppress the rise of any potentially autonomous basis of power within the community. Surely the products of such societies needed no instruction from Europeans in the arts of restricting and shackling merchants and displaying contempt for all those too obviously concerned with developing the state of the economy. The fundamental feature of most non-European traditional empires and kingdoms was the vigilant use of political authority to prevent the conspicuous growth of private enterprises. The principle of centralized authority was basic to the traditional system, and the practice of expropriating wealth, particularly that of foreigners and minority groups, as old as recorded history in Asia, was not inspired by the novel notions of European reformers. Even the practice of government-sponsored welfare enterprises came more from the standard practices of colonial regimes than from the doctrines of the socialist opposition parties of Europe.

In short, even the apparently radical ideas of socialism often represent little more than new titles for old practices, new ways of giving respectability to old attitudes, especially those of an elite toward the masses and any foreign minority element.

It is helpful, therefore, in characterizing the essential outlines of traditional Burmese politics, to organize the descriptive material around precisely the theme of a bifurcated society, divided between a distinctive elite and an agrarian community-oriented mass, which is typical not only of most traditional societies but also of transitional ones.

CHAPTER 5

Traditional Forms and Practices

The history of traditional Burma was one of ceaseless efforts of various rulers and kings to assert their hegemony over other potential kings and to establish some semblance of empire. Thus endless clashes took place between and within the various ethnic groups who now make up the population of Burma. Each of these peoples—the Mons, the Arakanese, the Shans, the Karens, the Chins, and finally the Burmans [1]—came from the mountainous north and pushed their way down toward the low plains and the delta.

Recorded Burmese history largely begins with the founding in 1044 of the state of Pagan during the reign of King Anawratha.[2] At the time the Burmese "were little more than a great tribe; even in the middle ages, at the height of their first supremacy, they can hardly have numbered a million; but they were a people of some power." [3] Pagan saw the beginning of both the propagation of Buddhism in Burma and the introduction of the forms and concepts of the Indianized state. The extraordinary achievements of Pagan are still to be seen in the miles upon miles of deserted temples and pagodas which must rank as one of the archeological wonders of the world.

1. Considerable confusion exists regarding the use of the terms "Burman" and "Burmese." English writers in general have tended to use Burman in referring to all citizens of the country and Burmese for the dominant ethnic group, but others have reversed the practice. We shall not attempt to bring order out of this confusion but shall use the terms interchangeably, trusting that the context will indicate which we have in mind whenever the distinction is relevant.

2. For the details of early Burmese history, see D. G. E. Hall, *A History of Southeast Asia* (New York, St. Martin's Press, 1955), and *Burma* (London, Hutchinson's University Library, 1950); G. E. Harvey, *History of Burma from the Earliest Times to 1824* (London, Longmans, Green, 1925).

3. G. E. Harvey, *British Rule in Burma* (London, Faber and Faber, 1946), p. 16.

The dry central zone in which Pagan was founded was unable to produce sufficient food for a dynamic empire,[4] and on the death of its
founder the empire began to wither. It was finally destroyed in 1287, to
be succeeded by a series of petty kingdoms, the most significant being
Ava, Toungoo, and Pegu. Not until the mid-eighteenth century was a
township headman of Shwebo able to piece together enough political
authority to establish again a commanding kingdom.[5] In finally con-
quering as far as Rangoon, which means the "end of strife," King Alaungpaya established in 1755 the last "but probably the greatest Burmese
dynasty." [6] The early European traders and adventurers thus came upon
Burma during a relatively high point in her history, not during a period of
decline as was the case with China and with most of the other countries
of Asia. Consequently we have substantial evidence from Western observers of both the strengths and weaknesses of the traditional system of
the Burmese kings.

Although Burmese dynasties began with men from the village, the system of the kings was characterized by a sharp division between the world
of the court and the way of life of the village-based multitudes. Those
who gained admission into the society of the court generally broke their
associations with the narrow and inhibited life of the village. At the center of the whole system was the god-king himself. In theory the king's
power was absolute and unlimited; in practice it was checked only by
"his inability to enforce rule over a country of thin population and poor
communication." [7]

As John F. Cady has pointed out, the concept of kingship in Burma
was buttressed by three important sanctions: the Indian concepts of
royalty involving the magical properties of the court regalia; the venerable
principle derived from Hindu cosmology that the divine status of the king
followed from his occupancy of the hallowed precincts of the capital;
and the popular belief in the king as the ultimate patron and supporter of
Buddhism.[8] The authority of the king rested clearly on other-worldly considerations, both magical and mystical. Within the court every facet of
life reflected awe of mystical forms and fear of the unpredictable potency

4. Maung Maung, *Burma in the Family of Nations* (Amsterdam, Djambatan,
1956), p. 11.

5. John F. Cady, *A History of Modern Burma* (Ithaca, N.Y., Cornell University
Press, 1958), pp. 3 ff.

6. Maung Maung, p. 9.

7. F. S. V. Donnison, *Public Administration in Burma* (London, Royal Institute of International Affairs, 1953), p. 13.

8. Cady, pp. 4 ff.

of magic. Ceremonies had to be conducted precisely according to rituals, and over the years the members of the court bound and hobbled themselves with an increasingly elaborate code of manners.[9] While the atmosphere of the court was heavy with a ubiquitous sense of other-worldly forces, the style of court politics was that of infinite calculation and inexhaustible scheming.

The world of Burmese officialdom was thus made extraordinarily unstable and unpredictable by a pervasive fear of both spirits and men. Men in power were concerned with seeking favor and avoiding destruction. The risks of politics were immense, but so were the rewards. "The great office-bearers—the ministers and the territorial governors—were not hereditary; they held office during the royal pleasure, and their tenure could be tragic as well as brief." [10] Although not untypical of traditional systems, the violence and cruelty of the Burmese kings is legendary: for example, Thisi-thu-Dhamana sought to increase his power through an elixir made of 6,000 human hearts procured by his officials; [11] the last Burmese king, on coming to the throne in 1878, sought to eliminate all possible contenders by executing his eighty half-brothers and sisters; [12] and throughout the last dynasty life was made more hectic for officials by the prevalence of insanity among the monarchs.[13]

Although the absolutism of the Burmese kings ensured that the court itself was always the crucial arena of traditional Burmese politics, the conflicts, while nearly always confined to relations among the king's officials, could extend into the country. It was assumed, as in most tradi-

9. For the details of the mystical properties of the kingship, see D. Mackenzie Brown, *The White Umbrella: Indian Political Thought from Manu to Ghandhi* (Berkeley, University of California Press, 1953); Robert Heine-Geldern, *Conceptions of State and Kingship in Southeast Asia,* Cornell University Southeast Asia Program Data Paper, No. 18, 1956; Michael Symes, *An Account of an Embassy to the Kingdom of Ava* (London, G. and W. Nicol, 1800).

10. Harvey, *British Rule in Burma,* p. 23.

11. He must have had some second thoughts about the elixir when a few months later his queen, seeking to increase her power, plotted with his ministers to kill him. See Maurice Collis, *The Great Stone Image* (New York, Knopf, 1943).

12. Since royal blood could not be shed, the relatives were all tied up in sacks and trampled on by white elephants.

13. Philip Woodruff has so described the sad endings of the last kings: "King Tharrawaddy, like his brother, had become insane and had been succeeded by King Pagan, the fourth in succession to be both bad and mad. But Mindon, who deposed Pagan in 1852, was a sensible man, tolerant and merciful, reported by European visitors to be 'every inch a king,' in spite of his custom of gazing at them through field-glasses when they came in audience. It was remarkable that anyone so normal should have come to be King of Burma." *The Men Who Ruled India,* 2 vols. (New York, St. Martin's Press, 1954), 2, *The Guardians,* 120–21.

tional societies, that the boundaries of legitimate participation in politics coincided with ranks of officialdom, for politics belonged to the elite, and the elite was defined as those possessing official status. All officials banded together to suppress vigorously the notion that any citizen, regardless of wealth or station, might have claims to make of the political process. The only crack they permitted in their monopoly was the influence they could not deny to the Buddhist monks, most particularly the *Sangha* or sacred order of monks.

The scope and focus of the traditional political process meant that all actions tended to be governed by a fairly explicit hierarchical pattern of relationships in which the issue of superior and subordinate dominated every move. Although it may be stretching that already extremely elastic term "bureaucracy" too far to employ it with reference to traditional Burma, it would not be inaccurate to suggest that Burmese officialdom was always straining to form itself into an essentially bureaucratic structure. The cardinal questions each official put to himself in all his dealings with others were "Who are my superiors?" and "Who are my inferiors?" Every action was designed to clarify the answers to these questions. A man acted with shameless servility before his superiors and poured out uninhibited contempt and disdain on inferiors.

Thus all in the system save king and commoner shared the same psychic experiences; all knew the meaning of fawning and abject obsequiousness, and all had opportunities of grandly displaying scorn and derision toward others. In a peculiar fashion, the significance of absolute differences in the hierarchy was mitigated by this bond of shared experiences; the lowest and the highest officials were drawn together by the knowledge of what it meant to treat both superiors and inferiors in the correct and satisfying ways. Indeed, there was even to some degree an inversion between absolute status and the frequency with which an official experienced the emotions of servility or contempt; high officials in their daily rounds might be forced to treat with superiors and royalty more frequently than with subordinates, while lowly officials might only infrequently encounter a superior and could therefore lord it over all they met.

Burmese officials, like most traditional elites, naturally developed infinite skill and delicate sensitivities in dealing with matters of prestige, status, and power. Indeed, there are probably few words less appropriate for describing traditional Burmese politics than "static," that term so frequently and thoughtlessly applied to traditional societies. Burmese officialdom was an extraordinarily lively community where men were constantly testing their wits, devising new ways to manipulate their fellows, and subtly scheming to do each other in. By comparison, modern men in contemporary Western bureaucracies seem to be psychically immobilized, lacking in vivid imagination, and capable of picturing themselves in new and higher positions only as a consequence of hard work and diligence.[14]

Much of the instability in the Burmese system, as in most traditional ones, stemmed from the extent to which an official's status was no more secure than the moods and whims of his superiors. At all levels the ultimate test of politics was the basic question of loyalty and personal acceptance. Loyalty is an absolute value in all forms of politics, but it is peculiarly basic to traditional systems in which men are moved by the sentiments of personal association and by an understanding of the appropriateness of rewards for services rendered. Under such circumstances, loyalty became honesty, and both could give a degree of predictability to political relationships. In a fundamental sense, the whole Burmese structure rested upon the efficacy of patronage. Men received their official posts as a reward for services or as a sign of their success in winning the favor of those in power.

In traditional Burma the calculation of rewards was in objective and not subjective terms, and hence there was a clear sense of precision.

At present in transitional Burma one of the difficult problems of adjustment has been the acceptance of more modern and less precise concepts of political loyalty. People hesitate to give up the traditional concept of rewards; they find disturbing the contemporary notion that people should render services to political leaders in return for nothing but the intangible reward of being told they have supported a good cause. They are not sure that they are not being taken in, especially when they are told that they should give up the old-fashioned principles of patronage and submit themselves to the manipulative potentialities of idealism. This sense of uneasiness is one of the major factors contributing to the widespread feeling that people are always being tricked, exploited, and cheated by dishonest politicians.

In contrast to, and in part as a reaction against, the arbitrary and personal qualities of authority, official society in traditional Burma was carefully regulated by sumptuary rules which dictated nearly every aspect

14. Possibly the best source on the spirit and the manners of traditional Burmese politics is the Burmese drama, for most plays have a court setting and deal with the relations within the elite circles. See U Htin Aung, *Burmese Drama: A Study, with Translation, of Burmese Plays* (London, Oxford University Press, 1937).

of a person's life, including "the style of house and clothing appropriate to his station in life; even the funeral ceremonies and types of coffins." [15] Some security could be found in these forms, but there was always an inverse ratio between security and status. Thus the only hereditary officials, aside from the king, were at the lowest level, the village headmen and the township headmen or *myothugyi*.

Once a man moved above the level of local government, his risks increased, but so also did the possibility for personal advancement. The most numerous officials were the *myosa,* which means literally "the eater of a town." They were given the right to enjoy whatever revenues they could extract from the towns or princely fiefs under their jurisdiction.[16] Indeed,

> until the reign of King Mindon (1853–78) no public servant was remunerated by a salary. Commission on taxes collected, or fees for services rendered, was theoretically the basis for remuneration. In practice, the local custom and public opinion allowed and remitted this through the *myothugyi* or other appropriate official to the royal treasury. A third to a quarter, more or less, was retained as remuneration by the local officials.[17]

The basic rationale behind the struggle of politics was the valiant quest of all to maximize their income while reducing their risks. Upon receiving quotas for revenue to be collected, officials would pass them on down, dividing and allocating the sums among their subordinates, who might in turn strive to negotiate an abatement and push the responsibilities onto neighboring districts. Once the revenues had been collected, the process reversed itself; each subordinate sought to keep as much as possible while each superior applied all the pressures he could to increase the amounts passed up. The strain on loyalties was often extreme, which helps explain the constant state of agitation and personal danger throughout the world of officialdom.

There are many Burmese sayings which reflect the dangers and insecurities of official life:

> In serving the king, one should act like waterplants swaying according to the blow of the wind and not like big trees.

15. J. S. Furnivall, Foreword to J. Russell Andrus, *Burmese Economic Life* pp. x-xi.

16. U Ba U, *My Burma: The Autobiography of a President* (New York, Taplinger, 1958), pp. 1 ff.

17. Donnison, *Public Administration in Burma,* p. 14.

A courtier's life is uncertain and unsafe like a tree which grows on the edge of a river bank.

Ministers are mere buffets, here today and gone tomorrow.

The four things which cannot be trusted are thieves, the boughs of trees, women, and rulers.

Be extremely careful and behave yourself when you are faced with fire, water, women, evil persons, snakes, and members of the royal family or else you will be courting death.[18]

Powerful forces for irrationality circulated throughout the traditional Burmese system. Belief in the god-king meant that it was *lèse majesté* to suggest or even to imagine any possible limits to his omnipotence. Anything and everything could be done by the mystical powers of officialdom. Faith in magic was a faith in the unlimited possibilities for change, and since magic and government belonged to the same sphere there were no conceivable limits to the capacity of politics to change the world.

The constant concern for status was another source of irrational behavior. Since the ultimate proof of high status was the capacity to act beyond the comprehension of mere reason, and the higher the official the less he had to account for his actions, there was a powerful urge at the ruling level to act in unaccountable ways. While lowly people were limited to the plausible and to the confining grip of ordinary common sense, the high official commanded respect for his actions and words no matter how implausible. Men put forward absurd ideas that defied all reason in an effort to claim or prove their high status. Since the test of relative power and influence was the ability to obtain unqualified support for one's views without relying on assistance from reason, people came to suspect that the more ridiculous the opinions, the more important the man.

The tone of traditional Burmese politics was thus greatly influenced by uncertainty, ambition, and struggles for prestige and status. Only at the two terminal points of the process were the tensions of officialdom slightly reduced. At the top was the *Hluttaw,* or royal council, which

18. For such sayings, as well as a superb analysis of the traditional Burmese attitudes toward government, see Maung Maung Gyi, "An Analysis of the Social and Political Foundations of the Burmese Executive, 1948–1956," dissertation, Yale University, 1958. Dr. Maung Maung Gyi argues that the absolutism and other authoritarian qualities of the Burmese kings contributed to the molding of a traditional pattern of Burmese thought in which government was seen as being inherently evil, a highly personalized and highly privileged hierarchical system, and not the business of the people.

literally means "the place of release." [19] The four senior ministers or *Wungyis* ("great burden-bearers") and their four junior ministers or *Wundauks* ("supports of the great burden-bearers") were to a degree protected from the endless struggle. However, even though they often became the wealthiest men in the realm, they still remained vulnerable to the whim of the king. Indeed, the *Hluttaw* never achieved "the independence and security of even a tsardom's cabinet . . . [for its members were] liable without a moment's notice to be flung into jail . . . merely because the king was displeased for some trivial reason." [20]

At the other pole were the hereditary township and village headmen, only marginal participants in the political process. All other officials could engage in the contest of diverting responsibility to others and seeking profit for themselves, but in the end responsibility rested with the headmen, particularly for actually collecting revenue from the citizenry. These men had to mix with the people and see how the requirements for maintaining the grandeur of government could be best met without unduly disrupting the processes of making a living.

The picture we have of traditional Burmese village life conforms remarkably well with Redfield's general model of a peasant community.[21] Agriculture provided not only a basis of life but also a way of life. The villages were relatively self-contained units, and people tended to live out their lives within the circle of known acquaintances.[22] The intimacy and the limited range of personal association meant that life could be bearable only if most activities were carefully surrounded by prescribed conventions. Everyone had to know where he stood, and all had at least to pretend to accept a common interest. Decision making in such a situation called for vociferous extolling of the virtues of cooperation, an ideal that was in form frequently attained. But the stress on cooperation was all too frequently, as in modern Burma, only the ultimate attempt to avoid responsibility for leadership and for the making of decisions.

19. For a general description of the organization of the traditional Burmese government, see Maung Maung, Chap. 1; E. C. V. Foucar, *They Reigned at Mandalay* (London, 1946); R. F. Johnston, *From Pagan to Mandalay* (London, John Murray, 1908); Symes, *An Account of an Embassy to the Kingdom of Ava*.

20. Harvey, *History of Burma*, p. 329.

21. Robert Redfield, *Peasant Society and Culture* (Chicago, University of Chicago Press, 1956).

22. The village unit, particularly in Upper Burma, was probably never quite as self-contained a unit as were the villages of, say, India and China. In fact, there was a tendency for particular villages to specialize along certain occupational lines, and thus from the earliest times there was generally some form of elementary trade among groups of villages. See J. S. Furnivall, *An Introduction to the Political Economy of Burma* (Rangoon, Peoples' Literature Committee and House, 1957), Chap. 3.

Within the village, formal administration was little needed, for only rarely did new problems arise calling for new approaches. Experience was thus a relatively accurate index of skill, and the older a man was, the more likely he was to be able to understand and solve problems. Normative standards sanctioned this fact by identifying status with age.[23] In the main, custom ruled; the government did not have to police the people, for they ceaselessly policed each other. The adjudication of conflicts was referred to the headmen and to the elders, and decisions were rendered according to the spirit if not the letter of the ancient Hindu code of Manu. In effect, this meant judgments according to old saws and folk wit and wisdom.[24]

The gap between the world of the rulers and that of the peasant masses might appear to have been too great to be bridged by any common psychic or emotional bonds. And yet there was a coherence to the society. In part it was achieved as a result of some unique functional relationships between commoner and royal court. A significant proportion of the population belonged to the hereditary *ahmudan* class, who owed personal services to the royal court in lieu of taxes and who were divided into numerous service units or "regiments" (*asu* or *athin*). Some of this class made up the military forces of the kingdom. Others inherited functions important for the general society, as for example the sluice-keepers on the irrigation canals.[25] Others were menials for the court—the masons, carpenters and gardeners, the cooks, the bakers, and even the keepers of the royal betel-chewing apparatus. Also passed down from father to son was the task of the bird shooers who perched on the top of every royal building.[26] All were rewarded with royal land.

The existence of these commoners scattered throughout the population but with their special ties to the royal system tended to reduce the gap between the court and the masses. Everyone knew someone who could claim a special connection with the god-king. This no doubt made it easier for the masses to feel a sense of identity with their ruler. The bonds

23. Age itself became a key determinant of status to the point that a difference in even a day is still considered to be relevant in present-day rural Burma.

24. For example, the code of Manu holds that if a husband bargains honestly with a father for a particular daughter as his bride, and if subsequently the father tries to pass off on him another girl, the offended husband shall immediately get both girls as his brides, and all should be friendly toward each other thereafter. (See Maung Maung, p. 16.)

25. Harvey, *British Rule in Burma*, p. 24.

26. Cady, p. 14. The Burmese kings apparently had a peculiar concern for roofs. One of the first and most conspicuous signs that the "Western impact" had reached Mandalay appeared after a traveling Frenchman sold the court galvanized iron roofing for the entire palace. Subsequent visitors were taken aback on finding, in the midst of grandeur, pomp, and mysticism, the roofs of a shanty town.

of religion and of a common ethnic and linguistic origin further reinforced the sense of a common identity. Differences in status and material well-being between elite and mass were thus not a source of envy but of satisfaction and even some pride. It has been observed that in traditional Southeast Asia the masses seemed to feel that their lords and kings symbolized a cultural well-being, reflecting the greatness of the people as a whole.[27]

The Web of Religion

In characterizing any traditional society, special emphasis must be given to the all pervasive sense of the sacred; a complete picture of traditional Burma would require an examination of both Buddhism and the more indegenous worship of spirits or *nats*. Here, however, we shall consider only how the web of religion helped to integrate and give coherence to the traditional political system.[28]

It is customary to suggest that religions were able to integrate traditional societies by providing the members with a common framework of values and a common orientation toward the basic problems of life. Yet the closer we examine the historical evidence from such societies, the more we are impressed with the divergences in the content of the religious beliefs. In Burma among some of the peasantry the worship and propitiation of all manner of animistic objects, malevolent spirits, ogresses, and *nats* were hardly modified by the teachings of Buddha, while among the elite were to be found men profoundly knowledgeable in the sacred texts. It would seem that the gap in outlook between the devout followers of the pure school of Theravada Buddhism and the adherents of *nat*-worship must have been nearly as great as that between the contemporary Westernized Burmese intellectuals and the more tradition-bound villagers.

How then could religion have provided the basis of consensus for the traditional order? The answer seems to lie in some extremely subtle

27. Cora Du Bois, *Social Forces in Southeast Asia* (Minneapolis, University of Minnesota Press, 1949), p. 31.

28. For an introduction to Theravada Buddhism, see Kenneth W. Morgan, ed., *The Path of the Buddha: Buddhism Interpreted by Buddhists* (New York, Ronald Press, 1956); Christmar Humphreys, *Buddhism* (London, Penguin Books, 1954); F. Harold Smith, *The Buddhist Way of Life* (London, Hutchinson's University Library, 1951); Huston Smith, *The Religions of Man* (New York, Harper, 1958); E. A. Burtt, ed., *The Teachings of the Compassionate Buddha* (New York, Mentor Books, 1955); Edward Conze, *Buddhism: Its Essence and Development* (Oxford, B. Cassires, 1951); F. L. Woodward, *Some Sayings of the Buddha, According to Pali Canon* (London, Oxford University Press, 1955).

and implicit sets of relationships which served as a chain linking together the most and the least sophisticated people in the society. A detailed examination of the structure of their religion reveals that the Burmese population was distributed among a host of different religious groupings in which there was always some overlapping membership. Each individual belonged in a very loose sense to some particular religious community or body, each of these groups in turn had some relationships with another one, and ultimately they were all tied into the structure of government.

Beginning at the top a very direct and uncomplicated relationship existed between Buddhism and the state. In fact, Buddhism and the concepts of the Indian-type state were introduced into the land as a direct means of supporting secular power. The Burmese kings not only became the defenders and champions of the Buddhistic faith, they even claimed as a basis of their legitimacy the myth of consanguinity to the noble house of Lord Buddha. The kings also supported other religions, in particular always keeping readily at hand various Brahman priests and astrologers to help them foresee the future.

The connection between secular politics and religion was made quite explicit at the court level through the god-king's appointment of a leading monk to the office of *thathanabaing,* which had a vague and unspecified degree of control over the monastic hierarchies and the *Sangha,* the order of the monks. The control was necessarily vague because Buddhism never developed an explicit church structure or organization. The concept of the *Sangha* was one of individuals following the disciplined life of the searcher for Enlightenment, and not that of a disciplining order controlling the lives of its members. Thus the picture of church-state relations in the European context is most misleading if applied to Burma.

Immediately below the *thathanabaing* were other venerable monks who, according to the rules of court etiquette and protocol, ranked with the members of the *Hluttaw,* with whom they freely associated. At the level of the district governors there were other distinguished monks called *gainggyoks,* and so it continued on down the hierarchy until reaching at the village level the leading *pongyi* of the local *pongyi-chaung* who was closely associated with the headman. Thus the structure of government tended to give some structure to the *Sangha,* and in return the sanctions of religion tended to encourage support for the secular authority.

The relationships both between the sacred and the secular authorities and within the sacred orders were extremely loosely defined. The monks themselves were not organized in a common hierarchy. Each individual monastery had its own pattern of authority, its own rules of conduct, and its own particular ties with other monasteries. Considerable differences developed both in organization and in the interpretation of Buddhism. Some monasteries upheld the pure doctrines of Theravada Buddhism, others were less strict and came to terms with traditional *nat*-worship, and still others concerned themselves almost entirely with the spirit world and were only marginally touched by the teachings of the Buddha. Among the lay population similar gradations existed, ranging from people who were deeply devoted to Buddhistic doctrines and practices to those who were much closer to the world of *nats* and malevolent spirits.

The loose structure of religion stemmed in large measure from the individualistic nature of Buddhism. There was no explicit lay organization, no organized basis of group worship. The monks had no rigorous priestly duties and no obligations to the laymen. Each monk was concerned primarily in his own self-development, his own quest for escape from the mundane world. Even within the monasteries little uniformity was to be found in discipline or organization, and the rules that did exist set minimum standards of individual conduct. Advancement occurred without any strict system of selection beyond the general principle that the older the monk, the higher his station. Leadership positions were filled without benefit of formal procedures or objective mechanisms of selection; the monks would just agree on the particular elders who seemed most deserving of being honored. This was largely necessary because the prime concern of monks was their individual advancement in "the way of mindfulness," and thus progress came through the subjective experiences of meditation. Few objective tests of ability could be applied.[29]

These considerations all militated against Buddhism providing either an explicit organizational framework or a common value orientation for integrating the society. Integration came instead from the fact that individuals could find some immediate group with which to identify and could believe that that group was in some way related to the highest centers of power. Each monk, in belonging to an order that consisted of a series of monasteries, could believe that he belonged to a body that eventually reached to the court itself. The common man, out of his as-

29. For an excellent discussion of both the relationship of religion to secular authority and the way in which "Buddhism" and "animism" are the two poles of a continuum which is Burmese religion, see E. Michael Mendelson, "Religion and Authority in Modern Burma," *The World Today, 16* (March 1960), 110–18.

sociations with his local monks, gained a similar sense of identity with something related to court circles. The important point is that the order and stability of the traditional system did not depend upon everyone having a shared outlook on life, but rather on the fact that all the different particular outlooks had some representation and were seen as having respectability in even the highest circles. People did not live under the illusion that all should subscribe to the same ideas and beliefs. Instead, in a very imperfect fashion, a form of pluralism, and oddly enough in religion, seems to have given the system strength and provided a genuine link between the sophisticated court and the less enlightened commoners.

This point is rather important. In contemporary Burma, as in many other transitional societies, it is widely believed that the traditional order was based on shared religious connections and outlooks on life; this false reading of history has encouraged people to believe that divergences in views must be suppressed for the sake of achieving again a sense of national unity. The stability of the traditional order in fact rested not upon the degree of similarity and differences in ways of thinking but upon the subtle means by which acknowledged differences in thinking and action were compatibly related to each other. The society displayed a strange tolerance for difference, even in that most vital of spheres, religion, in contrast with the impatience for ideological uniformity common to transitional societies.

The Traditional Order

From this brief survey of traditional Burmese politics we can derive some summary conclusions about the form and tone of politics in a society divided between a culture of an elite and one of the masses. Since this type of division is also characteristic of transitional societies, it is not surprising that many of the qualities of the traditional system are still permanent features of the contemporary Burmese political scene.

First, government in traditional Burma, closely associated with religion, was seen as the center of all society. The world of officialdom dominated all life and controlled all activities that might directly or indirectly affect social power and matters of status. The one secular industry in the society was government and politics. Those who belonged outside the realm of government might feel that they had been mistreated with respect to particular acts, but they never felt that they had either legitimate rights or valid claims on government. In particular, anyone engaged in private economic or commercial activities was controlled and hampered, for the dominion of officialdom was never allowed to be challenged by any other source of potential power.

Second, being in government was seen as personally rewarding. It was the one channel of social and material advancement, and a bright and ambitious village youth looking for ways to improve himself turned to government. Those who reached the top were expected to be wealthy and to live in a grand manner.

Third, government was seen as having mystical powers and as being closely associated with other-worldly influences. Beyond the connections with Buddhism, government was thought of in terms of a magical view of the universe. Government could achieve anything; the king was omnipotent; moreover, nothing had to be plausible. Government did not belong to a world of dull reason, of conventional cause and effect.

Fourth, government was accepted as an arbiter of customs and manners and of all social life. Government was society; it set the tone of all life. Everyone, in conforming to his immediate standards of propriety, was a conscious participant in an exciting and dramatic society which included the greatest and the best in the land. Government was all this because it was, above all else, concerned with matters of status. Ceremony and ritual, customs and habits, forms of speech and daily routines were all designed to reflect this central concern. Government gave legitimacy to all the gradations and distinctions in social positions.

Fifth, government officials were thought of as dangerous, ruthless, heartless people. Similarly, any man who calculated in terms of power was seen as being dangerous. If one could not be on the side of government, one would do well to be as far removed from its influences as possible. Indeed, the devout Burmese Buddhist to this day still prays every night that he will be spared from the five worst evils in the world, and at the head of the list he places government.[30]

Sixth, government was not concerned with problem solving or with the designing of public policies to improve the state of society. Issues common to the traditional process dealt mainly with questions of loyalty and status. The system as a whole was upheld and adjusted to any disruptions by the simple mechanism of all the members of the elite working to uphold their elite positions and their relative status.

Seventh, the system tolerated personal differences and ideological variety. The stress of all codes of behavior was on individual performance

30. The other four elemental evils in the Burmese Buddhist world are fire, water, thief, and malicious person.

and on the correct performance of particular roles. There was little explicit concern with the larger dimensions of society. It was assumed that if people concentrated on improving themselves, both in their spiritual inner life and in their social roles, they might best achieve a degree of security in an admittedly dangerous world. This focus on individual behavior minimized the pressures on public policy, for people worried about themselves and not the state of society as a whole.

These outstanding characteristics of traditional Burmese government would have made social life impossible if they had not been tempered by the influence of religion and social convention. As long as the Burmese government had a role in relationship to Buddhism and religion, it could command the loyalties and respect of the people. The British grossly underestimated the appeal of the Burmese kings when they assumed that the autocratic manner and the ruthlessness of government must have alienated the population. At the end of the Third Anglo-Burmese War the British were surprised to learn that the common people "had a real veneration for the throne and they loved the religious ceremonial that surrounded it. The street crowd wept as Thibaw was led into captivity, for, whatever he may have been, he was, after all, their king." [31]

31. Harvey, *British Rule in Burma,* p. 23.

CHAPTER 6

The Sovereignty of Politics
in Impeding Development

The ways in which traditional orders have been assaulted by the modern world have been almost as varied as societies are complex. That is to say, in some situations the attack occurred largely in the economic realm, in others it was in the sphere of religion or maybe of education, and in other societies it was another phase of life. Regardless of the particular emphasis, it seems that in this basic process of social change politics and government have tended to assume a sovereign role. The possibilities of the other social and economic processes generating orderly change from traditional forms to modern practices have been facilitated or impeded to an inordinate degree by the overarching place of power and authority in social relationships.

For numerous reasons this crucial role of politics is frequently denied either implicitly or explicitly in public discussions about the problem of nation building. Often it is hoped that the silent but profound effects of the more diffuse forms of economic and social change will almost stealthily prevail over the follies and irrational stubbornness of politics. Indeed, one of the more naive versions of the potency of American foreign aid has projected the vision of economic and technological advances in underdeveloped countries leaving in their wake increasingly benign, democratic, and intelligently liberal political processes. The bulk of the historical evidence points in the other direction and suggests that there is little possibility of escaping the consequences of actions taken in the political realm. In a sense, government and politics tend to perform a gatekeeper function in controlling the various dimensions of the modernization process. The dramatic demonstration of the power of politics is to be found in the abrupt reversals of trends that can occur when colonial governments replace, or in turn are replaced by, indigenous governments.

This is not to say that the effects of governments are likely to match their pretensions in matters of social change and development. The consequences of government and politics may have little relationship to the intentions of rulers. The point is only that in the process of nation building the implications of behavior in the political sphere cannot be readily circumvented by developments in the other dimensions of the society.

In seeking to bring out more clearly the complex relationships between the political domain and the processes of social and economic change, we shall need to survey the patterns of change in Burma during the colonial period. Our concern is not with history nor with an appraisal of colonialism. After briefly reviewing the political reactions to colonial rule, we can turn to some of the social and economic innovations which took place during the British period.

New Structures and Old Expectations

The early relations between the British and the Burmese followed the classic pattern of the clash between traditionalistic empires and the emerging European nation-state system.[1] The Burmese kings, trapped by the mystique of their view of the universe, and the British, equally trapped by the logic of their legal notions and their concepts of the appropriate obligations and duties of nations and governments, had to follow their particular courses of destiny, and neither could swerve to avoid the inevitable collision. Burma, like the rest of the traditional world, had to come in contact with the modern world; it had to be altered into the image of a state and become a part of the state system.

The essence of the colonial experience in Burma—as in all colonial countries—was the arbitrary introduction into a still traditional society of new structures, forms, and institutions which generated intended as well as unintended processes of change. These changes brought new demands on government beyond those fundamental to the traditional political system. In so breaking down the old order, colonialism dramati-

1. The best history of modern Burma covering the period of British rule is Cady's *A History of Modern Burma*. See also Harvey, *British Rule in Burma; The Cambridge History of India 5, 6* (Cambridge, Eng., Cambridge University Press, 1929); Donnison, *Public Administration in Burma;* Daw Mya Sein, *Administration of Burma: Sir Charles Crosthwaite and the Consolidation of Burma* (Rangoon, Zabu Meitswe Pitaka Press, 1938); Hugh Tinker, *Foundations of Local Self Government in India, Pakistan and Burma* (London, University of London, Athlone Press, 1954); Albert D. Moscotti, "British Policy in Burma, 1917–1937: A Study in the Development of Colonial Self-Rule," dissertation, Yale University, 1950.

cally highlighted the central question in the development of transitional societies: namely, what pattern of relationships is to emerge between new political structures and basic political functions? More specifically, will institutions which had their origins in the West perform the same or new functions in their new setting, or will new structures have to emerge in time? [2]

Within the realm of government the primary innovation under British rule was the establishment of a modern administrative structure which became the framework of the modern Burmese state. Conditions in Burma precluded the possibility of indirect rule, that is, of employing as far as possible traditional institutions, as in India, Malaya, and later in much of Africa. The elimination of the king brought down the old forms, and the British had no alternative but to establish a new form of administration. Thus, quite openly, British concepts of law and order, of justice and impersonal authority, of paternalism, and of cultural and racial distinctions permeated all aspects of the new creation.

In place of the monarchy appeared the governor-general, the direct representative of the viceroy of India, whose staff gradually increased until the Secretariat came to house all types of departments and ministries expected of a modern government. Burma proper was divided into eight divisions, each consisting of three or four districts. In a ruthlessly logical fashion two or three subdivisions were created in each district, two to four townships in each subdivision. The townships were each divided into nearly fifty village tracts which became the prime units of local government.[3]

This orderly arrangement of authority and the principle that authority should conform to geographical territory were quite different from the practices and concepts common to Burma under the kings. Too much, however, has probably been made over the conflict between the traditional Burmese practice of often maintaining several spheres of jurisdiction and authority in the same "circle" or "district" and the modern concept

2. With variations in emphasis and in language, nearly all students of colonialism and of the new states have been concerned with this central problem. For example, with respect to Africa this problem of institutional transferral is the subject of analysis in David Apter's *The Gold Coast in Transition* (Princeton, Princeton University Press, 1955); and the problems of terminal colonialism dominates James S. Coleman's *Nigeria: Background to Nationalism* (Berkeley, University of California Press, 1959).

3. For the details of British administration, see Donnison, *Public Administration in Burma;* J. S. Furnivall, *Colonial Policy and Practice* (New York, New York University Press, 1948, 1956), and *The Governance of Modern Burma* (New York, International Secretariat, Institute of Pacific Relations, 1958).

of a clearly defined geographical basis for authority. The traditional Burmese village headman and even the township headman or *myothugyi* were not necessarily responsible for all the people in the territory where they resided since there existed separate lines of authority according to the different service units or regiments. It is true that in the early years of British administration there was some difficulty in introducing the concept of a single line of authority in any area, but the Burmese soon managed to learn the new procedures.

British authority was generally seen as having the paradoxical character of being distant, lofty, and impersonal on the one hand and omnipresent, practical, and intensely personal on the other. These conflicting images of authority arose from the sharp contrast between the conduct of officials at the center of the administration and those in the district. The governor-general, as the direct representative of the viceroy of India, soon took on much of the pomp and grandeur of that office, which was without question more given to ceremony and splendor than most traditional roles and which was certainly the most imposing of all appointive offices known to history.[4] At the other extreme there was the Burmese equivalent of that most extraordinary of all British colonial inventions, the district officer. In Burma he was called the deputy commissioner, and supported by his senior police officer, his medical officer, and his public works officer, he embodied all the concerns of government in his district. There were no recognized limits to his interests or his involvement in his community. He was the chief administrative official, the chief magistrate, the eyes and ears of the entire government, conveying to the people the feeling that all problems could and probably should be referred to government. He was known as the "father and mother" of all in his district.

The British administration thus reinforced the traditional Burmese view that government was the center of all life, that its officials were the elite of all society, that its authority was omnipotent, and that there should be no limits to the concerns or interests of those in power.

4. The viceregal tradition was designed in part to numb the minds of Indians, to demonstrate the unqualified superiority of British power, and to put to rest any expectation that Western rule might only be concerned with the legal and rational approach to government. " 'I never tire of looking at Viceroy,' wrote Aberigh Mackay in 1880, describing the Great Ornamental. 'He is a being so heterogeneous from us! He is the centre of a world with which he has no affinity . . . He, who is the axis of India . . . is necessarily screened from all knowledge of India. He lisps no syllable of any Indian tongue; no race or caste or mode of India life is known to him . . .' " as quoted in Woodruff, *The Men Who Ruled India, 2, The Guardians*, p. 77.

British authority, like traditional Burmese authority, was seen as a hierarchy in which officials were intensely concerned with their own status and followed an esoteric logic in their decisions, characteristics that had the deceptive appearance of continuity. Although in its fundamentals the British introduced a profoundly different system, little change showed on the surface.

The significant historical fact is not that the Burmese had some difficulties adjusting to novel administrative forms but that they tended to accept the change in forms as being considerably less than revolutionary. Burmese often felt that they understood British ways, which seemed to resemble traditional ones, and later they were disturbed to discover that they did not after all comprehend fully the new order.

ASPECTS OF SOCIAL AND ECONOMIC CHANGE

Behind the appearance of a certain continuity the actions of the colonial government set the stage for tremendous changes in Burmese society. The introduction of a new system of law, new concepts of property, new ideas about the objectives of personal and social life, and new views of honor and morality all worked to weaken the bonds of the traditional order. Many of the changes were the indirect consequences of cultural contact, not the result of direct and conscious policies of government. In the process of cultural diffusion at least parts of the modern world were found acceptable, even desirable.

It would be both historically and psychologically incorrect to picture the colonial period as one of intense political hostility between a subjected people and a foreign oppressor. In a very basic sense colonial rule was accepted and an effort made to adapt to the rigors of a new order of relationships. Colonialism in Burma, as elsewhere, would never have been possible if it had rested only on force. It required some degree of voluntary recognition of the legitimacy of the new rule and of the validity of a dependent relationship. For several generations, as we shall be noting in detail, the ideals of the Burmese elite classes were heavily colored by their perceptions of the foreigner's world. Indeed, throughout most of the colonial era the British were seen as bringing to Burma not so much a new system of government as a new way of life. It was only in the later years, after change had first touched most phases of life and after the new system of government had been made more representative, that people began to see that the relationship was not primarily cultural but one of political domination.

In order to appreciate more fully the relationships between the political realm and the dynamics of change and modernization in other phases of life we must concentrate our attention in specific fields. For our purposes of understanding better the problems of nation building in transitional societies it is particularly useful to focus on three areas of change: in agricultural economics, in commercial and industrial activities, and in the development of urban life. The reasons for centering on these three fields are relatively self-evident. The peasant's life provided the basis for the traditional world, hence the peculiar significance of any changes in the field of agriculture as a result of contact with the modern world. Commercial and industrial activities are key aspects of the modern world culture which generally depend to a high degree upon the environment of the large city.

The Commercialization and Industrialization of Agriculture

History contains few more dramatic examples of the extraordinary power of economic motivations to change a society than the development of the Delta regions of Lower Burma under British rule. Under the kings, Burmese agriculture was only of a subsistence nature, and the Delta was swamplands and jungle. In a few years, particularly following the opening of the Suez Canal in 1869 and the resulting possibility of entering European markets, the Burmese countryside experienced a revolution unprecedented in Asia. The Burmese peasant became a mobile person, moving in response to economic calculations and fascinated with the possibilities of market operations. As agriculture became commercialized, the peasant abandoned subsistence farming and devoted all his efforts to raising a cash crop.

The dimensions of the change are to be seen in the figures for the acreage under rice cultivation in Lower Burma.[5] Whereas in 1830 there were only 66,000 acres in paddy,[6] by 1845 there were 354,000 acres. Thereafter the rate of expansion was about 45,000 additional acres a year until 1860, and the two decades after 1860 brought a two and a half fold increase from 1,333,000 acres to 3,102,000. By the turn of the century new lands were still being opened up at the rate of over 200,000 acres a year. World War I cut back the pace of new cultivation to only about 126,000 acres a year; by 1920 the total acreage had reached 8,588,000, and by the time of the Japanese invasion the figure was approaching 10

5. The following statistics were taken from Andrus, *Burmese Economic Life;* Maurice Zinkin, *Asia and the West* (New York, Institute of Pacific Relations, 1953); Furnivall, *An Introduction to the Political Economy of Burma.*

6. Paddy is to rice what wheat is to flour.

million. The exports of rice kept pace with this expansion until, by the 1930s, Burma was regularly exporting about three and a half million tons of milled rice a year. All this growth stayed well ahead of the rise in population: from the opening of Suez to World War II there was over a ten-fold increase in production and only a four-fold increase in population, including the immigration of a million Indians and 200,000 Chinese.

This spectacular expansion in the Burmese agricultural economy was possible partly because of the availability of new lands and a highly favorable relationship between population and cultivatable land. The decisive factors, however, were the willingness and ability of the Burmese peasant to adapt his way of life, the availability of adequate capital to finance the changes, and a government capable of providing the physical security and the psychological encouragement necessary for great adventures.

The human energy poured into the opening of the Delta lands demonstrated beyond any doubt the Burmese peasant's ability to adapt effectively to more modern conditions. Once the logic of the situation was clear to him in economic terms, he recognized with amazing spontaneity both the rational and nonrational components of the calculus of the market.[7] He quickly came to appreciate the short-run principles of supply and demand and the long-run principle that resources invested rather than immediately consumed would in time produce even more resources.

In adjusting to commercialized agriculture the Burmese peasant also showed a surprising appreciation of the function of capital, the importance of indebtedness, and the fact that only the indebted peasant could become the rich peasant. The great opening of the Delta required not only human effort but also great quantities of capital. The flow of capital into agricultural Burma is an extraordinary story which has yet to be told in its full details. The capitalization occurred through a complex set of institutions: in brief, European banks loaned capital to the Indian Chettyars, who in turn moved this capital into the hands of the agricul-

7. There was little evidence to suggest that the Burmese peasant had any peculiar characteristics which might have made him more adaptable than most peasants to change. Indeed, H. Fielding Hall who knew the Burmese peasant intimately before the opening of the Delta, advanced the opinion: "For myself, I think that the people generally would resist any change if that change applied to the land. No people are more attached to their ancestral fields than they [the Burmese] are. No one feels more the dignity of being a landowner, if it be only a hundredth part of a field from which he can never reap any benefits." *A People in School* (London, Macmillan, 1906), p. 234. And yet within a few years after these observations the Burmese were buying and selling their lands as casually and as unsentimentally as any entrepreneur exchanges his goods.

turalists; this flow was supplemented by the rice mills, which on the basis of their hedging sales on futures were able to provide further capital; finally the process was marginally assisted by more traditional sources such as local moneylenders and Chinese retail merchants. The government also assisted in financing agriculture by passing the Land Improvement Loans Act of 1883 and the Agriculture Loans Act of 1884. Through these mechanisms the Burmese countryside received the highest influx of agricultural capital that any Asian country has known except for Japan in the post-World War II period. In 1929–30 the Banking Enquiry Committee estimated that the Chettyars were advancing capital to finance agriculture to the extent of Rs 500 million or about $180 million at the rate of exchange current in 1930.[8] Before the Depression, and during the height of the expansion of new lands, the flow of capital probably reached nearly a quarter of a million dollars a year. By the time of the Japanese invasion the total advanced to agriculture in Burma exceeded all the British capital investments in shipping, mining, banking, oil production, and retail imports.

It is, of course, often hard in a rural setting to distinguish indebtedness that represents wealth and investment from indebtedness that represents poverty. Certainly some peasants were thriftless, and many loans were made to satisfy the classic needs of peasants to keep body and soul together between harvests. But there was more to the actions of the Chettyars than this; the loans represented a substantial capitalization of agriculture which had dramatically increased production. Many social costs were being paid for these developments. Some observers were distressed by the disruption of the traditional patterns of life and felt that the Burmese peasant was becoming a less social being, more materialistic, more given to crime and immoral ways. Some also felt that the peasant was being unjustly exploited by the workings of an impersonal market and by the clever, and presumably selfishly evil, manipulators of finance and credits. Although the Burmese peasant appreciated the functions of capital and indebtedness, he also preserved the traditional distrust of agriculturalists for those who deal in money and not goods. He was willing to go into debt in order to open new lands or expand his operations, but he never ceased dreaming that somehow his debts would miraculously disappear.[9]

8. Andrus, p. 75.
9. An extraordinarily complex pattern of relationships, built upon conflicting as well as complementary attitudes, brought the peasant, the Chettyar, and the government official into a three-way game situation. The peasants first of all were

The importance of capital and government policy in permitting these tremendous changes in the prewar Burmese countryside can be seen from what has happened since the Japanese occupation. Just before the war the Burmese peasant was conceivably on the brink of becoming a farmer and experiencing a significant improvement in his standard of living. The amount of land under paddy was stabilizing to an expansion rate only a little in excess of population growth, but the flow of capital into the countryside was continuing and beginning to finance a revolution in technology that would have led to increases in per-acre yields. Throughout the period of the opening of the Delta the Burmese peasant had retained the practice of working nearly twenty acres of land as an individual or family unit, and thus he was in a good position to benefit dramatically from improvements in technology. In the only country in Asia where peasants have become farmers, in postwar Japan, the average unit of operation is only two acres.

The Japanese invasion destroyed the whole structure. When the exporting of rice stopped, the peasant lost the market for his crops, and so he cut back production. When imports ceased, and he could no longer obtain his textiles, tools, implements, and other consumer items, he turned back to the life of the self-sufficient village. Consequently, land

---

ceaselessly trying to get as much from the Chettyars as possible with the least possibility of repayment, and to do this they would seek government sympathy against the Chettyars. At the same time the peasants solicited Chettyar assistance in avoiding as best as possible the payment of land revenue to government.

Government officials tended to have little understanding of the principles of capital expenditures and saw the peasant's indebtedness in highly personal terms as though it were the same as their own personal indebtedness; therefore they tended to moralize the problem and see either the Burmese peasant as thriftless or Indian Chettyars as scheming and heartless usurers.

The Chettyar was caught in dynamic situations in which he had to make hard judgments about risks, with little prospects of security, while worrying about his notes that were coming due at the bank.

On balance this complex of relationships was a remarkably efficient way of getting capital into agriculture. The sensitivity of the operations, as well as the small margins of profits, were illustrated by the fluctuations of interest rates which always showed tendencies to be responsive to changes in the European money market, the prospects of rice futures, the policies of government, and the degree of security the peasant could offer. For example, whenever the government adopted a lenient attitude towards defaulting peasants and did not rigorously support the claim of the Chettyar, the interest rates rose, and whenever the government either forced foreclosures or apprehended those who borrowed and moved on, the interest rates immediately dropped. Government never was able to decide what was the most desirable policy, and there was always considerable difference from district to district according to the personal biases of Deputy Commissioners, magistrates, and police officers.

that had been taken from the jungle reverted to jungle, and people who had moved into the complex world of a modern market economy and may have been on the verge of realizing its full potentialities, reverted to the ways of a subsistence economy.

Since the war, economic stagnation has continued. At first this could be attributed to the insecurities and disorders associated with all the various insurrections against the newly independent government, but now it is evident that deeper problems exist which probably cannot be overcome in the foreseeable future. In spite of an increase in population of nearly five million people during the last two decades, rice production is still below prewar levels, and Burma is exporting hardly half as much rice as she normally did before the war. The Burmese peasant is now tenaciously clinging to his nearly self-sufficient village economy, which resembles more and more the Burmese village under the kings than the partially modernized rural scene of the immediate prewar period. He is not prepared to change because the two features that made the prewar expansion possible no longer exist: capital is no longer available, and the government has different sympathies.

Foreign capital is no longer available to finance Burmese agricultural development; the Chettyars are gone, and European capital knows that it can be used more effectively elsewhere. The government has sought to provide rural credit through its own agricultural loans and through the State Agricultural Banks.[10] But these sources are not nearly adequate to finance growth: the total capital provided in the entire postwar period to date hardly equals the amount of a normal prewar year. By 1958 the Burmese government was only providing between 40 and 50 million kyats of credit out of the nearly 300 million kyats needed merely to maintain existing levels of rural subsistence.

The situation seems more serious when viewed in terms of the total Burmese economy. Assistance to agriculture has been a drain upon the urban sector of the economy, and thus resources have been taken from potential urban industrial development. Confronted with a situation in which both countryside and city have been desperately short of finance

10. State Agricultural Banks have been established in most districts and provide loans at 12 per cent and up to 20–25 kyats per acre. Cooperatives have provided further credits with governmental assistance, but since April 1958 most of their lending functions have been taken over by the State Agriculture Banks. The interest rates at the state banks are insufficient to cover costs; they would have to be raised to nearly 18 per cent to break even, but there is strong political pressure against this because this would mean that the bank would be charging about the same rates as the Chettyars did before the war.

capital, the government has tended to respond in the classic manner by allocating its extremely scarce resources not by the economic calculus of marginal efficiency but according to the political calculus of optimizing loyalty. Loans to the peasants have gone through political channels and have been used mainly to build up political support of particular politicians and especially the All-Burma Peasants' Organization. The political calculus has called for the acceptance of a high proportion of defaults on loans and on relaxed principles of lending.

The basic difficulty has been the fundamental attitude of government toward the commercialization of agriculture. Although Burmese officials recognize that rice is basic to the country's economy, they have little appreciation of the need for capital in agriculture. They are Westernized to the point of having an urbanized outlook on life and biases in favor of urban forms of industrial development. At the same time, they are still too close to the traditional views of the old Burmese elite; they tend to think of agriculture as the natural work of the poor man, as something that anyone can do naturally without benefit of either training or capital. At most they believe that the peasant should need financing only to help him through till the next harvest. In their view what the peasant needs is to work hard, to receive frequent moral exhortations, and to be taught where his political loyalties lie. This view, of course, does not conflict with the also traditional assumption that the peasant should provide the economic support for the entire elite culture and the world of government; thus, since the war, the difference between what the government (through the State Agriculture Marketing Board) pays the peasant for his rice and what the government obtains for that rice when sold abroad has been the prime source of government revenues.

Commercialization and Industrialization

The social changes in Burma that came as a result of commercial and industrial activities were essentially typical of those in most colonial lands. European firms assumed the leading role in developing the prime export industries (timber, oil, silver and tungsten mining, and rubber) and basic services (river transportation and electric power). The main importing firms were also European, while most of the retail trade, particularly in the rural areas, was in the hands of foreign Asians—Chinese and Indians.

The foreign firms represented enclaves in Burmese society. The larger of them were quasi-governmental in that they established very distinct forms of order within their properties. The physical domains of the foreign firms bore a striking similarity to army posts: the grounds were generally well maintained, movements were orderly and even subdued, and outsiders were carefully excluded. Burmese workers, both laborers and staff members, had to adapt to the spirit and traditions of each particular company. Status and position within the enterprises usually followed ethnic and racial lines, but all had to adapt to the basic standards and conventions of the organization. The various firms thus presented themselves to the outside world as nearly autonomous societies or communities.

Burmese employees often developed exceptional skills and performed crucial roles, but they needed the environment of the enclave to be efficient. Burmese who were able to perform as effectively as British or Indians in the atmosphere of prewar firms have now found, with the enclave setting destroyed after the war, that some of their effectiveness has been lost. Thus the Burmese have come quite generally to perceive commerce and industry as being identified with the distinctive cultures of autonomous enclaves. This view is directly related to the present situation. It explains the tendencies of postwar Burmese politicians to confuse the economic task of creating new industries with the objective of making each state enterprise a separate and autonomous enclave.

The assumption that enterprises must of necessity have a quasi-governmental quality has also apparently encouraged the practice of treating the different state enterprises and industries as fiefdoms of individual politicians. The association of enclave qualities with industrial activities has tended to make the Burmese politician think of enterprises in political power terms rather than according to economic or market considerations. This helps to explain why the Burmese politician's distrust of foreign enterprises springs from more than just his suspicion that they may be exploiting Burmese wealth. Foreign firms are seen as discrediting the government by performing more effectively within their domains the prime government functions of maintaining law and order. The desire to eliminate foreign companies is basically a desire to eliminate, if not a potential competitor, possible examples of more effectively ruled communities.

To summarize, British investments in industry, which totaled over $260 million by 1940, created organizational structures within which large numbers of Burmese drastically changed their modes of behavior but with very little permanent effect. Once the environment disappeared, the people lost the bases for their effectiveness, and therefore the early industrial enterprises failed to set the stage for subsequent expansion of economic activities. Involvement in commercial and industrial activities created fewer class problems than issues of acculturation, of loyalties, of form and propriety in personal conduct. Since for the Burmese the social rather than the economic dimensions of industries were the most conspicuous, industrial activities seemed to pose questions of social control and political relationships. Conversely, the Burmese came to expect that any organization which appeared to have the qualities of a government should be effective as an industrial enterprise.

Thus we are led to the conclusion that the early experiences of commercial and industrial activities tended to impress the Burmese more with the forms than with the rationale of such economic pursuits. Instead of accumulating experiences that would increase their capacities to organize their own enterprises, the Burmese have tended to conclude that trade and industry are quasi-governmental endeavors and hence appropriately handled according to the logic of Burmese political calculations.

Urbanization

Modern life is related to the city, and in any traditional society the attack on the old order is most intense in the large cosmopolitan cities which become vital links both in the flow of world commerce and in the diffusion of the world culture. The people who move to the new cities know that they are taking on new jobs and new habits of life; they see new possibilities. The outward flow of trade calls for concentration of people at the port city, people who are willing and able to change their status, to accept new roles, and to learn new skills.

In Burma the district towns under British rule only expanded slightly since they were largely limited, as in traditional Burma, to the population needed for the administrative functions of government and possibly for the activities of some particular local industry of significance. The phenomena of urbanization were largely centered in the growth of Rangoon. That port city, a mere village at the beginning of the British period, attracted a diversified population of Europeans and Asian immigrants; it became an "Eastern" city which reflected more the common culture of Asian ports than Burmese culture. Rangoon became not only the center of commerce and government for the whole country, it also became the center of fashion and manners, and by the 1930s urban life in Rangoon was providing for its citizens a rich array of social, cultural, and educational outlets. Before the war, however, the development toward a more plural society was checked; and since the war, although Rangoon has continued to grow in population, psychologically and sociologically the process of urbanization has slowed down, and even in some respects reversed its direction. The assumption that increase in the density of population would be enough in itself to bring about all the other developments associated with urban life has not held. The progress toward an open, plural society has given way to a pattern of growth in which Rangoon has become a large number of village communities crowded close together.

The explanation for this retardation in modern urbanization seems to lie in the manner in which certain forms of social and political controls have developed. In essence what happened was that the pace at which Rangoon was beginning to become an open society began to outstrip the pace at which the appropriate modern forms of social control could be introduced; hence there was a tendency to revert to more traditional forms of social control, which turned out to be increasingly effective because they could now be reinforced by modern professional police control methods.

Very briefly, the difficulty seems to have arisen from the fact that in the face of tremendous population changes—first the influxes of people in the immediate prewar years, then the turnover of people under the Japanese occupation, and finally, and most significant of all, the floods of refugees from the postindependence insurrections in the countryside who became colonies of squatters in Rangoon—the authorities have come to rely upon headmen in each quarter for information and assistance. Rangoon is divided into thirty-five wards, each consisting of two or more quarters, with each quarter averaging about a dozen streets. The police have found it useful to appoint a headman for each quarter and to have from one to four representatives for each street to assist the headman. The headman is expected to communicate regulations to the people and to report to the police all who move into the quarter or even spend a night in it. The headman is also called upon to vouch for individuals; in almost every dealing a citizen may have with government, from applying for a driver's license to obtaining permission to engage in certain forms of trade, it is necessary to obtain the signature of the headman.

As a result of these forms of control refugees have been kept together in what are essentially village communities, and any individual who has moved into the city has had to have some relative or friend to vouch for him. Each quarter has thus become a peculiarly intimate association, composed not only of people who know each other but also often of people originally from the same district and possibly following the same occupation. Paradoxically, therefore, even as the city has expanded it has tended to become increasingly composed of separate but highly homogeneous communities in which face-to-face relationships are all-important. The solidarity of the quarter is reinforced by several forms of associations ranging from sports clubs to one or more religious clubs or *"phongyi* feeding associations" which collect food for the monks of a particular monastery.

Three types of association in the quarter are especially important politically. First, there are the institutions peculiar to Rangoon known as reading clubs. Each quarter may have half a dozen such clubs, each with from a dozen to over a hundred members who have banded together to subscribe to one or more newspapers, magazines, and journals. Burmese generally find it more interesting to read their newspapers with an audience close at hand; the opinion leaders among them appreciate the opportunity to explain the meaning behind the almost invariably garbled versions of the news conveyed by the casual Burmese press, while the uninformed derive satisfaction from being able to put their questions immediately to their intellectual betters. Needless to say, the headmen and the other politically active citizens of a quarter generally take a very serious view of the political orientation of the journals and newspapers to which each club subscribes. The result is a degree of uniformity of views in each quarter which would be remarkable only if it were assumed that individuals made autonomous decisions.

Second, there are the consumer cooperative societies. These grew out of the arrangements established by the British Military Administration immediately after the war to distribute essential relief items, mainly milk, sugar, and other imported foods and necessary consumer goods. This distributing system remained intact after independence and became the Civil Supply Board. Within the quarter, as within the rural districts, the stores themselves have been politically significant. The managers of the stores tend to be political appointees, and they have generally taken a keen interest in maintaining unambiguous political loyalties and sentiments among their customers; those who prove to be the most conspicuously loyal usually receive credit and a choice of scarce items.

The third type of organization which has tended to give a village-like quality to the quarter has been the political parties and their affiliated groups. During the period immediately after independence when the cities were dominated by the single nationalist party, the Anti-Fascist People's Freedom League (AFPFL), the party politicians were usually either the headmen of quarters or their immediate associates. The quarter was thus, in an odd way, more directly linked to the national scene than to the city administration, and it was also brought under the domination of both police and party controls. After the AFPFL split in 1958 each quarter, like each rural village, was generally taken into one faction or the other by its leadership, and its politically monolithic qualities were preserved. Within each quarter the street representatives kept careful track of how well each family was meeting its quota of political participation by attending rallies, parades, and other "spontaneous" demonstrations.

Thus the pressures for conformity in the quarter have been quite as strong as those in the traditional village. Although the possibilities of exposure to new and conflicting ideas are clearly greater in the city, the techniques of control within the quarter are also greater. Consequently, many of the dynamic qualities generally associated with the urbanization process seem to be effectively countered by political practices.

In this chapter we have noted some paradoxical relationships between the rates of social and economic change and political development. During the colonial period, although they were experiencing profound social and economic changes, to a deceptive extent Burmese could believe that there had been few fundamental changes in the nature of government. It still seemed to be dominated by a distant elite with its own culture and its own logic about what was reasonable in human affairs. As the pace of social and economic change accelerated, however, restraints began to build up mainly in the realm of politics. Significant and even rapid initial changes which tended to bring Burma more in line with the modern world have all been countered by the dynamics of the transitional political process.

An examination of other areas of social change would have revealed much the same pattern. For example, Rangoon University began as an institution devoted to the highest standards of modern education, and yet increasingly over the years, particularly as the university graduates have come to play more important social and political roles, the university has found itself nearly defenseless against political pressures. As university life has become increasingly politicized, the university has been less and less capable of producing people with modern skills and knowledge, and as the quality of graduates declines, the pace of effective modernization is likely also to decline.

In every instance the impetus for change initially came from the political realm, but ultimately the single most important factor contributing to economic and social stagnation in postwar Burma has been the attitudes and practices that govern Burmese political behavior. This has not been a simple equilibrium situation in which a system responds to the threat of change by always seeking to maintain its basic characteristics. The old system was too completely destroyed for there to be any pull in that direction.

In seeking to explain the primacy and indeed the sovereignty of politics in the modernization process it would be also incorrect to equate agricultural, commercial, and urban growth with colonial rule and stagnation in this field with Burmese rule. This would be to praise colonialism falsely and to criticize the postwar Burmese politicians unjustly; such a one-sided view of the process of diffusion of the world culture would be quite untenable.

The basic point is that government can be a relatively easy enterprise as long as traditional forms of social order give a society coherence, but once the process of social change has gone far enough to disrupt the old order, the task of creating a new one becomes increasingly difficult. Hence the problems of contemporary politicians are hardly comparable to those of either the colonial rulers or traditional Burmese officials. This is the case above all because the diffusion of modern culture affects the capacity of people to associate with each other in effective organizational efforts, and because politics and government are, of all the areas of social life, the most sensitive to problems of association and collective behavior.

The changes in all phases of Burmese life which affect the potentialities for association are felt most keenly and in greatly magnified forms in the domain of power relationships, that is, in the domain of politics and government. The conspicuous problems of government are only symptoms of the general difficulties found throughout all aspects of social life, but, in a sense, these symptoms are so dramatic that they become contributing factors to further problems of social organization. Hence both the sovereignty of politics in the developmental process and the vicious circle leading to stagnation.

When those involved in the political relationships in a society understand themselves and each other, they are capable of encouraging, directing, or even merely tolerating a wide range of change in the other spheres of social life. When those involved in political relationships are unsure of themselves and are searching desperately for their own as well as their society's sense of identity, then they are likely to use their powers to inhibit further changes. In a sense, all significant social life must await the search for political identity. This search must center in the dynamics of political development to which we must now turn.

CHAPTER 7

New Structures and the Clash
of New Political Roles

Political structures are not rigid, static forms but dynamic processes involving the complex interrelationships of people performing complementary as well as conflicting tasks. The problem fundamental to all
transitional societies is the creation of new structures of authority. New
kinds of activities and skills, new outlooks and standards of conduct, and
new expectations about the behavior of others all have to be fitted together
to give form and substance to new institutions.

The evolution of traditional societies toward constitutional government
and democratic practices requires a host of radical changes in the actions
of those involved in government and politics. It is convenient to sum up
all these necessary changes by speaking of the need to create both men
who can perform as modern administrators and men who can serve as
popular politicians. The creation of the administrator's role means in
essence the development of civil services and bureaucratic structures. The
politician's role, on the other hand, is more related to the dynamic processes of mobilizing power and opinion, of articulating and aggregating
interests, and of fulfilling the affective, and basically emotional, dimensions of politics. In a transitional society the politicians must above all
struggle with the problem of giving expression to the identity of an entire
people. They thus have to grapple with the subtle and paradoxical tasks
of finding common interests while respecting particular interests, of creating the myths of a society while being held accountable for the realities
of policy.

All political systems generate tension between the ethos of those who
administer public programs and the ethos of those who deal in choices

97

and values. In transitional societies that tension tends to be peculiarly acute and a chief cause of disillusionment with democratic institutions. This conflict has certainly been the key issue shaping modern Burmese politics. Yet the process of nation building depends to a crucial degree upon bringing stability and trust to that most central political relationship for a democratic society.

In large measure the peculiar intensity of the clash between administrator and politician in transitional societies follows directly from the fact that the two roles have usually been introduced at different times, under different circumstances, and with little regard for their relevance to each other. For reasons basic to the process of modernization the role of the administrator has usually appeared before that of the politician, generally during a colonial period when there was no legitimate open and competitive political process. More often than not, the politician's role has taken its definite shape in the revolutionary atmosphere of nationalist movements, which for much of Southeast Asia meant during the disruptive years of war and Japanese occupation. Each role thus was developed in isolation, and neither was shaped by a continuous process of confrontation and interaction with the other.

Administrators and politicians developed in a setting in which each group could realistically conceive of itself as appropriately and rightfully holding a monopoly over the realms of significant and modernized politics. Out of the colonial experience administrators came to see themselves operating the full machinery of state and to regard politicians as emotional, corrupt, irresponsible disrupters of the orderly processes of government. The politicians, on the other hand, were able to consider themselves more than adequate for handling all aspects of government, and they felt little need for, but great uneasiness about, the skills of administrators.

So basic has this conflict been to the evolution of Burmese power patterns that it readily becomes the organizing theme for our discussion of the problems of political change. In surveying the Burmese experience in political development, we shall therefore focus on the introduction of these two roles and on the basis for the struggle between them.

THE INTRODUCTION OF THE ADMINISTRATOR'S ROLE

Politically, the dominant characteristic of the diffusion of the world culture has been the greater ease and effectiveness in transferring the authoritative or formal institutions of government as compared with the institutions for representing, articulating, and aggregating interests. The fact that civil bureaucracies and armies have had longer histories than political parties and interest groups in all transitional societies is probably of less significance than the fact that, with the same amount of effort, it has been easier to create modern authoritative structures. In large measure this has been true because there has been no concealing the need to change, quite explicitly and with concerted direction, the habits of mind and behavior of all who are recruited to authoritative services. There are considerable ambiguities about how natural and unaffected people should be in performing as party politicians and organizers, but there is nothing spontaneous, natural, or untutored about membership in civil service and military establishments. Members of the authoritative services are under no illusions about being trained and changed. Hence they are likely to see themselves as being in closer touch with the modern world than popular politicians, and they are likely to be instilled with the notion that they are being of service to their society, that they are helping to build a nation.

These, in general outline, are some of the considerations that seem to underlie the paradoxical set of attitudes common to the Burmese administrative class, as well as to administrators in most other transitional societies. They see themselves as being vested with a fundamental responsibility for the well-being of all the people of their country, while also sensing themselves to be different and distant from the common people. The typical Burmese administrator's attitude can be traced to the spirit of the early British colonial service, which tended to emphasize precisely these two qualities of a concern for social welfare and a coldly impersonal approach to the common people.

The image of a government with limitless concerns, which was first reflected in the pretensions of omnipotence of the governor and the endless activities of the deputy commissioner, became in time increasingly related to British colonial involvement with welfare measures. Indeed, an odd aspect of colonialism was the extent to which the majesty of a foreign authority became bent in the direction of initiating and supporting welfare functions which were generally not only far in advance of the economy of the colony but also, on occasion, more advanced than those of the mother country. As J. S. Furnival observed near the end of the British period, "Care for native welfare is nothing new; it dates from the earliest days of British rule and there have been repeated endeavors to bring the machinery of welfare up to date." [1] For example, in the field of medicine and

1. Foreword to Andrus, *Burmese Economic Life,* pp. viii–ix.

public health, the Rangoon General Hospital provided free services to the citizens of the capital, and civil surgeons and government dispensaries functioned in all the districts.

Among the many reasons for this emphasis upon welfare, two closely related ones were of special importance in shaping the attitudes which became basic to Burmese administrators. First, the British officials became very quickly a distinct class of men with extremely strong feelings for their profession, which they saw in terms of the rationalistic standards of public administration. The colonial society, in which they were never challenged by the conflicting demands and emotional pressures of an open political process, offered a unique opportunity for pure administration, for rational and efficient government. British officials were able to convince themselves that good government was essentially an administrative phenomenon in which routine service functions were the ultimate test, that in the good society, specialists and technicians could apply their skills without being harassed by the irrational acts of popular politicians. In short, they saw themselves as administrators who should properly be judged according to the skill with which they provided services for the community. Second, the British attached high importance to the welfare functions of government precisely because they felt politically isolated from the people. They felt that the only way they could reduce Burmese hostility and make their rule more acceptable was to ensure that the Burmese were better off than before. Lacking any sense of common identity, there was no purely political way of reducing the psychological gap between ruler and ruled. Since the only justification for British rule was good government, the Burmese people were looked upon more as clients than as citizens.[2]

The British emphasis upon welfare was not, however, matched by a warm or humane approach to government. British rule was extraordinarily impersonal, partly because it represented the novel concept of a rule of laws and not men, but above all because it took place in a political vacuum, for it was unresponsive to an open and acknowledged political process. G. E. Harvey, the historian and former official, has observed:

> What we gave Burma was not a government but an administration. Political direction, so far as there was any, came from the Indian government, with the British parliament in the background. It was a curiously impersonal system. As in other tropical dependencies,

2. For an interesting introductory analysis of how the cult of efficiency became a part of the British colonial tradition, see Eric Stokes, *The English Utilitarians and India* (London, Oxford University Press, 1959).

officers retired at 55, they were always liable to transfer (often just as they were beginning to know their charge), and they rose to power, if at all, only when they were within a few years of leaving the country forever. And the people they ruled were inarticulate. Thus the forces at work on both sides, Burmese as well as English, were impersonal.[3]

The paradoxical combination of impersonal administration and widespread welfare functions appears to have facilitated the creation of the distinct subculture of the Burmese administrator class and to have encouraged the Burmese public to develop somewhat cynical feelings about the nature and functions of government. As Burmese administrators began to learn the ways and the attitudes of their British superiors, they found that the process of becoming removed, if not alienated, from their own people and their old culture was made easier by the moral reassurance that they were doing the right thing for the welfare of their people. To be distant from the people was both morally and intellectually justifiable for men who were sure they were serving their country. The Burmese public, on the other hand, came to see government as supposedly providing them with services, but at the same time they felt no need to identify with government. The result was that while they expected much of government, they sympathized little with its problems, a basically critical view of government that has persisted to this day.

Building the Community of Administrators

The distinctive class of Burmese administrators began to take form very early in the British period. Within a decade after the Second Anglo-Burmese War the British succeeded in establishing the tradition that township officers (*myo-ok*) were salaried officials who could expect to be periodically transferred to any district in the country.[4] These men were the entering wedge of what in time became a sizable community of Burmese officials who developed a strong sense of profession and were among the most modernized elements in the entire society.

Later the British divided their administrative services into three main classes. Class I was the elite level of the Indian Civil Service (ICS). Its members set the tone of administrative life and commanded the key posts. They totaled only between 120 and 130 men, of whom approximately a third were Indians and the rest predominantly Europeans. Al-

---

3. *British Rule in Burma*, p. 30.
4. Donnison, *Public Administration in Burma*, pp. 23–24.

though technically a part of the Indian service and thus liable to assignment anywhere within the Indian Empire, in practice most of those who began their career in Burma could expect to remain there.

The Provincial Civil Service (Class II) was popularly known as the Burma service and was predominantly Burmese and Eurasian, most of its personnel being locally recruited. It was disturbing to some Burmese to think of the superior service as being Indian and the inferior service as Burmese. On the other hand, the members of the Provincial Civil Service felt that they belonged to the same general class of government official, and in their daily operations they all performed much the same kinds of operations as the members of the ICS.

The Subordinate Civil Service (Class III) supplied the clerks for the entire government. Before the end of the nineteenth century local schools were providing practically all the members of this service. Its character was determined by the peculiar institution of the branch, the basic unit of all administration in Burma. The practice of organizing the clerical staff into cell units of four or five men began with the British East India Company in Bengal, and to this day the atom or cell unit of the Burmese administration is not the individual but the branch; departments expand or contract in terms of number of branches. Each branch now consists of four men: a superintendent who directs and disciplines the group, the assistant who does much of the drafting, an upper division clerk who also drafts reports and communications, and a lower division clerk who does the filing and the most routine functions. The position of the individual in the branch is usually determined by the grading he received at the time he was first admitted to the service, and in most cases the individual stays in the same branch throughout his entire career. The same men must thus work together over the years; and, needless to say, personal relations become extremely critical as each gets to know the other's strength and weakness, and all tend to store up memories of slights, injustices, and all the other forms of irritants to harmonious relations.

The pressures for Burmanization of the higher civil services increased in direct proportion to the increase in the number of Burmese with university degrees. There were about 400 graduates in the country when, largely in order to train civil officials, the University of Rangoon was established shortly after World War I. Within a few years of its establishment, the University was graduating about 200 students a year, and competition for government service steadily increased, with only the best candidates being accepted.

The administrator class included not only civil servants and bureau-

THE CLASH OF NEW POLITICAL ROLES

crats but also those connected to the courts, the judiciary, and the legal profession, those involved in the educational and medical services of government, and those who held positions in the railway administration and the harbor authority. In short, it included all those who held offices dependent upon the government and the particular pattern of British rule.

They could think of themselves as belonging to the ranks of the *min-myo* or the society of officialdom. Their status depended upon the view that government was and should be the center of all society, a view which they naturally encouraged and which most Burmese readily accepted. As a distinct social class, they had their own way of life and even to some extent their own language, for they were the most Westernized and acculturated people in the country and they all had some command of English.[5] A significant proportion of the administrative class had traveled abroad, either to India or England, where many had passed through the training colleges.[6]

The members of the administrative class came from the better families as defined by the traditional social order. They were thus accustomed to an elite role, and they combined traditional concepts of leadership with a command of new skills. Their sons received the best education; they had considerable pride in their standards of English usage; they were on personal terms with important officials; they had been posted to many districts and knew much of their country; they could talk knowingly of short and long leaves, of pension and of retirement. They lived in a world of widespread personal ties and associations; wherever they traveled in the land they could find acquaintances and other people who were just like themselves.

The Structure of Administrative Politics

It has been customary to picture societies under colonial rule as having been politically dormant for a long time and then suddenly awakening when the silent effects of gradual social change dramatically came together to strike a spark over some handy political issue. Thus it has generally been assumed that before the 1920s the Burmese were largely apathetic to government and that the pace of change quickened only after World War I. This conventional view has been well summarized by the historian Harvey:

5. By the early 1930s nearly 2 per cent of all Burmese males were literate in English. "These were concentrated chiefly in the larger towns, but thousands of villages have one or two persons each with a smattering of English." Andrus, p. 37.
6. Donnison, p. 61.

It was only after the First World War that the predominance of foreign capital showed signs of becoming a political issue. Until then
the Burman was content to jog along in his village, seeing little and
caring less; even if he had wanted to get about, there were hardly any
roads. But after 1918 roads developed, and country buses too. And
now there was a parliament; its sessions brought the representatives
of every district to Rangoon the capital, the one modern city in
Burma, the port where all the wealth of the country was concentrated. And there, as they went through the streets, they discovered
that only a third of the citizens were Burmese, that the houses of
the merchant princes were almost exclusively English, Indian, or
Chinese. The effect on the mind of a generation which had forgotten
the seamy side of native rule can be imagined, especially as they
were just beginning to read the literature of the Left, in a crude form,
at third or fourth hand.[7]

It is true that before the 1920s there was no open and manifest political
process in Burma. However, that does not mean that Burmese society
lacked all ways of influencing governmental decisions or that its people
were uninterested in the interplay of power and values and did not seek
to get what they wanted. The process by which an administrative class
was created also set the stage for a latent but extraordinarily intense form
of politics which revolved around personal relationships of officials and
the informal associations between official and citizen. It was inconspicuous, undramatic, and highly privatized—but politics nevertheless. We
may call this a form of administrative politics to contrast it with the later
period of popular or agitational politics.

Under the pattern of benevolent administrative rule there were no possibilities for people to organize and articulate their demands so as to
change specific rules or laws. Lawmaking, in a formal sense, was reserved
by the colonial authority.[8] Although the citizens might expect the laws to
be more explicit, more constant, and more predictable than under the
traditional authority of the kings, the source of lawmaking was just as far
removed as ever. Relations of citizens with the government tended to

7. Harvey, *British Rule in Burma*, p. 66.
8. Even from the beginning of British rule, the governor was assisted by a form
of council that in time developed into a legislative body which was the origin of
the present Burmese parliament. It was only in the later stages of the British period
that the machinery existed for openly communicating popular demands to government. The best detailed account of the evolution of these institutions is Cady, *A
History of Modern Burma*.

congregate at the level where specific policies were being applied. This simple fact of structure, which determined the point of access of the citizen to the realm of government, determined the entire pattern of political behavior. It also encouraged many practices that still color Burmese political behavior.

We have already suggested that when access to government is primarily at the law enforcement or application level rather than at the formal legislative level the consequence is a latent rather than a manifest form of politics. Burma, during the era of administrative politics, provides strong evidence in support of our hypothesis. Burmese with problems tended to proceed in unobtrusive and informal ways, insisting that their interests were minor exceptions which were only of a highly particularistic nature. No private citizen would presume to argue according to a universalistic ethic that might cast doubts on the wisdom and justice of the supreme and unapproachable lawgivers. Wisdom seemed to lie in not giving formal or conspicuous organizational form to any interests within the community.

Although this spirit discouraged the development of an open and manifest political process, it did stimulate numerous practices and attitudes which survived the rise of popular politics. Three of these have been especially significant in forming the contemporary Burmese political culture and in creating problems for nation building.

First, the era of administrative politics produced among the general population a widespread fascination with the workings of the formal law, and among the administrative class a deep anxiety over legal forms and formulas. In part, this development was merely a reflection of the rise of a lawyer class as the country's new elite, for modernization meant a Western education, which in turn usually meant, in its highest form, training in the law.[9] To a remarkable extent, urban and educated Burmese came to take an intense interest in the decisions of courts and the reasoning of judges. Even before World War I many Burmese were knowledgeable about the idiosyncrasies of each personality in the high court, and they could discuss endlessly among themselves the wit and wisdom of each justice. There emerged a class of politically conscious Burmese who perceived the modern world of government as being on the one hand remarkably stable, even static, since it was defined by a given framework of law, and yet on the other hand as offering considerable opportunities for unexpected and uncertain turns of events since so much seemed to hinge

9. The feelings of the Westernized Burmese toward legal training are well documented in the autobiography of the former Burmese president; see U Ba U, *My Burma.*

on the personalities of colorful English judges. The result was a somewhat sporting attitude toward government: the general rules were firm and stable, but the outcome of any encounter was pleasantly uncertain.[10]

In seeking to impress upon the Burmese the impersonal nature of justice and the firmness and predictability of an independent legal system, the British constantly stressed the majesty of the law. Consequently, in Burmese eyes form became quite as important as content and spirit. Indeed, the realization that any error in procedure could change the entire outcome of a case contributed to a feeling that the potency of the law must lie in the rituals associated with its every manifestation; hence deference for law eventually became a powerful inhibition against novel and unprecedented measures.

The concern with legalistic forms appears to have been a reflection of a deeper anxiety over the very nature of an explicitly defined legal system. The British system, with its stress on the mysterious potency of the *sa-ok-gyi*, or "Big Book," seems to have tapped all the anxieties a semiliterate people can have for the concepts relating to "The Word," "The Sign," "The Letter," "The Book," "The Message." The Law was distant but demanding, different yet majestic, subtle but explicit, manipulatable but unchanging, frightening but just.

Both the administrative class and the general public sought restlessly to come to terms with the Law by seeking some humanizing relationship with it. The Law could become unbearably dangerous if it were allowed to become too impersonal, too firm, too soulless, too "un-Burmese." Yet there was always the equal danger that a changeable Law might be exploited by others to do great harm to the self. Better to keep the Law equally unpredictable for all, pull its teeth, leave it impotently benign. But this was still an unhappy solution, especially for the members of the administrative class, for the Burmese elite possessed a powerful sense of the explosive and unimaginable dangers that may be set loose in a society if people are left unrestrained and uncontrolled. A latent fear of anarchy and a suspicion that all people must be controlled against dangerous and aggressive impulses are basic elements in Burmese political thought. These ambivalences toward the very concept of law seem to have encouraged in the Burmese political class an oddly inverted set of responses: to this day their reaction to crises has been to search for the rigid security of legalistic forms while in more normal times they have tried to per-

10. It was a well-established practice for firms and even individuals to set aside sums of money each year so as to "play the courts." They would hire lawyers to explore possibilities for profitable law suits.

sonalize and "Burmanize" the law and hence corrupt its ability to give predictability to human relations.

A second lasting consequence of the era of administrative politics was the tendency of the Burmese to associate politics and influence with career considerations. Members of the administrative class came to see power and influence as measured largely in terms of career advancement, and citizens learned that those with power and influence were highly sensitive to such personal calculations. The hierarchical structure of politics, which in the traditional system revolved around status and personal loyalties, now took on an added dimension involving prospects of promotion. In their relations with each other officials soon learned how to apply wisdom and discretion to advance themselves, and such wisdom and discretion was assumed to be the essence of political skill. More significantly, the operations of administrative politics, in contrast to the traditional process, made officials aware that their relations with civilians could have decisive consequences for their own careers. The officials were forced to recognize that, even though they were still in the eyes of all the people far more important than mere citizens, prudence called for them to treat the citizen with greater care. For the private citizen could now find ways to retaliate and damage the career prospects of the official. It was in the light of such threatening possibilities that the Burmese official first came to see the citizen as a source of power.

The positive aspect of this step in bridging the gap between officialdom and population was more than balanced by the negative consequences of greatly expanding the number of people wrapped up in a politics of petty scheming and rascality. For the tendency to relate politics to career considerations was also a step in the direction of making politics into an intensely personal and essentially crafty activity.[11]

A third enduring consequence of the system of administrative politics was the prevalence of both the practice and the criticism of corruption. The British system of law and order eliminated a host of abuses common to the traditional system, but it did not eliminate corruption in the dealings between officials and citizens. On the contrary, the concern with legal forms and the connection between politics and career interests may have encouraged an increase in corruption, not only in the civil service but also in the lower courts.[12]

11. This dimension of the era of administrative politics has been recorded with great honesty in George Orwell's novel *Burmese Days* (New York, Harcourt Brace, 1930).

12. *Report of the Bribery and Corruption Committee* (Rangoon, Government Press, 1941).

Many of the forms of corruption became so institutionalized that the administrative system became functionally dependent upon them, but they were never openly acknowledged. Thus the ideals of the system bore little relation to reality, and almost from the beginning the introduction of modern forms of government was associated with a need to adopt hypocritical positions. The Burmese learned that in a modern system it was inappropriate and indeed impossible to discuss the realities of politics. The gap between public attitudes and private practices, firmly established during the colonial period, only took on a different form in the postindependence period when democratic claims were used to cloak the realities of one-party rule and authoritarian practices. The problem of widespread petty administrative corruption also left a heritage of anxiety about Burmese capabilities to operate a modern and democratic system of government. To this day, Burmese leaders give periodic utterance to their fears that their entire system of government will collapse from the evil effects of corruption.

INTRODUCTION OF THE POLITICIAN'S ROLE

Faith in the potentialities of spontaneity, which we observed to be so basic to the Western liberal view of the process of nation building, takes its highest form in the Western conception that politicians are born, not trained or educated. We have tended to assume that out of the efforts to establish modern nation-states and modern political processes there will somehow miraculously emerge politicians displaying all the skills and performing all the subtle functions essential to that role in a representative system. Therefore, wherever modernization has been encouraged under the auspices of Westerners, all the emphasis has been on training administrators and soldiers, while the training of politicians has been left to chance.[13]

A dominant theme in the story of the introduction of the popular poli-

---

The problem of corruption is also well analyzed by Harvey, *British Rule in Burma,* pp. 34–38, 80–90.

13. It is important to observe that this has been the case not only with colonial rule but also with American foreign aid. To the extent that American aid has been directed to political development it has been focused almost entirely upon strengthening the role of the administrator and ignoring that of the politician. In this sense American aid places us in the tradition of the colonial rulers. In contrast, the Communists have concentrated more on building up the politician's role. For this comparison see my "Communist Strategies and Asian Societies," *World Politics, 11* (October 1958), 118–27.

tician's role into transitional societies is the extent to which the emerging politicians have developed ambivalences about their own positions that mirror Western feelings about the democratic politician. Given the attitude of leaving to chance the development of the actors most essential to the effective operation of a democratic system, it is not surprising that the record of introducing the politician's role into transitional societies is one largely of disappointments and disastrous consequences.

Politicians without Organizations during the Era of Administrative Politics

Although in Burma, as in all colonial countries, the brunt of the Western impact occurred in the administrative realm, the British did try to introduce formal machinery for legislative decision making. Each decade of British administration saw significant steps in Burma's constitutional development.

The Legislative Council was established in 1897 when, ten years after the annexation, the country was elevated from a mere chief commissionership under the governor-general of Bengal to a lieutenant governorship, With the Government of India Act of 1909, the Legislative Council had its first elected member, but he represented only the British commercial and retail communities; until the Government of India Act of 1917, which was not put into effect in Burma until 1923, the council remained essentially an advisory board for the governor. When the British finally induced the Burmese in 1923 to accept dyarchy—a system effectively employed in Indian constitutional development whereby some ministries became the responsibilities of the elected members of the Legislative Council while others were retained under the direct control of the governor— the Legislative Council was expanded to include 77 popularly elected members out of a total of 103. In 1937, when the country was separated from India and given the forms of a national government, a bicameral legislature was established, consisting of a Senate elected by the lower house and a House of Representatives of 132 members, of whom 91 were from general constituencies and the rest from communal, labor, commercial, university, and other special constituencies.

The introduction of the machinery for representative legislation led to considerable uncertainty over the sources of governmental responsibilities. Both British officials and Burmese members of the administrative class agreed that the new Burmese politicians displayed little skill or competence in utilizing their opportunities for influence, and that they actually set back the evolution of modern government.[14] A former president of the Union of Burma reflected:

> It was a great blot on the Administration's record that it did practically nothing in the way of social welfare work. As the Government was by then in a sense fully representative, it was the duty of our political leaders to see to the improvement of our peasants' lot and to provide for the care and training of waifs and strays. I regret to say that they did nothing and took no interest whatsoever.[15]

The Burmese politicians, on the other hand, denied that they were responsible for government and in fact insisted that until independence was realized they should not be judged by any standards of responsibility. But their protestations were not convincing, and the Burmese still tend to look back upon them as a group of self-seekers, deserving of little respect.

How was it that from the very beginning the Burmese politician was seen in a negative light? In essence, the difficulty arose from the fact that he was caught up in a world which was made by others and in which he seemed to cut an awkward figure. The Legislative Council was designed by administrators to serve the purpose of administrative order. Although the subsequent House of Representatives was a true deliberative body, the standards of performance, the criteria of personal competence, and the expectations of excellence were all defined by those who belonged to the legalistic tradition. The aspiring Burmese politician found himself criticized not only by British officials but also by his fellow countrymen who were at home in a setting that emphasized legal procedure and form. Often he did not know what was proper and correct, and, worst of all, he knew that others knew his failings.

Consequently, the first Burmese politicians tended to favor the extremes. They either sought to become indistinguishable from those trained in the law and the administrative tradition and thus tended to become agents of the civil service, or they sought to strike back by challenging and even denying all the adminstrative tradition represented. Placed in the uncomfortable situation of having to choose between being servile to and controlled by the administrative system or appearing bent on annihilating it, they sought to escape their dilemma by ignoring the rest of the world and concentrating on their relations with each other. Thus originated the

---

14. For a good example of the spirit in which the British officials observed the emergence of a Burmese political class, see Harvey, *British Rule in Burma*, pp. 87–95.
15. U Ba U, p. 139.

tendency of Burmese politicians to look inward to realms of intra-elite relationships, a tendency which remains a cardinal element of the Burmese political scene.

The crucial vulnerability of the Burmese politicians in their first confrontations with the modernized administrative system was their lack of any firm foundations or binding commitments within the society. Through the arbitrary acts of a colonial regime they were suddenly placed in the center of power as ministers in charge of government departments before they had had to create a popular basis of power in the society. Thus, since they could aspire to high office and serve as prime ministers without paying the cost of organizing popular parties, they appeared to be free agents whose actions could be guided by their own personal preferences. They could hardly plead that their freedom of action was constrained by party considerations or commitments to constituents, for they appeared to be untouched by the conflicting social and economic forces which in democratic societies are recognized as inhibiting and compromising the actions of politicians. Naturally, since they acted as individuals, it seemed fair that they should be criticized and held accountable as individuals for their public actions.[16]

The Burmese politicians could, however, advance one argument to make the case that they were not free agents and hence not fully responsible for their actions: they could deny the entire legislative system and proclaim it unworkable until the country was sovereign. They could aver that until complete independence was achieved they could not be expected to meet any test of responsibility. The result was a curious blending of unselfish appeals for independence with intensely personal and petty struggles to make or break governments. Thus the second contribution of the early politicians to modern Burmese politics was the practice of articulating idealistic positions presumably unrelated to the quest for personal power. As the resulting gap between public discourse and private calculations steadily increased, the Burmese public came to see their democratic politicians as men without programs for gaining their announced objectives, without policies for the machinery of state, but with

16. In fairness to the early Burmese politicians it should be noted that their British and Burmese critics were making unrealistic demands of them. They were, in fact, never quite the free agents they appeared to be, for they were dependent upon sponsors. For example, one of the reasons why the Burmese politicians felt it necessary to adopt the strange position of opposing the British proposal in 1937 to separate Burma from India and develop it as a potential separate nation was the fact that Indian financial interests were a prime source of support for the activities of Burmese politicians.

inordinate skills in parliamentary maneuvering and personal calculations. In the five years from the time Burma was separated from India
to the arrival of the Japanese, the country had four ministries. From
1937 to 1939 Dr. Ba Maw and his Sinyetha party, with only sixteen members in the House, were able to establish and hold together a government
that depended mainly upon the support of Indians, Karens, Arakanese,
and Europeans. The next two governments, of U Pu (1939–41) and U
Saw (1941–42), were monuments to personal ingenuity and to the irrelevance of public policy in the creation of cabinets. The ministry of Sir
Paw Tun represented a last-minute return to administrative rule just as
the Japanese conquest was about to begin.

Political Agitators and the Rise of Popular Politics

The development of an effective form of articulate and popular politics
in Burma occurred largely independently of British efforts to introduce
the role of the responsible politician. The early Burmese politicians very
soon found that their main competitors as spokesmen for the Burmese
people were a group of modern intellectuals who belonged on the fringe
of the administrative class. These men were concerned with what should
be the character of a modern Burmese society. Interestingly, many of
them were led to a concern with Burmese traditions by the heavy emphasis their British acquaintances placed upon the importance of British traditions in modern Britain. They conceived of modern European society as
being the logical product of traditional Europe. Thus in an odd fashion
they were led to believe that to become modern one first had to stress one's
traditions and that there were elements of their heritage which should be
preserved but would soon be lost if each generation of Burmese continued
the pace of modernizing. In other words, they were at heart transitional
people; they wished to see changes in Burmese life, but only those which
were not inconsistent with the old Burmese traditions.

In their search for tradition, and for other reasons relating to the fact
that they had not yet broken decisively from the world of custom, they
turned to religion as a basis for viewing their society. As in most of the
other Southeast Asian countries, the first Burmese explorations in social
ideology took the form of religious discussion groups. The tendencies of
a people still close to tradition to delve into questions of religion were reinforced by the obvious prudence of staying on the right side of the colonial authorities by adopting an apparently nonpolitical approach to social
thought and criticism.

More specifically, these developments took the form of the establishment in 1908 of the Young Men's Buddhist Association (YMBA), which its leaders expected would be essentially the same type of movement as its model, the YMCA. The YMBA, however, soon developed into a debating club in which status, prestige, and honor were closely related to forensic skills and command of English. In spite of its name, it also became a vehicle for producing secular leaders. By the end of World War I the YMBA had dropped its rigid bars against outright political discussions. But once this change had been made, it did not survive long as a political force. It was supplanted in 1921 by the General Council of Burmese Associations (GCBA), but even this larger and more diffuse organization failed to endure more than a few years, and by 1925 had become fragmented into a host of splinter groups.

The difficulties the YMBA and the GCBA experienced as political movements touch the very heart of the problem of modernizing transitional societies. Almost invariably in such situations, the pattern seems to be that as discussion moves from generalities toward specific strategies for modernizing and developing the nation, those involved begin to recognize the inescapable fact that change does not affect all in the same fashion, and that with any policy some will gain while others lose. When the initial group of modernizers is small, the prospects of division and fragmentation increase as the issues become more concrete. On the other hand, unless the issues do become concrete there can be no hope of significant progress.

In the early years of the YMBA people with quite varying degrees of acculturation to modern life could participate with enthusiasm in the general and diffuse deliberations of the association. Once the question of action became linked to ideological discussion, sharp disagreements emerged, for some found that they preferred to adhere to British policies for modernizing—particularly since these meant maintaining and expanding their own positions within the administrative system of rule—while others felt that their interest would best be served by opposing every measure of the British and demanding a completely different pattern of political develoment. In 1920 the YMBA broke up over the issue of participation in the elections for the Legislative Council. One group, speaking for the tradition of the civil service, argued against participation because their continued membership in the association would be compromised once the YMBA lost its nonpolitical quality; a second faction pressed to exploit the opportunity offered by the British, arguing that it would be appropriate for the organization to contest the elections; and a third group opposed participation in the hope of sabotaging the British experiment and forcing the government to even greater concessions. All who opposed participation sensed the danger that elections and change would disrupt and weaken the comfortable atmosphere of unity which had previously characterized the modernizing elite. Although calling for more extreme changes, they were in fact hesitant to accept any significant change.

Much the same problems and arguments beset the GCBA in 1921 when the issue of participation in District Council elections irrevocably split that body. The Party of 21 was formed of those who favored participation in any kind of election, and the remainder of the GCBA became known as the Hlaing-Pu-Gyaw Party after its three leaders, U Chit Hlaing, U Pu, and U Tun Aung Gyaw. Further splits left it consisting of little more than the personal followings of individual personages who, in varying degrees, fell increasingly under the influence of the Buddhist monks or *pongyis*. The general pattern was one in which the modernizers first fell out among themselves whenever they were confronted with demanding choices of policy, and then tended to seek support from among the more traditional elements, which in time gained the ascendancy.

The early efforts of the YMBA and GCBA to organize popular political movements contributed some remarkably lasting traditions to subsequent Burmese politics.

First, they encouraged a strong interest in discussion of ideological matters. The search for a new world view was recognized as essential for Burmese political growth. Even more significant, ideological discussions were seen as comforting, secure, and, above all, innocuous. As long as discussions remained at this level there was little danger of serious conflict. Out of this experience the Burmese also came to recognize the irrelevance of ideological issues where actual choices and personal decisions were concerned.

Second, these early experiences convinced many Burmese that the practical problems of political development and modernizing were highly dangerous and likely to threaten the social and political security of precisely those who found the greatest comfort in ideological discussions about the need for development. Action and practice suggested almost certain sources for conflict and disagreement. Friendships could be threatened by the need for decisions.

Thirdly, the early political experience suggested that persistent efforts at programmatic actions could lead to splits and divisions which invariably opened the door to an increase in the influence of the traditional elements

of the society, particularly that of the Buddhist monks. Once the modernizers divided among themselves, the temptation was always great for one
group to seek temporary advantage by appealing to the monks for support, with the result that all the forces for modernization were set
back.

This pattern—which assumed a remarkably regular and cyclical form
of moving from a politics of grand ideologies to one of personalities,
to an appeal to religious powers, and then back to new ideological formula-
tions—characterized both the immediate prewar and the entire postindependence periods. In the immediate postwar period, when Burmese
politics were under the domination of the AFPFL, much attention was
given to ideological considerations, but the pressure toward concrete
policies created tensions among the leaders to the point where the united
party finally split in 1958. A politics of personalities and positions continued until U Nu was able finally to regain the ascendancy in the 1960
elections by appealing to religion and the monks.

The Contemporary Clash between Politicians and Administrators

The history of postindependence Burmese politics represents a con-
tinuation of the frustrating conflict between administrator and politician.

The success of the young leaders of the Anti-Fascist People's Freedom
League (AFPFL) in achieving independence for their country represented the triumph of a new group of politicians who had not been
systematically inducted into the prewar Burmese political process. They
had had relatively little experience in the command of power and the
manipulation of legal authority. In a sense they inundated the open
political process, monopolizing all offices and assuming direct charge
of all operations. Those who were not with them were soon pushed aside
as they sought to monopolize the political arena as legally defined by
themselves.

They were soon confronted with substantial opposition groups, all
of whom turned to violence and insurrection. First, and most important,
came the revolt of the Communists; then most of the minority ethnic
groups also turned to insurrection.[17] The threat of the insurgents began

17. For accounts of these numerous "multi-colored" insurrections, see *Burma
and the Insurrections* (Rangoon, Government of the Union of Burma, 1949); *Is
It a Peoples' Liberation: A Short Survey of the Communist Insurrection in Burma*
(Rangoon, Government of the Union of Burma, 1952); Hugh Tinker, *The Union
of Burma: A Study of the First Years of Independence* (New York, Oxford University Press, 1957); Cady, *A History of Modern Burma;* Brian Crozier, *The
Rebels: A Study of Post-War Insurrections* (Boston, Beacon Press, 1960).

to decline by the summer of 1950 when it was apparent that they were incapable of coalescing into a single rebel force. Although a decade later the various rebel forces were still in being, it had become increasingly clear that political development rested on the ability of the AFPFL leadership to guide the country.

After the war the administrator class found that its basis of influence had been largely destroyed by the Japanese occupation and the triumph of the AFPFL politicians. As individuals and as a group they felt themselves powerless and victimized. They also had a host of self-doubts, for they could not be sure that they had not possibly loved British culture to well, found too much to respect in the image of rational government, and been too ready to reject their own traditions. Few were able to stand up to the politicians' charge that they had worked too enthusiastically to maintain the colonial system of government.

On the other side, the politician, while appearing to be supreme, lacked confidence in his ability to operate the machinery of government. Posing as the man of the people, he was himself not too sure that he really was of the people, for he too had been affected by the process of acculturation. He knew only that he had to strike back against the administrator, who, employing all of his legalistic and bureaucratic jargon, seemed determined to show up and unnerve the untutored politician.

In time the administrators' fear of the politicians gave way to resentment and then to contempt, for many began to feel that the AFPFL politicians were bringing shame and disgrace to Burma. The politicians increasingly found that they were dependent upon the skills and knowledge of the administrators. They were, however, able to preserve their monopoly of influence as long as they remained united. The decline in the insurgents' threat reduced the pressures toward unity and opened the way to a more personalized politics among the AFPFL leadership. The result was the dramatic split in the AFPFL, announced openly on April 28, 1958.[18]

Once the politicians fell out among themselves, the administrators sought to reassert their position, but the deterioration had gone too far. Into this situation stepped the soldiers in order to end the squabble among the politicians and to re-establish the influence of the administrator. The period of army rule which lasted in Burma from October

18. For accounts of the split see Frank N. Trager, "Political Divorce in Burma," *Foreign Affairs, 37* (January 1959), 317–27, and "The Political Split in Burma," *Guardian, 6* (January 1959), 13–16; Furnivall, *The Governance of Modern Burma*.

1958 to April 1960 represented in a sense an effort to build up again the basic administrative framework of the Burmese state.[19]

The establishment of what the Burmese called a "caretaker" government under the direction of General Ne Win demonstrated that armies in transitional societies can play a stabilizing role at moments of extreme crises.[20] The experience also demonstrated, however, that armies cannot deal effectively with all the complex problems of nation building. The army could re-establish to a degree the conditions of prewar colonial government, but the basic problem of introducing the role of the popular politician remained. Thus army rule in a sense gave the Burmese a second opportunity to move out of a system of administrative politics and create a democratic government based upon the partnership of the politician and the administrator. In April 1960, when the army relinquished authority to U Nu and his "clean" AFPFL, which was soon to be renamed the Pyidangsu or Union party, the country faced again the test of building a modern state in the democratic tradition.

It was in the months following the split of the AFPFL into the clashing "clean" and "stable" factions and during the first phase of army rule that the field study was undertaken for this book. On the basis of these general observations about the historical origins of Burmese politics, we may turn now to the substance of the Burmese political culture.

19. For analyses of the period of army rule, see Richard Butwell, "The New Political Outlook in Burma," *Far Eastern Survey* (February 1960), and "U Nu Returns to Power in Burma," *New Leader* (March 28, 1960).

20. For a study of the phase of army rule in the context of the role the military can play in underdeveloped countries, see the author's contribution to the forthcoming symposium sponsored by the RAND Corporation and edited by John Johnson.

PART III

The Political Culture

THE SPIRIT AND CALCULATIONS OF BURMESE POLITICS

CHAPTER 8

The Political Culture and Transitional Societies

The preceding analytical-historical survey of the introduction of modern political roles into traditional Burmese society provides us with a basis for an over-all view of the salient qualities of contemporary Burmese political culture. In Part III we shall seek to outline the critical patterns of behavior and the fundamental orientations and feelings toward action that underlie the Burmese political process and determine the course of nation building. We shall be exploring in depth the origins and bases of these patterns with respect to, first, the general culture and the process by which the individual is inducted into his society, and then the processes by which the members of the political class are selected, recruited, and trained to their political roles and hence are socialized to the political culture.

By proceeding in this fashion, we emphasize the various interrelated processes which combine to give form and substance to a society's political culture. In particular, this approach should make it apparent that the political culture is shaped on the one hand by the general historical experiences of the society or system and on the other hand by the intensely private and personal experiences of individuals as they become members of first the society and then the polity. Indeed, by interposing a bold and generalized description of the essentials of Burmese political culture between our macro-analysis of Burmese political development and our micro-analysis of the development of the individual Burmese political actors we hope to highlight the manner in which these analytically separate processes in fact mirror each other to produce what we have called the society's political culture.

The concept of political culture as developed by Gabriel A. Almond stems from his observation that "every political system is embedded in a particular pattern of orientations to political action." [1] Since a political culture is built out of the cumulative orientatations of a people toward their political process, its dimensions include the limitations imposed by the realities of the power and authority structures of the society, modes of calculation and of estimating causality, constellations of values, and patterns of emotional responses. Most significantly, a political culture includes:

1. *The scope of activities, issues, and decisions which are perceived by people as relevant to the management of political power.* The scope of the political may be regarded in some societies as legitimately wide and diffusely defined and in others as properly limited and rigorously delineated.

2. *The body of wisdom and knowledge of the people which makes it possible for them to comprehend, find meaning in, explain, and predict those behaviors which they perceive as being relevantly political.* Some political cultures rest upon highly elaborate theories of cause and effect which make it possible for the people to feel that most of the events affecting the individual and collective well-being of the members of the society are appropriately traceable to political actions. In other political cultures people act on the basis of more empirically tested knowledge and hence intellectually expect less diffuse but more specific consequences from political acts.

1. Almond, "Comparative Political Systems," *Journal of Politics, 18* (1956), and republished in *Political Behavior: A Reader in Theory and Research,* ed. by Eulau, Eldersveld, and Janowitz, pp. 34–42. In Almond's usage the political culture is not coterminous with the political system, but usually extends beyond it, so that in his view "the United States, England, and several of the Commonwealth countries have a common political culture, but are separate and different kinds of political systems." In this study we shall conceive of the political culture as being intimately related to the subtle patterns of the particular set of political actors, and thus in our thinking it is possible, and even likely, that there are several competing or possibly relatively autonomous political cultures within any particular country. Consistent with this view and using Almond's example, we would be inclined to think of the United States, England, and several of the Commonwealth countries as representing the same kind of political system, but having significantly different political cultures. More specifically in relation to the subject of this study, we are inclined to think of the transitional or non-Western political processes as representing a common category, but we assume that each country within the category has its own distinct political culture or cultures. We are therefore centrally concerned with the problem of how these individual political cultures either facilitate or impede progress toward nation building.

3. *That faith beyond substantive knowledge which is governed by the prophetic words of those perceived as appropriate spokesmen of the future.* With respect to this dimension, all specific political cultures can be classified along a continuum and according to a typology. The continuum would range from societies in which people's expectations are affected by little beyond the deductions they draw from empirically tested knowledge to those in which the people are readily influenced by the claims of nonempirically tested knowledge. The typology would be according to the social status and occupational skills of those most commonly accepted in each society as probably possessing prophetic insights. In some societies, they would be priests and divines who specialize in other-worldly considerations; in others, businessmen who calculate in terms of the market; in still others, scientists who are adept in the techniques of intellectual investigation. The point is that each political culture is colored not by firmly tested knowledge alone but equally by the pretensions to knowledge and foresight which are always utilized by some in order to manipulate the predictions of others and hence to control them. This is because the man who claims to be able to see beyond the ken of others is also claiming to be their legitimate superior and thus claiming the right to have his predictions accepted as the governing guides to current actions.

4. *The values assumed to be most sensitive to political actions.* In a sense, the entire array of basic values of a society are reflected in its political culture, but there are always some values which are peculiarly significant for the political culture because they are assumed to be the appropriate concern of those with political power and responsibilities. Likewise there are values which are seen as much too precious, sacred, or personal to be touched by the crude and profane character of political action. The determination of suitable values for political concern does not appear to be necessarily governed by the scope of the practical. In traditional China, for example, the frequency of rainfall was a political matter for it was assumed to be related to elite behavior; in the American political culture of a few years ago it was believed that politicians were more competent guardians of motherhood than of the economy.

5. *The standards accepted as valid for appraising and evaluating political conduct.* These are divided between the moral and ethical standards assumed to be appropriate for guiding and evaluating political behavior and the criteria of skill and competence employed in appraising performance. Although moral and technical judgments usually rest upon

different systems of evaluation, the relationships between the two are of peculiar importance in shaping the political culture, for they may be seen as either conflicting or complementary. Is it assumed that highly moral behavior is likely to be inconsistent with effective and competent political performance? And similarly, to what extent are those highly skilled in commanding political power expected to be paragons of virtue or allowed to conform to a more relaxed and elastic code of ethical standards?

6. *The legitimate identities people can assume in contending for power and the common identity which the polity provides for all.* What range of choices does the individual have in selecting the larger self in terms of which he may act politically; and what is the content of the self-image of the people as a whole when they picture themselves as a political collectivity? This issue of identity of both the individual and the collectivity is of great importance in transitional societies, for from it emanates that note of uncertainty, of anxiety, of frantic searching and passive acceptance which is so characteristic of this particular class of political culture.

These dimensions of the political culture may help suggest and illustrate the nature of the concept. It should be noted that many objective factors, by imposing an unambiguous logic on the situation, may be crucially important in determining aspects of the political culture. For example, the configurations of a political culture invariably reflect both the technologies the society has developed for organizing and manipulating power and the structures and institutions created to reinforce and advance politically relevant values. The very forms of power available or absent in the society and the matter of access to legitimate instruments of influence are of course of fundamental importance. On the other hand the essentially subjective nature of all political behavior is of overriding importance in providing the specific content of a political culture, in large measure because politics involves values and norms of behavior. Thus a political culture can be found only in men's minds in the patterns of action, feelings, and reflections which they have internalized and made a part of their very existence.

The subjective dynamics of the political culture also follows from the need of the political man to impose an element of order upon a mass of seemingly unrelated events and happenings. He is expected to see causality where others only notice coincidence; he can see the import of danger in clues that the nonpolitical man fails to perceive or comprehend; he can give warnings or reassurances to the people because within his own personality he has an ultimate means of testing the significance and validity of all he perceives. Indeed, the substance of much of his profession is ideas and abstractions, calculations, predictions, threats and promises, exaggerations and ambiguities, subtle degrees of amity and enmity, and ceaseless evaluations of the endurability of specific human relationships, none of which can be seen or grasped in the physical world and all of which rest upon a sense of empathy. Political man must thus find in his own personality the guides for his actions and for his understanding of the political sphere, a sphere never clearly defined and composed of processes which can never be fully seen.

The importance of the subjective, and the need for people to look inward in order to grasp the outward realities, means that feelings and sentiments are of crucial significance for the political culture. What may first appear to be only subtle attitudes and latent feelings can turn out to be the key considerations shaping political behavior. This is particularly likely to be the case in unstable and changing situations in which patterns of behavior have yet to be fully institutionalized.

Anxiety, Aggression, and Charisma

When we turn to the subjective dimensions of the political culture of transitional societies and to the people who are still struggling to find their identities in the nation-building process, questions relating to anxieties and aggression usually seem to occupy a peculiarly important place. This may be because the host of social and personal mechanisms which in most stable and integrated societies control, divert, channel, and sublimate feelings of interpersonal aggression have been weakened or broken in transitional systems, with the result that aggression is far less effectively predicted and controlled.

The expectation of unpredictable or aggressive behavior tends to create an undertone of anxiety in interpersonal relations, which in turn tends to increase the likelihood of aggressive behavior; thus a vicious circle is established impeding effective communication among people. In well-structured and firmly institutionalized settings, compulsive, irrational, and even fanatical behavior can drive individuals into greater economic productivity or to higher standards of excellence even while destroying them as individuals. In transitional societies, however, this possibility is less likely; such behavior tends instead to be destructive of both the individual and the collectivity. Without that minimum degree of trust and mutual confidence which makes possible complex organizational life, the emotions of aggression can rarely serve socially productive purposes. Here again we see the basic problem of lack of trust which is the most fundamental obstacle to effective organizational behavior, and hence to the modernizing of the society and the building of a secure nation-state.

In this context, it is important to observe that the prevalence of charismatic leaders in transitional societies is not solely related to the need to rely upon basic emotional appeals at a time when other modes of communication are blocked by a lack of consensus on values and on the reasoning appropriate to political thinking. The charismatic personality is itself reassuring, for of all the types which might manipulate power, the charismatic leader is likely to seem the most safe, the least threatening, the least dangerous in his relations with others. Power in the hands of the charismatic leader can be seen as power neutralized, for it is the art of being and not the art of doing which makes him what he is. Thus, when the problems of aggression and anxiety color to a high degree interpersonal relationships, there is a readiness and even eagerness to settle for the leader who is a bit removed, who seems detached from the emotions of personal relationships, who is comforting in words, and who appears concerned only with the good and the ideal.

This pattern of relationships among aggression, anxiety, and charisma seems to provide the basic theme when we turn our sights to an overview of the Burmese political culture.

In outlining the spirit of Burmese politics, we must analyze first the nonrational components of behavior, an enterprise which can easily be misunderstood, especially when the analysis is directed to a foreign culture. Since we cannot treat all societies at the same time, readers may falsely conclude that we are suggesting that the nonrational bulks larger in Burmese politics than in the politics of other societies. This is most decidedly not the case; the spirit of American or British or Russian politics is as far removed from a narrow concept of rationality as is the spirit of Burmese politics. What we are pointing out here is only that, although elements in the Burmese political culture also appear elsewhere, their sum total and the ways in which they are combined are unique to Burma, and its people clearly have their own distinctive spirit of politics.

Another warning is in order. One should never make the false deduction that because a political culture contains much in the way of follies and irrationalities the people who make up the system are individually lacking in an appreciation of good sense and rationality. Nor should one conclude that if the individuals were more at home in the rational spirit their political culture would reveal less of the nonrational. The absence of any such simple relationship between the individual and his political culture can be readily appreciated by a moment's reflection on, say, the spirit of American academic politics and on the wonderfully preposterous ways in which men devoted to the advancement of enlightenment and clear thinking can end up organizing their professional life.

With these qualifications in mind, we may now examine the spirit of Burmese politics in an effort to locate attitudes and practices which inhibit and impede the processes of modernization and nation building.

CHAPTER 9

The Imperfect Communications of Politics

Politics is an activity peculiarly dependent upon communications. Neither participants nor observers can acquire knowledge on their own of all the events and actions that make up the political process; everyone is at the mercy of the particular web of communications to which he has access for his understanding and appraisal of public affairs. To the degree to which a society possesses a coherent and open communication process, it has one of the necessary elements for an integrated and rationally oriented political process. That is, to the extent that people share the same information they have a tool necessary for reasoning together and for arriving at common conclusions. When the communication process is fragmented, as it is in most transitional societies, the political culture is likely to be colored by uncertainty; instead of actions being based upon reliable and shared information, the margin for imagination is widened to the point that decisions and policies are likely to be guided more by fantasies than by realities.

The Gap between Public and Private Discourse

There is an opaque quality to Burmese politics. Observers of the Burmese scene customarily experience frustration in trying to locate reality and separate the significant from the irrelevant in the daily flow of events. The real game of politics seems to be played far from the public view, and outsiders usually feel that they receive only the vaguest hints of the considerations that are in fact influencing developments. Even the earnestness or levity of the politicians usually fails to coincide with the apparent character of the situation. Extreme developments can take place with little or no warning; major changes can be long advertised but never occur. Even after the fact it is difficult, often impossible, to reconstruct with confidence the precise sequence of events, for, more often than not, key facts and considerations are never brought to light.

During the week leading up to October 28, 1958, when U Nu supposedly asked General Ne Win to form a caretaker government, there was hardly a hint in the Burmese newspapers that such a dramatic development might be in the offing. Through the open channels of communications the public was informed only that U Nu had returned to Rangoon, radiant and elated, from a triumphant campaign tour of the dry zone, that the prospective election would be close, and that the competing "trade unions" representing each faction of the split AFPFL were not above using violence. The private and informed elements during the same period abounded with all manner of rumors; people in coffee shops were discussing whether SEATO troops might not have invaded the country and if it were true that the Chinese Communists had dispatched two divisions to assist the Burmese Communist insurgents. Then came the dramatic radio statement by U Nu, consisting of only one sentence, informing the people that he was asking Ne Win to assume the responsibilities of government. Since that date there has been no complete public report on all that happened during that action-filled week, and Burmese politics has continued without all of the participants sharing even a common understanding of the most dramatic and significant single event of the postwar period.

It is, of course, the very essence of politics that those involved have imperfect information about each other and all must attempt to fathom uncertainty. However, the situation is even more extreme in transitional systems such as Burma's; although it is difficult to measure the gap between public and private discourse on politics in any society, it is not unlikely that in Burma this gap is unusually large.

First, Burma illustrates the tendency that whenever a society feels that external events and foreign powers, rather than domestic efforts, will be decisive in shaping the country's future, a substantial gap is likely to emerge between public and private opinions.[1] Public utterances of the politically active class of Burmese are generally tempered by considerations of their possible impact on foreign governments, while private communications are likely to reflect more accurately the realities of domestic power relationships and also the frustrations over having to be constrained

1. Hans Speier has observed this phenomenon with respect to Germany in his *German Rearmament and Atomic War: The Views of German Military and Political Leaders* (Evanston, Ill., Row, Peterson, 1957), p. ix.

by foreign considerations. The belief that their own decisions may not be of ultimate significance also seems to dull the Burmese elite's sense of reality and to reduce their ability to resist the comforts of pleasant illusions. Feeling that they may not have ultimate responsibility for their own national fate, they are tempted to seek security by publicly articulating an image of their nation's development in which they do not fully believe.

Second, the gulf between public and private views is widened in Burma by the anxiety common in transitional societies about meeting the routine standards of Western and modern performance of government. There is need to impress the outsider, and yet there is a sense of failure among some of the important elements in Burmese politics. The need to put up a good front tends to blur the sense of realism of a people and makes it easy for them to escape the ultimate discipline of politics, that of facing facts.

Partly as a protection against failures and partly for reasons deep in their culture, the Burmese tend to create a highly idealized picture of the present, which is always identified as being the "best of all possible Burmas." The immediately preceding period is usually depicted as having been an extremely unpleasant one, filled with all manner of dangers; more important, many of the negative qualities of the present, which cannot be publicly articulated, are attributed to the earlier period. Thus, for example, during the first postwar years the public image of Burma was of a united AFPFL heroically struggling to bring about socialism and utopia, while the preceding period of British and Japanese rule was depicted as one of uninhibited autocratic rule. Then, after the split in the AFPFL in the spring of 1958, a new public version of the situation was advanced, depicting the country as emerging into a new phase of freedom in which administrators could speak their minds and the press could engage in democratic debate. At the same time, the earlier period of united AFPFL rule was then characterized as having been a one-party dictatorship in which free expression was denied and public policy was guided only by the personal interests of politicians. After the transfer of power to the army, the public image became one of a united people purposefully re-establishing efficient government, while the preceding period was now described as one of near anarchy, widespread fear, and frequent and unpredictable arrests. Finally, with the restoration of civilian rule the public front was one of the country returning to its true self, especially with the acceptance of its traditional stress on religion, and the phase of the caretaker government was described as a close brush with dictatorship.

These are the public images. In private the Burmese have had quite different views. Specifically, they tend to be hypercritical of all those who have power, and they generally expect very little of significance to come out of the efforts of their own leaders. The leaders themselves communicate in private this same lack of confidence in Burmese performance, and even those with formal responsibilities for particular activities will speak as though they had no influence and are at the mercy of "theys" who always do things wrong. The mark of political sophistication is to be able to indicate subtly that one is not being taken in by the public image, but that one knows how to use it to personal advantage. For members of the Burmese political class the important thing is to keep the public and private images of political events separated. The Communists have persistently followed the practice of saying in public what other Burmese would say only in confidence, and hence are considered boors beyond the pale of respectability. At the other extreme, some Americans are considered rather artless by many of those who would be the intellectuals of Burma, because they do not make a sharp distinction between the public and private versions of Burmese realities and continually employ aspects of the public image in their private conversations. Fringe members of the Burmese political class—journalists, students, traders in government licenses, and subordinate members of the bureaucracy and army—are inclined to see their society's hyprocrisy before seeing their own; while the core members of the political class find their hypocrisy bearable because they know that all must share in it if the system is to be maintained.

In this connection it is worth noting that the Burmese tend to have a highly tolerant response to nonsense. Even when they are quite capable of seeing through the illusions and pretensions of others, they are more often than not prepared to go along with them. They can thus take a detached view of hypocrisy and rascality and feel that it is unimportant to separate, say, cant from faith and religiosity from hogwash in the minds of others. Given their sense of tolerance, Burmese generally find human relations considerably easier and more accommodating if there is an idealized picture of the present to which one can pay lip service until one is able to learn the personal opinions and convictions of the person with whom one is dealing.

As a consequence, the small talk of Burmese politics, the carefully contained conversations designed to minimize potentially aggressive re-actions of others when treading near a potentially dangerous subject, tends to be of only two types: first, the apparently naively optimistic and idealistic, and second, the apparently unqualifiedly cynical and pessimistic. In a sense, the Burmese in seeking a posture of casualness toward his politics tends to reach for a position that is detached in the sense of being more extreme than either the idealized official view of affairs or the more critical operational view of reality.

Lastly, it should be noted that the practice of maintaining a large gulf between public and private opinions about politics has the effect of protecting the Burmese from the judgments of outside observers and critics. Those who accept the public image too readily can be quickly dismissed as naive souls, while those who treat publicly what should be only private views are considered to be ill-mannered and unnecessarily hardheaded and crude. Thus no outsider can effectively criticize Burmese political developments.

Imperfect Information and the Powers of Secrecy

Those involved in the day-to-day operations of Burmese politics have remarkably little reliable information about the course of developments. There is considerable groping and stumbling on the part of most of the participants, and when decisive action does take place it is usually accomplished by completely disregarding the position of others.

A major factor in limiting the extent of shared political information is the intensely personal nature of Burmese politics. Individual whim or mood, personal ties, or accidental associations can be the prime molders of decisions; they do not necessarily stem from the more manifest and concrete features of either the social structure or political history. Since to calculate moves and maneuvers means fathoming the depths of individual personalities and not just tabulating the professed positions of stable groups, actions must be based on flimsy and scarcely articulated clues. In turn the lack of a common source of information encourages the participants to act according to intuition which adds to the unpredictability of developments and forces people to rely even more on subjective rather than objective considerations.

The problem of imperfect information in Burmese politics is further complicated by the political elite's keen appreciation of the extent to which information is power. Indeed, this consideration receives so much attention that Burmese are in constant danger of confusing the fact that they know something that someone else does not with the notion that they have power over that person. Thus information becomes something to be collected and withheld until it can be properly used to advance one's interests, and a mark of political skill is the ability to tell exactly who is in the know with respect to individual pieces of information.

The connection which the Burmese political elite make between information and power tends to make them highly suspicious of the intentions of anyone who seeks information and knowledge. The notion that the problems of the world could be reduced by the spreading of enlightenment and information is basically distrusted by the members of the Burmese political class. The link they see between information and power helps explain their inordinate fear of foreign intelligence; they tend to assume that any effort to learn the facts about another country is really only preparatory to attempts to control it. Conversely, their expectation that others are likely to misunderstand their intentions along this line explains why the Burmese government often follows extraordinarily devious means to acquire routine information relating to foreign countries.

The way in which information is distributed is often the decisive factor in Burmese political maneuvering. Leaders of political parties and even cabinet members are apparently not completely candid even with their closest associates. U Nu, for example, has followed throughout most of his political career the tactic of never giving complete information to any of his immediate associates while assuring that no two have identical information. This has made it possible for several individuals to believe simultaneously that they were personally closer to the Prime Minister than any of their associates, because each thought that he know something the others did not. At the same time, no single person knew enough to be a source of danger. This situation helps explain why at times the Burmese cabinet has appeared to be going off in all directions at once, each minister having jumped to his own conclusions about the prime minister's intentions.

Although such manipulative use of information often results in administrative inefficiencies, at a more fundamental level secrecy serves a crucial function in Burmese elite politics. The Burmese place such a high value on personal power that they would tend to be endlessly preoccupied in quest of it but for the dampening effect of the lack of reliable information. Moreover, the compulsive desire of the Burmese to be above others or, more accurately, to have no superiors, is a primary cause of interelite tensions which lead to the constant splintering of political groups. In the final analysis then, the particular balance between secrecy and information at any time is an extremely important factor in giving order and structure to elite relations. If all the aspiring leaders felt that they had a complete picture of the situation, they would all be equally tempted to assume a commanding role.

The fact that order is maintained by keeping key participants uninformed does, on the other hand, contribute greatly to the already high state of tension common to Burmese elite relationships. People are constantly learning, with shock and resentment, things that others already appear to have known. In this setting the skilled politician is one who can absorb new information while making it appear as though he had already known all about it.

It is not just manipulative considerations that encourage Burmese leaders to keep information from their subordinates. The Burmese seem to have an intense distaste and even fear of criticism, and throughout Burmese life superiors generally find it desirable to employ great care in not exposing themselves to any possible criticism from their subordinates. They generally assiduously check all unnecessary downward flow of information. The subordinate or staff member who is even tolerably well informed about his superior's actions and plans is extremely rare, the true confidential secretary or alter ego is almost unknown.

Most Burmese have a craving for warm and intimate relationships in which all inhibitions that might limit candor can be safely cast aside, but they feel that such relationships are almost impossible except when one is prepared to become completely submissive. For, in a sense, the act of telling all is the same as throwing one's self at the feet of a superior. It cannot usually lead to completely equal and reciprocal relations, and if one holds back some information and knowledge he always has the upper hand; the desire to tell all is in conflict with the fear that doing so involves a serious threat to the self.

Thus deep in Burmese thinking is the belief that to have secrets is to be on the side of power. This view is consistent with Burmese feelings about nature and about the relationships of the supernatural to daily life. In nature it is the invisible not the obvious that dominates life, and for most Burmese the world of the *nats,* or spirits, is a very real world, in part precisely because it is invisible. The conviction that power operates out of the public view is coupled with a feeling that power is likely to act in unexpected and often malicious and treacherous ways; therefore the Burmese tend to expect that those with power may act in an unpredictable fashion. Similarly they appear to derive a great deal of satisfaction and genuine enjoyment out of being able to arrange a completely unexpected development. For example, most Burmese take considerable pride and satisfaction in the fact that during the war Burmese leaders were able to plot and execute the sudden reversal from cooperating with the Japanese to attacking them. To be able to surprise the unsuspecting is more than just an indication of cleverness; it suggests to the Burmese that one has real power.

To some extent the degree of imperfect information common to contemporary Burmese politics is simply a reflection of the conspiratorial quality of their politics in modern times. During the last days of the Burmese kings, those actively involved in high-level Burmese politics had to proceed with skill and caution just to stay alive. In more recent times the emergence of nationalist politics had to take place at the margins of legality under British and Japanese rule, and under the AFPFL, politics remained an extremely tough and brutal enterprise.

CHAPTER 10

The Contradictions of Politics

Basic to the concept of a political culture is the assumption that the feelings and attitudes which are the elements of that culture are in some deeply human and social fashion meaningfully related to each other and not a mere congeries. This does not, however, preclude logical contradictions, for much of behavior escapes the constraints of systematic reason; indeed, the dynamics of much of a political culture may be closely linked to certain paradoxical patterns because they are likely to reflect some fundamental and disturbing ambivalences in the character of the people.

Transitional societies may hold more room for contradictions and paradoxes than other societies because people may share not only the ambivalences produced by the process of acculturation but also those inherent in the traditional culture itself. In all cases, however, the assumption remains that there is an explanation for all contradictions and that, in some sense, each paradox represents only two sides of the same coin.

Gentleness and Violence

Burmese politics is divided between two distinct levels of activity, and any study that concentrates on one to the exclusion of the other will give a distorted picture of its total range. One level is characterized by gentleness, religiosity, and a compelling need to elucidate the qualities of virtue. The other is characterized by violence, malicious scheming, and devious thinking.

If attention is focused on only one set of data, one cannot but be impressed with the self-righteous, middle-class, and even puritanical quality of so much of Burmese political behavior. Enemies of the state are not treated in a harsh manner but quickly welcomed back into the society. Much of the public political discourse carries the gentility and apparent earnestness of contemporary British politics. All politicians are at great pains to stress their interest in spreading happiness, encouraging welfare, and supporting all the nice things in socialism.

Political articulation in Burma is devoted to illuminating all aspects of virtue and goodness. Often such discussions take the form of expounding a feature of Buddhism, even though they are based entirely upon secular considerations. There seems to be genuine appreciation of skill in expostulating on the nature of virtue; those who are thus skilled are highly respected regardless of their private conduct. "In Burma political slogans and catchwords such as Pyidawtha, Socialism, Communism or People's Democracy are Utopias chiefly used to incite in the public a sense of well-being." [1] This attitude appears to be related to the Burmese belief that intentions are more important than mere deeds.

Viewed from only a slightly different perspective, Burmese politics appear to be rife with violence. Few governments in history have had as many groups of its citizens take up arms against it as has the newly independent Burmese government. Political murders appear to be fairly frequent, and, even more important, Burmese believe them to be frequent. People will discuss in private, with little sense of shock, the possibility that their cabinet ministers use violence and hired thugs to advance their political fortunes. They find it not implausible that leaders of political parties may have raised the funds for their political activities through armed robberies.

The Burmese press constantly emphasizes this quality of violence in its efforts to delineate the Burmese national character:

> In these days of rampant crime, it requires a good deal of savagery and barbarianism for any particular piece of crime to receive notice. A double or triple murder committed in the heat of a mass dacoity would hardly raise one's eyebrows. [2]

> Ten years of indiscipline and centuries of ignorance are responsible for the people of this country being completely confused as to what constitutes freedom. [3]

> This country, after many years of indiscipline, is rather like an unruly classroom. [4]

1. *The New Times of Burma* (August 22, 1958).
2. *The Burmese Review and Monday New Times* (September 1, 1958).
3. *The Nation,* Rangoon (December 16, 1958).
4. Ibid. (April 20, 1959).

> The crime index in this country is one of the highest in the world, and there are all types of criminals . . . the fault for all this does not lie in the religion but in our own innate mental aberration.[5]

Behind all these acts of violence lies not only a tradition of dacoity but also the significant fact that Burma has possibly the highest per capita murder rate in the world. A juxtaposition of violence and gentleness seems to run through Burmese society. The two extremes of behavior seem to come together within the individual Burman.

There are those such as J. S. Furnivall who feel that the violence in Burmese life stems largely from the disruptive effects of the Western impact and British rule upon traditional Burmese society. Certainly the old restraints were greatly weakened with the elimination of many of the traditional political and religious institutions. However, the fact that other traditional societies have been disrupted without a comparable degree of violence in interpersonal relations suggests that there are other factors contributing to the prevalence of violence in Burmese life. If we pry deeply enough into the dynamics of Burmese behavior, we find that the source of much of the violence seems, paradoxically, also to be the source of Burmese gentleness.

As Burmese move through life they usually display a degree of uneasiness and also unsureness in interpersonal relations. They tend to act as though they would like to have human relations so elaborately structured that uncertainty could be reduced to a minimum in all their dealings with others. But Burmese society, particularly since the Western impact, does not provide the basis for such clearly defined relationships. As a consequence, the Burmese tend to apply such a refined calculus to their interpersonal relations that they are constantly reading meaning into the actions of others when none exists.

The Burmese feeling of uneasiness in human relations may be traced back, first, to the relatively unpredictable emotional basis of the Burmese mother's relationship to her child and, second, to the manner in which the acculturation process appears to have threatened the modernizing Burman's sense of identity.

Briefly, the anthropological evidence seems to be that the Burmese mother on occasion provides warm and uninhibited affection for her child and on other occasions acts in a cold, distant, and even teasingly cruel manner toward him. The mood is the mother's; it is determined by her

5. Ibid. (April 7, 1959).

whims and is not governed by the behavior of the child. At best the child learns that he can be the cause of the negative reactions of his mother but not the cause of her positive and loving responses. Thus the Burmese may constantly seek warm and close relations, but unconsciously he tends to expect that he cannot control others in any positive fashion and that his actions are only likely to produce hostile responses. Hence, at the root of both the violence and the gentleness is a deep-seated fear of provoking others.

To exaggerate the picture somewhat for the sake of clarity, it can be said that the Burmese tend to seek in life those warm and close personal associations they occasionally experienced with their mothers, but their behavior is governed by the expectation that any human relationship may hold great dangers. The basic outlook is that people can be easily provoked to hostile responses. Behind every sign of friendliness there always lies the possibility of precisely the opposite pattern of behavior. And in an even more complex fashion, the acculturation process tends to reinforce a sense of distrust toward precisely those who would appear to be anxious to help, for helping is the same as controlling; when people are being changed from traditionals into moderns, they are likely to be hypersensitive to the deeply felt sensation of being changed and manipulated by others who always protest that they are only being helpful.

The Need for Controls and the Fear of Provocation

The basic Burmese fear of provoking others rests upon the assumption that within most people the restraints against violent outbursts are extremely tenuous, that people are not likely to be able to control their hostile emotions if they are in any sense attacked. This fundamental Burmese attitude is possibly best expressed in U Nu's observation and warning, "Even insensate stone, if kicked often enough, will rise up. Therefore let none of us try the game of exploiting another." [6] Consequently those who commit acts of violence are not severely censured; rather, it is the one who does the provoking who is considered something of a fool and probably deserving of uncontrolled violence. Since people are like buzz saws, anyone who pokes his finger too close deserves what he gets. U Nu suggested that his control over his own emotions was limited and that the consequences of exploitation could not be predicted when

6. U Nu, "The Road to Unity," speech delivered on National Day, November 8, 1947, in *Toward Peace and Democracy* (Rangoon, Suptd. Govt. Printing and Stationery, 1949), p. 11.

he said, "Therefore my anger against these people is rising. Let them take what is coming to them." [7]

Coupled with the belief that people have only a weak grasp of their emotions is the Burmese feeling that emotions are generally dangerous, destructive, evil, but if expended they will leave the individual exhausted and harmless. U Nu has on many occasions articulated this basic Burmese anxiety about emotions:

> Even before the attainment of independence, I had, in the capacity of a leader, deeply pondered on the ways and means of relieving the chests of our nationals, especially the younger set, of the pent-up feeling so long suppressed during the days of the British and Japanese rules. Such feeling can be really dangerous. For example, if a man entertains very strong feelings and has to suppress them against his will, he will not only experience the greatest discomfort but his suppressed feelings are likely to result in uncontrollable outbursts. With these thoughts in mind, I devised ways and means of subli- mating the energy of young people and directing them towards the rehabilitation of the Union. While the plans were being formulated, however, the outburst came. But in the hurly-burly of fighting, run- ning and shouting a part of this pent-up feeling has been relieved. We have definite information that in many parts of the turbulent areas, many insurgents have been overcome with exhaustion and desire both openly and secretly to cut themselves away from their methods. [8]

On another occasion U Nu vigorously criticized Burmese authors for writing about what was "in their heads" which must be "bad," and not writing about what was "outside themselves" which must be good:

> The majority of them only give out what is in their heads and they do not care to take in what is worth taking in. . . . Therefore I ear- nestly appeal to you not to drain your heads by giving away what you have, but to acquire whatever knowledge you can assimilate so that we may be able to overcome this love mania [9]

On still another occasion, when discussing the political threat of the army, U Nu further revealed the common Burmese feeling that most dan-

7. Ibid., p. 16.
8. U Nu, *From Peace to Stability* (Rangoon, Suptd., Govt. Printing and Sta- tionery, 1951), p. 13.
9. Ibid., p. 4.

gerous behavior comes from people being unable to control their inherently dangerous emotions by suggesting that the source of all such danger was soldiers who "default in their legitimate duties either through hate or love or fear or bribery or laziness or failure to control the urge for stealing or looting." [10] Note that in his view love is as dangerous as hate, and that there is a fundamental urge toward acts of extreme violence.

In political relations these same sets of expectations play a very important part because so much of political life involves situations that can easily be interpreted in terms of provocation. A basic characteristic of the Burmese spirit of politics is the feeling that one must always be careful not to provoke others, that one must at all times appear to be gentle in overt actions. At the same time one must be constantly prepared for violent attacks from others. Fundamentally one must follow the strategy of never provoking others until one is prepared to destroy them; otherwise it may be oneself who is destroyed. As an editorial in the leading Burmese newspaper once observed, "In Burma, political parties work on the basis that the opposition exists only to be crushed, and whichever party gets into power sets about this task as systematically as it can." [11]

Thus there is a tendency for the manifest level of Burmese politics to be characterized by a high degree of friendliness and the latent level by considerable tension. The result is that violence and intense animosities may erupt with very little warning; it is a fundamental expectation in Burmese politics that when someone is not crushing a possible rival he must be merely biding his time for a better opportunity. In a famous Burmese play, a mother who was the second queen, in seeking to advance her son over the position of the legitimate heir to the throne, advised him:

> Use your cunning. Use your wisdom, my love. Err not, lose not in your anger. Control yourself, hide your feelings and take what comes in good part.

> Listen, my loved one, follow not your intention, your inclination. People can guess your intentions, your plot will be discovered.

> Do not be rash, my son, do not follow one side of your mind. . . . Your men are not many, your officers are few. Why not bide your time, and wait at least until your might is equal to the kings.[12]

10. Ibid., p. 7.
11. *The Nation*, Rangoon (August 31, 1958).
12. U Kyin U, "Parpahsin"; trans. by U Htin Aung, *Burmese Drama*, pp. 194, 198.

Fear of provocation explains a fundamental passivity toward danger in the manifest level of Burmese politics. Once a threat of danger has been identified, the basic expectation is that since it probably cannot be effectively controlled, one can only hope that it will in time expend itself against others. Faced with a threat, the classic Burmese response is to avoid provocative actions and seek to become inconspicuous. Thus, for example, the Burmese have little faith that their neighbor Communist China can be controlled by outside forces or even by her own leaders; therefore everything must be done to avoid in any sense provoking her until, as is hoped, she will finally have dissipated her dangerous emotions and become a safe neighbor.

While awaiting such a happy denouement, the only open positive actions permissible would be the use of moralistic pronouncements. It is not that the Burmese have great confidence in the restraining powers of moral precepts. People are constantly violating basic Buddhist precepts in their daily lives. It is rather that the Burmese are oddly insensitive to the possibility that moralistic injunctions could appear provocative to others. For all the care the Burmese show in avoiding any provocative act, they seem peculiarly unaware that many non-Burmese dislike and resent being preached to. The Burmese insensitivity to the fact that their moralizing might be annoying to others suggests that such activities are designed less as a means of possibly controlling others than as a means of suggesting the innocence of their own intentions. For in their view people who sermonize are not really trying to change the behavior of others but are only seeking to reveal their own pure hearts and nonthreatening qualities.

The acceptance of the unreliable nature of controls on human emotions also means that when action is planned against dangerous people it is generally done in the spirit of revenge and not of punishment and discipline. In U Nu's words, "Retaliation is inevitable in politics." [13] The strong positive act comes when one is prepared to crush those who have threatened or damaged oneself. The basic contest of politics is thus seen as one in which the contenders maneuver about with fine and scheming calculations until the initial moment when, releasing the tenuous controls on their deadly emotions, they strike out against each other. There may be great care and preparation, but the ultimate act is one of blind fury. This is basically how the Burmese understand the Cold War and Russian-American relations.

That the Burmese lack a fundamental appreciation of the logic of punishment or the utility of discipline is revealed in their common attitudes

13. U Nu, *Toward Peace and Democracy*, p. 42.

toward police powers. If the authorities act vigorously against any particular criminal, the general reaction is that the police must be motivated by a sense of personal revenge. The more appropriate approach is for the authorities not to seek the punishment of the criminals but to arrange to make them less threatening. Illustrative of this quality in the spirit of Burmese politics is the retired police officer's account of how he dealt with a gang of 80 members who were "responsible for no less than 50 heinous crimes such as murder, dacoity, arson, rape, kidnapping, looting of guns and what not." [14] Instead of seeking to capture, try, and punish the criminals, the police officer took pride in having "shattered their morale" by firing over their heads and then, through the cooperation of *pongyis* or monks, promising a complete amnesty to all members of the gang. When the gang "came into the light," an evening of entertainment was arranged during which "the *pongyis,* the police, the villagers, and the gangsters were merged into one fraternity from that day." Thereafter a dozen of the gangsters were "ordained into Buddhist priesthood for a duration of 10 days to make atonement for their past misdeeds," and the two former leaders of the gang "were given a shotgun and 25 rounds of cartridges each for self-defense. Thus law and order was restored once more in the Yenangyaung sub-division, Natmauk and Nyaunghla townships, without any bloodshed. This was the outcome of esprit de corps and teamwork displayed by the district police and the flying squad, plus the benediction of the 'sayadaws' whose cooperation and coordination never lacked. May the area still enjoy peace, and the Rule of Law prevail." [15]

Inaction and Overaction

The tempo of Burmese political life is characterized by vacillation between extended periods of inaction and short periods of frantic action, between a stage of lethargy and great outpourings of energy. It would be tedious to illustrate the many ways in which this is true. It need only be noted that it is within the formal structure of government, where responsibility can be most sharply defined, that we find the spirit of inaction most firmly entrenched. Officials hesitate to use their authority in order to avoid provoking others or exposing themselves to the criticism of their subordinates.

The outbursts of activity seem to be associated with a spirit of breaking down all inhibitions, of recklessly striking out without fear of conse-

14. "Memoirs of a Retired Police Officer: The Roundup of Nga Dwe-Naga San Gang," *The Guardian*, Rangoon 7 (July 1960), 19–20.
15. Ibid., p. 20.

quences. It is significant that they usually take the form of the physically bold act and have a dramatic and emotional character. Action is thus a characteristic of the virile man who can fearlessly cast aside all inhibitions, who desires to be firm, decisive, unambiguous, and resolute, to demonstrate the qualities that are rare in daily Burmese life. Outbursts of political activity may have a hostile and aggressive undertone which is usually coupled with a feeling that some enemies must be crushed.

Although the psychological dynamics of the vacillation between inaction and overaction seems to stem from the Burmese personality, the forms it takes seem to be related to the images of British colonial leadership. On the one hand was the image of the high-level colonial official who appeared to live in undisturbed quiet and dignity, and whose conduct therefore suggested that power and position were associated with a sheltered and inactive existence. On the other hand was the image created by the British military or other official in uniform, a man of vigorous and decisive action whose every move conveyed the impression of sureness of mind and steadfastness of purpose. Fundamental to this image was the feeling that command and decision rested on a highly emotional base: the higher the authority, the shorter the temper.

This latter image has great appeal for many Burmese who wish they could conquer their fears by dominating others. For it is a model of authority in which powerful emotions can take an overt form and be fully expressed; feelings of fear and inhibition can give way to those of conquest and domination; uncertainty and self-doubts disappear in favor of self-assurance and a resolute manner; and feelings of hostility and aggressiveness are confused with sensations of glory and honor. In sum, a world of fear can be replaced with the world of the charismatic leader.

This image of authority which gives form and direction to the Burmese outburst of action has strong authoritarian overtones. By its very nature such action is not conducive to innovating activities. On the contrary, Burmese outbursts of political activity tend to be effective only when directed toward restoring a former state of affairs or achieving well-defined and widely understood goals. For example, there was little real enthusiasm for the various developmental projects under the AFPFL government, while, on the other hand, there was considerably more effective action under army rule when the goal was that of recreating the Burma of British rule.

CHAPTER 11

Sentiments about Power and Action

The realities of power within a society are crucial in shaping its political culture. The structure and distribution of power and authority constitute the basic framework of political life; they provide the inescapable logic of the situation for all the actors and thus represent the basic elements of realism that must color all political choices. The capacity of a people to perceive in common the realities of power in their society is a most important factor in support of the role of rationality in politics. For people to reason together about politics they must first agree to the facts of power in their society. Political behavior, particularly to the extent that it is guided by intelligent choices, is thus fundamentally influenced by the situation of power in the society.

The fact that power relationships can change, even suddenly and dramatically, and that people can be led to make new calculations and new alignments does not lessen in any sense the fundamental importance of the structure of power in governing political action at any particular historical moment. It does, however, pose problems for the student of political cultures. He is faced with a dilemma: if his analysis takes fully into account the structure of power, his study (particularly if it is about a transitional society) will soon be outdated by the flow of events; but if he should slight the significance of the power situation his study will not only lose an important ingredient of realism, but also unduly exaggerate the limitations of reason in guiding political behavior. There is no happy escape from this dilemma.

Behind changes in power relationships there are, however, more fundamental feelings and sentiments about power, authority, and action which are also of the essence of a political culture. These deep cultural sentiments outlast the transitory shifts in power structures, and they condition the entire approach of a people in their dealings with and manipulations of power. In transitional societies where the structures of power have not been well institutionalized, it is appropriate to focus upon these fundamental sentiments in characterizing the political culture.

The Thrill of Power

There are few cultures that attach greater importance to power as a value than the Burmese. Considerations of power and status so permeate even social relationships in Burma that life tends to become highly politicized. The fact that Buddhism is a central feature of Burmese life only makes the quest for power more subtle and more indirect.

The lack of a well-defined class structure, with the consequence that no one can assume he is secure in his station, may provide some explanation for the Burmese emphasis upon power and status. Even in traditional Burma the class structure was not rigid enough to permit status to be taken for granted; now the disruptions of the Western impact have created further insecurities, especially for those in the Westernized elite who tend to be hypersensitive to instability of status.

Burmese place such a value on power that they are capable of genuine emotional appreciation of pure, unadulterated power. To have power is to experience an inner thrill and to find true happiness. The Burmese themselves recognize that their elation with power is "a fundamental trait of the Burmese character. He [the Burmese] loves kings and princes. If he cannot be a king himself he'd like to be a follower so that he can enjoy some of the perquisites. He is not averse to doing something difficult or dramatic, but he wants to do it just the once and live happily forever thereafter." [1]

The appreciation of power is in many ways similar to the American feeling about love: namely, it is a thing of the highest value, to be pursued, but once grasped it is far too precious to be used for any material gain, at least not openly or explicitly, for it is an end value in itself. The American in love is forgiven if he acts on impulse, is slightly impractical, or does not consider ultimate consequences; the Burmese with power is expected to act on impulse and to be above concern with practicalities or ultimate consequences.

Since the Burmese concept of power is in fact a concept of status, it is hard for Burmese to make a distinction between the two. Power without high status is thought of as brute force and immoral behavior; once power is related to status, however, the personal qualities of status tend

1. *The Nation,* Rangoon (February 22, 1959).

to dominate the concept of power. In American culture there is something indecent about seeking power in the context of personal satisfaction or status. Indeed, in the spirit of American politics one is expected to show disinterest toward power itself and find satisfaction only in helping others to realize their values; one can admit to enjoying power only to the extent that it makes one appear to be a better and more efficient representative of the hopes and ambitions of others; one can work for one's principles but not for one's personality. By contrast, in Burma power is fun, and so the Burmese have ambiguous feelings about the appropriateness of relating it to anything as commonplace as policies and programs; as a consequence, in Burmese politics power and programs tend often to be unrelated.

Much of the complicated Burmese view of power is contained in their concept of *awza,* only the more salient aspects of which we can summarize here. *Awza* is a function of relationships, the important thing being that in every group there is someone who has *awza.* In every family, class, community, office, organization, political party, nation, there is one person who has *awza.* Burmese often display considerable skill in being able to enter a new group or situation and identify that person immediately. The components of *awza* include the characteristics we would normally associate with power, influence, and prestige—among them, respectability, wisdom and knowledge, a degree of religiosity, a commanding presence, and skill and ease in handling authority. But *awza* also implies a likable personality, a touch of modesty, and usually considerable sex appeal. Wealth in itself may not be absolutely essential, but one must give the impression of being above worries about matters of daily living, of being able to live beyond one's visible means, or, best of all, of having no visible means of support but still living comfortably.

Age and wisdom also are generally recognized components of *awza.* Although one must always show respect in proportion to chronological age, the *awza* of extremely elderly people is likely to decline. The important quality seems to be the appearance of being slightly older than even one's contemporaries, to be the elder brother or the still vigorous father. Some Burmese contend that the component of wisdom requires formal education, while others argue that just the appearance of being scholarly and profound is quite enough. The element of wisdom is critical, however, for Burmese do not feel that authority without superior wisdom can claim to be legitimate.

The relationship between *awza* and religiosity is extremely subtle and complex. The excessively devout man, one who seems unable to leave a life of meditation, is unlikely to have *awza*. The superior abbots or *saya-daws* in a monastery who have *awza* are usually the ones who appear to have firm and hard minds and to understand the inner workings of the upper levels of the secular society. On the other hand, a man who displays no sensitivity to religious concerns is likely to lose all claims to having *awza*. Some Burmese have said that one with real *awza* always gives the impression of being slightly impatient with religious practices not because he is irreligious but because he really knows more about the true doctrines of Buddhism than ordinary monks.

Above all, *awza* has a powerful physical dimension. It is the complete image of leadership in a highly personal and physical sense. Those with *awza* show with their every move that they can handle authority with skill and a light touch. Since *awza* implies a likable personality, a touch of modesty, and composure, it becomes in its full manifestation much the same as charisma.

In the Burmese political culture the sense of *awza* puts emphasis upon the style of power holding. Careful attention must be given to form and manner. Judgments about the quality of an act are far more sharply held than judgments about its probable consequences or effects. Discussions about those in positions of influence tend to become detailed and elabo-rate criticism of their mode of behavior, with little emphasis given to the substance of their policies. Since in the concept of *awza* form is more closely tied to the basic properties of power than are consequences, there is little possibility of the logic of the situation imposing some clearly recognizable limits on aspirants to power. In political cultures where the possession of power depends upon effective performance in decision mak-ing, it is difficult for a person with no record of action to have pretensions of power. In Burma, however, since much of the essence of *awza* is be-lieved to emerge out of the careful cultivation of one's inner self and of one's personal manner in dealing with others, everyone can aspire to *awza* and therefore to power.

In any fluid situation there is likely to be an extremely vigorous quest for *awza*. Indeed, stable social life would be quite impossible if it were not for some important restraints that prevent the development of unin-hibited quests for *awza*. The most important of these is another distinctive and fundamental Burmese concept, the feeling of *ah-nah-deh,* which can-not be translated into a single English expression. *Ah-nah-deh* is an emo-tion that wells up inside a Burmese, paralyzing his will, in particular pre-venting him from pushing his own self-interest and compelling him to hold back and accede to the demands of others. Burmese will claim that only they of all the peoples of the world are capable of *ah-nah-deh* and that it represents both the glory and the tragedy of the Burmese people. Apparently the Burmese feel that the considerations of *ah-nah-deh* are appropriate in any situation in which one's interests might conflict with those of others or in which one might feel some sense of obligation or indebtedness to another. A man may patiently save up his money to make a special purchase, but if his neighbor then asks him to lend him some money he will feel compelled, out of his sense of *ah-nah-deh,* to do so. Similarly, a man will be bound by his sense of *ah-nah-deh* not to offend or in any way disturb the peace of mind of one who has invited him into his home.

Burmese businessmen will claim that they are disadvantaged by their feelings of *ah-nah-deh* because they cannot behave in the same "ruthless" and "business-like" fashion that foreigners can. Government officials similarly claim that considerations of *ah-nah-deh* make it impossible for them to act in a completely impersonal manner in upholding the principles of the law. There is hardly a fault in Burmese performance in any field which some Burmese will not attribute to the workings of *ah-nah-deh.* The Burmese notion that they are laboring under a more compelling need to consider the feelings of others makes them also feel that there may be something soft or weak at the core of the Burmese personality. Thus Burmese will often explain an exaggeratedly harsh, firm, or thoughtless act as one impelled by a need to overcome the restraints of *ah-nah-deh.*

Burmese females generally describe *ah-nah-deh* as a very pleasant sensation of yielding to the wishes of another. Burmese males, on the other hand, often describe the sensation of *ah-nah-deh* as a highly unpleasant one. In particular, Burmese males may frequently sulk and build up strong resentments toward anyone who they feel has exploited their feelings of *ah-nah-deh.* Ultimately they may find it impossible to control their rage any longer and turn with violence against the very person for whom they had previously made a sacrifice. Thus the question of who is exploiting whose feeling of *ah-nah-deh* frequently guides the course of personal relationships, and a consideration that began as a mechanism for regulating and pacifying human relationships frequently tends to become the very source of personal conflicts.

In Burmese character there seems to be a constant struggle between a quest for *awza* and the pull of *ah-nah-deh.* Within the individual Burmese the conflict between the two is often very strong; no one can have *awza* without giving the impression that he is capable of feeling *ah-nah-deh,* while on the other hand anyone who seems excessively susceptible to the restraints of *ah-nah-deh* cannot expect to command *awza* or, for that matter, even a modicum of respect.

Both the desire for *awza* and the capacity to feel *ah-nah-deh,* like the traits of violence and gentleness, probably spring from the same source in the Burmese personality: that is, the lack of trust in human relations, the expectation that the friendly and kind may suddenly become capable of destroying. It is not hard to see how a sense of fear and uncertainty in personal relations can contribute to the type of feeling described by the term *ah-nah-deh*. Unsure of the basis of one's relations with others, and expecting the unpleasant, one is likely to feel inhibited and restrained in a relationship with anyone who seems to have clear demands and a set purpose and to fear provocation if the demands are not met. But the Burmese craving for power and their peculiar emotions about power also reflect a sense of insecurity in human dealings and a desire to escape from interpersonal relationships. Fear that others may harm and even destroy one leads to fantasies about unlimited power.

Thus the Burmese feeling for power is in a sense the desire to glide through life without being touched or affected by the acts of others, to have one's personality encased in a protective shell of omnipotence so that nothing in the world can hurt or threaten it. In a way, the dream of power is the dream of being able to strike out in any direction according to whim and never encounter encumbrances or obstacles, to walk toward blank walls and have doors suddenly open. A distinguished Burmese statesman has observed that the fatalistic element of Buddhism which holds that one's lot in life has been largely determined during one's previous incarnation makes it easy for Burmese to take to power as if it legitimately belonged to them.[2] No matter how one might have come to power, it is always possible to rationalize that it was entirely proper. One must accept one's fate even if it means being greater than all others, including the apparently more deserving.

The Chore of Decision

In the context of politics, it follows that the Burmese emotional concept of power makes policy making seem a dreary chore. For a people as concerned about the attitude of others and as fearful of personal relationships as the Burmese, political decision making is an extremely difficult task. Moreover, given the fear of provoking others, to make political decisions that may offend or even hurt some people becomes a highly displeasing activity except when it reflects unanimity or when it involves crushing

2. U Ba U, *My Burma,* p. 178.

someone in a weak position. Thus, although power is thrilling and exciting, decision making is at its best a chore and often a source of real danger. Only if a man has tremendous power can he make decisions without a sense of fear or difficulty; and very rarely does a member of the Burmese political class feel that he has such power.

The common Burmese connection between power and decision making is that a powerful figure will have a staff or an entourage about him to do the worrying over the necessary decisions and make sure that nothing happens to weaken the power or status of their leader. If possible one hires "technicians," invariably low status people who have no hope of gaining greater power or prestige, to make the unavoidable decisions. The classic model of the "technician" is the astrologer whose advice is respected but who always remains outside the round of normal social and political life. The Burmese, including high government officials, still rely upon astrologers who not only can see into the future and thus take the uncertainty out of decision making but can also make the actual decisions and thus relieve the power holder of responsibility.

The Burmese distrust of, and even distaste for, decision making is so strong that at times they will pretend that decisions have not been made even when the fact cannot be hidden. For example, the Burmese government has on occasion asked that announcements about agreements with the United States be made only in Washington. The government in Rangoon can thereby keep quiet in the hope that attention will not be attracted to the decision even though everyone knows the wire services will carry the report.

Intentions rather than Deeds

Since the Burmese assume that people will always try to hide their real intentions and that much of human behavior is unrelated to intentions, deeds are in a sense viewed as dust to be thrown in the eyes of the unsophisticated. Thus the essence of skill in Burmese politics is the ability to calculate the intentions of others and not be taken in by their manifest actions.

This emphasis upon intentions rather than deeds was clearly illustrated after the split in the AFPFL when preparations were being carried out for the expected election in the fall of 1958. If the army had not intervened, a key issue in the election would have been the question: "Is U Nu power-mad?"; the electorate would have been presented with a clear-cut choice involving the intentions of the national leader toward that most prized of values—power. Had U Nu treated power in a crass and materialistic way? Had U Nu, as the opposition charged, done that most questionable of things in Burmese culture, "sought to take short cuts to power"? [3] Was his intention to obtain so much power that he could be above fear and thus be uninhibited in crushing all who might stand in his way? Both factions of the AFPFL agreed that U Nu's political acts should not be taken as a reliable basis for finding the answers. The test should be in terms of the qualities of the inner man, and not in terms of anything so marginal as his substantive contributions to government policy and Burma's national development. This point of view is even held by Burmese critics of their government's record of inaction and failures.

The Burmese concern over intentions can be traced back to the underlying elements of tension and aggression in the Burmese personality. Fear of the destructive impulse in others, doubts about the strength of restraints and inhibitions in others, and the expectation that others may act suddenly in a violent and hostile way all contribute to a concern for fathoming the inner personality of others. Experience suggests that one should always distrust the manifest and seek to understand the latent.

By stressing intention rather than deeds, the Burman is able to avoid responsibilities and thus reduce the possibilities of dangerous attacks and criticism. The Burmese view is that if one's actions should in any way provoke or anger another, there still should be hope of safety since one can always claim that one's intentions were good. In a very real sense a Burmese never intends to attack or provoke another if it will threaten his security, and then he knows that his intentions are much more important than mere acts, which can be misinterpreted or can be simply unfortunate accidents.

The emphasis on intentions rather than deeds also seems to stem from the fact that in Burmese culture stress is placed upon the present, upon the act of being, and upon self-development. The focus of Burmese Buddhism is on gaining merit for the self; the social significance of an action is less important than its effects upon the inner self. Pagodas are built with little thought of developing art forms or of realizing exacting standards of achievement; the concern is entirely with protecting the inner well-being of the self. The all-important consideration of improving the inner self can range from efforts to insure a better life in one's next incarnation

3. U Nu is very conscious of this form of original sin in the Burmese character. He has said, "I have repeatedly stressed the fact that the evil tradition of wresting power by short-cut methods has been inherent in us from the days of our forefathers." *From Peace to Stability*, p. 13.

to contemplation about the state of one's inner self, and even to a fascination with body-building exercises.

It can be seen that the emphasis upon the act of being is related to the sense of insecurity in interpersonal relationships. Hesitation to commit oneself to works that might be judged, criticized, and attacked seems to be greatly reinforced by the feeling that the world is full of dangers and that others are always primed for attack.

Politically this all means that value is placed not on deeds, programs, or records of performance but upon finding self-realization, gaining authority and *awza,* and, above all, suggesting that there is greatness in one's inner self—another aspect of a politics of charisma. In terms of political behavior it means that the Burmese politician tries to avoid any action that can be easily evaluated. If one must do something, it is hoped that others will not take it too seriously as a basis for judging one's worth. Thus Burmese who have achieved some status in the bureaucracy are extremely hesitant to initiate programs or act in any way that would expose them to criticism from their subordinates. And clearly any serious political action which is bound to provoke someone is danger-laden; it requires great care, detailed calculations, and, above all, strict secrecy.

Actions without Consequences

There is, however, in Burmese politics a second category of acts which follow from efforts at self-fulfillment and which are not expected to provoke others. Since their effects are entirely limited to the actor's self, they are unrelated to other people and are acts without consequence as far as society is concerned, Similarly, since they are not likely to cause danger to the self, they are generally the acts that bring the greatest happiness to the actor. In a sense it is precisely the ineffectualness of these actions which makes them so satisfying.

Most such actions involve efforts as self-expression, and more often than not they take the form of oratory. Generally Burmese orators seek to strike the bold, the heroic, the daring posture. They tend to project themselves as fearless men who are unconquerable but also capable of expressing modesty. But in the Burmese self-image even the simple rural folk are not expected to be taken in by the words of politicians "because they, like all other intelligent citizens, know that speeches and promises of our leaders are made more as exercises in oratory than for serious implementation." [4]

4. *The Daily Guardian,* Rangoon (July 17, 1958).

In acting out their roles of self-fulfillment, Burmese politicians can often make extraordinary statements that seem to be the very height of irresponsibility. U Nu, for example, in the heat of his oratory has said that the British assassinated Aung San and that they had encouraged not only the Karens but also the Communists to revolt. But he would have been surprised and disturbed if he thought that the British had taken his statements seriously and been in any way offended by them.

This kind of political irresponsibility is further encouraged by a rarely articulated belief that political action can have little influence over fundamental developments, that history is controlled by forces quite different from those at the command of the Burmese politicians. In part their doubts about the significance of their own powers stem from the fact that they are not taken in by their own propaganda; they know, for example, how little they really had to struggle for their own independence. And the attitude must have been encouraged by the conditions under which the politician learned his profession in Burma; he knew that it did not matter how irresponsibly he acted since the colonial government would make sure that nothing would go seriously wrong. But the feeling seems above all to be related to the belief that the only satisfying actions are those that can have little consequence.

Naturally, therefore, in Burmese politics effort tends to be concentrated in inverse proportion to the social significance of a problem. For example, rice is the basis of the Burmese economy, and the entire well-being of the land depends upon the annual export crop. Nothing is more important; consequently politicians avoid becoming involved with, and indeed do little about, the exporting of rice. It is too serious, too precious a matter to be tampered with, and the politicians have arranged that the agency responsible for handling rice exports is so organized that it can rarely make new decisions. Decisions require the unanimous agreement of five directors, who have contradictory interests.

The underlying hope of the Burmese political class that political action may somehow not be too closely related to fundamentals is revealed in their approach to economic development. Since political action is regarded as incapable of either greatly advancing or impeding important matters, it appears largely irrelevant to economic development; programs are announced with the apparent expectation that results will follow automatically and little need be done to assure their success. Comforting themselves with the hope that their actions are not decisive, politicians feel free to view the various projects in the same light as the building of pagodas: they provide opportunities to demonstrate purity of motive and to realize self-expression. Politicians have customarily regarded development projects not with an eye to eventual output as industrial managers or economists might, but as opportunities for leaders of a society to maximize their glory and power and to find their own self-realization. The various projects have consequently tended to become the private preserves, almost fiefdoms, of individual leaders, within which each can freely build his personal following through acts of patronage and not feel guilty that the economy may be harmed in the process.

In sum, then, political action can govern the fate of an individual—it can determine whether he is to gain *awza* and status or become a subordinate of others—but it cannot influence history. The record of the Burmese independence movement is one of repeated surprise on the part of the leaders that their actions and demands could have such effect. Indeed, there are those who believe that the propensity of the Burmese to underestimate the effectiveness of politics may have been decisive in putting the country outside the Commonwealth; since the Burmese leaders did not believe their demands would be granted, they made exaggerated claims that did not accurately reflect their real desires.

Ideologies as Unexceptionable Sentiments

The Burmese seem to have an inordinate fascination with formal political ideologies. They have been very articulate about socialism, Marxism, Buddhism, and the elements of a welfare state. Rangoon was the location of the Asian Socialist Conference. However, it is nearly impossible to demonstrate any connection between the manifestations of ideology and significant Burmese political behavior. In the Burmese self-image ideology occupies little importance: "in Burma, more than perhaps in any other part of the world, people join parties or break away from them more for personal than ideological reasons." [5] Indeed, the Burmese are so attuned to their politics that they can sense full well the implications of any increase or decrease in the political power of leaders or parties without needing to rely on ideological distinctions.

The interesting question is why the Burmese seek to give the impression that they are interested in matters of formal ideology when in fact their politics revolve mainly around personalities. At the more obvious level the answer seems to be that the very intensity of the personal clash means that for the sake of respectability they need some form of fig leaf to clothe the power struggle. It may also be that the British are responsible for the Burmese belief that respectability is associated with a preoccupa-

5. *The Nation* (September 14, 1958).

tion with ideological questions. Over the years the British were tireless in telling the Burmese that a politics of principles, which the Burmese tended to confuse with ideological politics, was superior to a politics of personalities. Only in recent years have the Burmese come to appreciate the extent to which British politics hinges on class considerations and personalities rather than abstract principles.

At a deeper level the Burmese use of formal ideologies seems to be related to their concern with articulating the nature of virtue. Given the uneasy feelings the Burmese have about interpersonal relations, and their fear of provoking others, it is understandable that their more calculated public statements tend to take the form of unexceptionable sentiments. In the emotion of oratory they may make the startling statement, but otherwise they usually prefer the safe and respectable idea. This encourages politicians to discuss religion and secular concepts of virtue. The result is the use of ideologies not as fully developed programs of action but as safe subjects of discussion that will reflect favorably on those articulating them.

Ambivalence toward Personal Independence

In the spirit of Burmese politics there are strong ambivalent feelings toward independence, toward being isolated and uncontrolled. On the one hand the Burmese craves to be the autonomous actor free to carry out any whim or desire. On the other hand he desires to nestle under the protective wing of another and to be inconspicuous and unprovocative. The only well-recognized roles in Burmese politics are those of the personal leader and the devoted disciple, either complete independence or complete submission.

These two extremes in attitude, like most paradoxes in the Burmese character, seem to stem from a common source. The desire to strike out and be independent is coupled with the hope that nothing one does will hurt one's self and that in the final analysis one will be protected from the consequences of one's acts regardless of what they may be. This feeling is related to the belief that intentions are more important than deeds and that acts will have no significant consequences. To be independent is to be safe from all criticism and danger of attack. Or so it is hoped. To be completely under someone's wing is also to be safe from attack and criticism. Thus independence and complete dependence have much the same emotional character: they both can be seen as providing a haven of security in a dangerous world.

The quest for independence in Burmese politics does not generally promote a strong attachment to particular public policies. Rather it tends to be more closely associated with a basic need for self-respect and the positive recognition of others. This recognition gives the individual a sense of security and well-being, hence of dependence. This pattern of emotion and response is very much like that of the young Burmese boy who, in seeking to gain the warmth and protection of his unpredictable mother, tries to assert himself, to prove his manhood, to gain her attention and even respect so that he can be fully accepted by her and thus realize the security of a stable dependent relationship. At the same time, however, the Burmese boy is distrustful of the dependent relationship itself because his mother's behavior has been too unpredictable.

This complex of attitudes seems to underlie Burmese feelings about "neutralism" in the sense that the Burmese did not expect their "independent" foreign policy to leave them in an isolated position. Rather they seem to have expected that out of their assertions of neutralism they could gain respect for being intelligent and reasonable, thereby achieving a warm dependent relationship in which they would be fully protected from all dangers. The Burmese have consistently expected everyone to react in a most positive fashion to what they consider to be the sweet reasonableness of their policies. Just as they seem to be peculiarly blind to the possibility that moralistic pronouncements will have a provocative effect, so too they seem to expect that they will win support and backing rather than alienate people by pushing the "reasonableness" of their positions. In private Burmese will confess to disillusionment toward neutralism because it has meant that Burma must be alone in a hostile world. Somehow they crave a new arrangement, a new status, in which they can feel that they are secure under a protective wing, while at the same time remaining independent, unfettered, uncontrolled, and unrestrained.

A quality of unfulfillment thus lies at the heart of the Burmese spirit of politics. The absence of a basic sense of independence has in turn colored the Burmese ability to deal with others. The inevitable result is a pervasive and self-destroying suspicion of others, of all that is foreign. This basic dimension of the Burmese political culture reflects the experiences of the Burmese political class in personally facing the challenge of the modern world. It is therefore only possible to appreciate in full the complexities of Burmese feelings about their relationships with the outside world after more has been learned about their experiences in acculturation.

CHAPTER 12

The Perceptions and Judgments
of Burmese Politics

In dividing our treatment of the political culture between the spirit of politics and the calculations of politics we are suggesting that the former may be more closely related to the processes of the basic culture that shape its modal personality types while the latter stem from the cognitive processes through which people learn about the operations of their polity. Thus we are assuming that in a broad sense the spirit of Burmese politics derives from the fundamental socialization and personality formation processes of Burmese culture, and that the calculations of Burmese politics are the product of the later experiences of being inducted into the realm of politics.

This distinction is not a rigid one, and behavior cannot always be classified by this means, for it is difficult to say whether any particular aspect of the political culture is more directly related to earlier experiences than to later ones. More often than not, the dominant features of a political culture reflect both socialization processes since particular patterns are created and given firm form out of the accumulative ordering of total life experiences. Thus the constant and basic effort of humans to find some element of order and meaning in experiences makes for a degree of coherence in all aspects of the political culture. On the other hand, the very essence of the human condition is that people are quite capable of living in repose while clinging to grossly illogical and contradictory points of view.

In turning now to the calculations that appear to underlie Burmese politics, we shall be relying primarily on information derived from interviews with Burmese politicians and administrators in which they discussed how they came to understand and participate in the politics of their society.

Interviewing the Practitioners of Politics

It was striking how frequently an interview terminated with the respondent commenting that this was the first time he had ever had an opportunity to reflect seriously upon the matters under discussion, and that he had been articulating points of view which he had never had a chance to discuss with anyone else. Often during the conversation the respondent's views would suddenly shift from one position to another as he groped to find respectable postures and opinions which he felt would reflect well on him and his country. Also, as we came to know the individual better and he developed a sense of confidence in an interview situation, the discussions often moved from a superficial and saccharine treatment of problems to a realistic, even bitter, approach. The capacity to move from one extreme to the other and then back again was quite as important as the substance of their attitudes. Obviously, we would have been misled if we had taken seriously as firm attitudes many of the answers we were given.

It is unrealistic to expect that direct questions will elicit from busy political actors direct answers about their understanding of politics. Politics is far too diffuse and too complex a phenomenon for people generally to have clearly developed concepts about it which they can readily articulate. The researcher and scholar must piece together the political philosophies of individuals who, although they actively shape a country's political culture, do so without following a clear design. We therefore had to employ indirect approaches in exploring the attitudes of Burmese administrators and politicians.

We could discuss with administrators how they came to be recruited to the administrative service, their memories of their early years of apprenticeship, and their reactions to their initial assignments and their first promotions. It was possible to talk to politicians about their first interests in political careers and in the role of political leadership. From the answers they gave as they discussed and criticized political institutions, from the ways in which they explained the events of history, and from the criteria they used in justifying or denouncing the behavior of others, we gained a basis for inferring their political philosophies, their ways of comprehending political phenomena and of judging and evaluating behavior in the domain of political action. As they discussed their experiences we were able to learn what excited—or worried—them about politics and what they expected could or could not be achieved through the utilization of state power.

In essence, our approach was to treat seriously what our respondents said, but to try also to find behind their words the logic and patterns of emotion and reasoning which underlay their basic orientations toward life and politics. Thus, for example, as we listened to the politician describe why he believed that his group was likely to have success in the coming elections, we began to get at his methods of calculating power, his ways of interpreting political justice, his sense of the relevant factors in determining history, his emotions toward the tangled web of political relationships. As the administrator described the development of particular programs, we could sense how he interpreted control and command, what he felt to be the relationship between plan and action, between official and civilian, between politician and administrator. Point-blank questions on any of these areas might have led to professions of ignorance or conventional textbook phrasing of views which an American might be expected to appreciate.

THE SCOPE OF POLITICS

The number of people perceived as involved in the political process is in itself a powerful factor shaping a person's understanding of the process and coloring his expectations about policy actions. The answer he gives to the simple question, "How many people have to be moved in order for significant developments to take place?" tells much about his feeling for the possibilities of rationally controlling events. The number of categories he feels it necessary to construct in order to describe all the significant participants in the process reveals the degree of refinement with which he can make his political calculations.

A Small but Dangerous World

Our Burmese respondents displayed a remarkably uniform feeling that the scope of politics is small with respect to participants but unlimited as to permissible issues and content. With a few noteworthy exceptions, they tended to picture themselves as standing at the boundary of the political arena in the sense that they thought of no one beneath themselves as being significantly involved in the political process. They were all looking inward and upward to locate the small group who could move events. In short, they held the highly elitist view of politics that the function of the people as a whole is to control itself, behave properly, and respond to the leadership cues of the elite.

This understanding of the scope of politics appears to encourage the assumption that all events in any way traceable to elite action must be the consequence of rational and purposeful calculations, while all events which stem from nonelite behavior and thus come from outside the proper scope of the political process must be emotional, irrational, and highly dangerous to all. Members of the political class in Burma, despite their vocal commitment to democracy, seem to be continually surprised when those they consider beneath them actually influence events, something which in fact happens quite often.

The assumption that important politics belongs to the few seems to make members of the Burmese elite feel that institutions run by people they do not personally know cannot be really significant. One of our informants remarked, "I do not believe that parliament is of any importance at all for I do not know by name any of the members below the rank of ministers." Another informant dismissed an entire ministry as insignificant on the grounds that, "I do not know anyone over there and therefore they can't be important."

Attitudes about the substantive scope of politics appear to be far less clearly defined. The respondents shared a general feeling that certain types of issues should not be the subject of political deliberation, that they involved matters "too important for politics." However, there was also a widespread expectation that anything and everything is likely to become politicized, an attitude which reflected the Burmese feeling that there are no specialists and that all problems fall within the competence of the one real elite of the society, the political elite.

The feeling that politics involves only a small number of people but a large number of problems leads also to the calculation that the political elite can be properly criticized for nearly everything that occurs within the society. This helps explain the basically defensive posture of most Burmese politicians, who tend to assume that they are always vulnerable to criticism on some score, and the deep anxiety of many who feel that they must be lacking in certain skills since they are not able to control events as completely as they themselves and others expect them to. They seem to be unable to reconcile their elitist view of politics with their limited effectiveness in changing their society.

Conflict and Cooperation

The most significant consequence of the Burmese view of the scope of politics is revealed in their calculations about conflict and cooperation. In well-established societies, where interests have become institutionalized and governmental departments are well established with a continuity in history, it is possible for individuals to clash and still assume that their controversy represents merely the interplay of impersonal forces, not an expression of personal animosities. Societies in flux apparently lack the protective shield of impersonal institutions which can shelter the individual from the full force of controversy. Our interviews revealed clearly that in Burmese politics it is almost impossible for people to represent their controversies as conflicts of social and not personal interests.

Since whatever interests may exist within Burmese society have not been adequately organized, they have no recognized political roles. Particular political leaders claim to be the representatives of, say, the trade unions, the peasants, the students, and other such groups commonly identified in modern societies, but no one believes that in their controversies with other politicians they are speaking only for others and not in defense of their own personal points of view. Consequently, whatever conflicts of interest may appear invariably take the most acute personal forms. All the leading figures assume that this is the natural course of political controversy; however some are more ready than others to move quickly to the inevitable conclusion, to assume the initiative in personalizing controversy, and then to claim that they have done no more than what is natural and inevitable.

Burmese politics and administration in this respect suffer all the problems of the closed community. The intimacy with which the participants know each other, their ambitions, and their customary modes of behavior makes it almost impossible for any form of controversy to be perceived as other than an expression of aggressive, personal hostility. Out of the logic of such a situation come tremendous pressures to ensure that everyone suppresses aggressive feelings. The calculations of Burmese politics are thus those of a small club, a small town, an academic community. To make life bearable, leaders have to adopt as a permanent political posture an attitude of seeking cooperation and unanimity.

Unfortunately, however, the Burmese government is not the government of a small town or an intimate club. As a national institution, faced with all the domestic and foreign problems inherent in modern governance, it cannot escape the host of issues which create controversies and which in established societies are played out in clashes between institutions. Thus in Burma there must be controversy, but it takes place in an atmosphere and setting that seem to demand unanimity. The politics of the small world constantly proves itself inadequate for the problems of the real world, a dilemma which takes on a psychologically threatening form for Burmese politicians.

Knowing that the acceptance of open controversy and debate is basic to the democratic ideal, they constantly feel that they should be able to accept controversy and conflict. The fact that they find it so difficult in their intimate community to prevent political controversy from becoming personal aggression forces many of them to suspect that as a people they are possibly unprepared for or incapable of managing democratic institutions.

Thus the scope of Burmese politics seems to compound the problem of cooperation and controversy which, as we have seen, is in any case a basic and peculiarly complex problem in terms of Burmese personality and culture. Burmese politicians are always ready to extol the virtues of the two extremes, but they seem to be perennially dissatisfied and distrustful of whatever state of affairs may exist at the moment. For example, before the split in the AFPFL, political leaders constantly spoke of the values of cooperation and unanimity but were disturbed that their country had so little democratic competition in ideas. After the split, they swung to the other extreme of openly championing the values of controversy and competition while anxiously worrying in private about the need for cooperation and conformity.

The effect of these considerations has been a steady erosion of sympathy for democratic practices and a rising belief that authoritarian ways based upon a spirit of unanimity are likely to be easier to live with. This is a diffuse sentiment which comes into conflict with the more particularized fear of being dominated or controlled by others. The Burmese political class is prepared to accept the tyranny of rigid consensus but not the tyranny of the openly dictating leader.

THE TENSION OF POLITICS

The outsider is likely to be impressed by the subdued, and in fact lethargic, atmosphere of Burmese government offices, in which little seems to be accomplished. However, both Burmese administrators and politicians seem to share a desire that their government and political activities become less tense. They tend to imagine themselves caught up in extremely high pressure situations, and they will argue that the nation's business might be better managed if the atmosphere of politics were more relaxed.

The exaggerated sense of tension in politics is probably related to the ingrained Burmese feelings about power and the danger common to inter-personal relations. It is therefore interesting that in spite of their professed wish for less tense political activities, most members of the political class seem to be made happy by dramatic and publicly exciting political events. They say that during political rallies and demonstrations "everyone is happy together and nobody is off by himself plotting and scheming against us." Thus the excitement of popular politics is pleasurable because of its innocence. Also, popular rallies are reassuring because they seem to establish a harmony between public and private levels of political calculation; at such events it is possible to proclaim freely and openly the seriousness, the importance, and the basic sense of violence that is a part of all private estimates of politics.

Basic to the Burmese feeling about the tenseness of politics is the concern with violence that we have already noted as such a fundamental part of the spirit of Burmese politics. The current generation of Burmese politicians began their public careers during a period of extreme violence. They learned about the nature of power first during the war and the Japanese occupation and then in the period of disorder and insurrection which followed independence.

It is noteworthy that almost without exception both administrators and politicians treated as interesting and important the query we put to most of our respondents: "Leaving aside casualties related to the insurrections, how many political murders would you say take place each year in Burma?" The actual numbers they gave, which tended to run between ten and seventy-five, are of less significance for our purposes than the opportunity the question gave for the respondents to express their feelings about the place of violence in Burmese public life. Many of the administrators clearly saw in the question a chance to express their hostilities toward politicians:

A prewar British trained official:
> The number of political murders a year tells the whole story of our politicians. They are a hopeless lot and no wonder there is no peace in our country.

A member of the Planning Commission:
> Our politicians in the districts spend all their time thinking up ways to tear down law and order. They are the worst problem we have, and they cause us more trouble than all the other thugs and dangerous types.

A young member of a clerical staff:

Our politicians do not use ideologies, they're always using murders. If you could find out how many murders really took place a year in this country, you would find the truth of Burmese politics.

The enthusiasm of the administrators in describing the violent ways of the politicians reflected their need not only to discredit the politician and undermine his new and superior status but also to justify their own inabilities to act more effectively. They felt that by accenting the prevalence of violence they explained fully why rational administrative programs are impossible in Burma.

An official in the railway administration:

Everyone knows in Burma that the main reason our country has not been able to develop is because of the breakdown of law and order. Our politicians say that this is because of the many insurrections. The truth of the matter is that we as administrators have not been able to carry on our programs not because of the insurrectionaries, but because of the politicians who are always threatening our programs and disturbing our people who are trying to work in the districts.

A senior official in the Secretariat:

It is impossible to maintain discipline within the civil service. We give orders to Deputy Commissioners; and when they fail to carry them out, they only have to say they were threatened by the politicians in their district. As long as they can claim that their lives have been endangered, how can we insist that they carry on our programs?

Burmese politicians, in their turn, are equally frank in acknowledging the frequency of political violence, and in the main the leading politicians find that the fault lies with their underlings and with the local politicians. U Nu has repeatedly proclaimed that "all manner of bad hats and thugs and other evil characters" have crept into his political party.[1] By identifying violence with the lower ranks of the party politicians, the national leaders are able to represent themselves as dikes holding back the waves of violence that might otherwise sweep the land. On this score the senior politicians tend to share the administrators' attitude that violence is an inherent characteristic of the more traditional Burmese people and that

1. U Nu, *Toward Peace and Democracy*, pp. 16–17.

its prevalence is likely to decline among the more modernized, more urbanized groups.

Significantly, the facts do not suggest that there is such a clear connection between acculturation to the modern world and a decline in violence. As we have noted, there are grounds for accepting the opposite pattern. Therefore, the belief that the less acculturated are more dangerous than the more acculturated seems to reflect a sense of isolation and unsureness in the leading members of the Burmese political class. With noteworthy exceptions, most of them are not entirely confident of their own ability to control the masses while leading them in new directions. The feeling that distance exists between themselves and the more traditional people tends to create anxieties and fears, and they tend to suspect precisely those of whom they are least sure as being dangerously prone to violence.

As a group the politicians can see a positive aspect to violence which the administrators do not generally appreciate. The politician often thinks of himself as a romantic child of revolution, working always under the shadow of violence and having to prove constantly his personal courage in a calling that requires brave men. One of the common charges that Burmese politicians make against the civil servants is that they lack the physical courage and nerve to perform effectively in the inherently dangerous political arena. In part the Burmese politician seems to choose to see politics in these terms because it reassures him about his manhood. In part he chooses to picture politics as extremely dangerous because to do so provides him with grounds for rationalizing his own sense of ineffectualness and for insisting that his critics fail to appreciate the dangers, and hence the limitations, of his profession.

The undesirable frequency of extreme acts of physical violence in Burmese society makes the less extreme and more subtle forms of danger seem all the more likely, for if political murders are possible, then all other forms of aggressive and hostile behavior seem plausible and even probable. Thus the administrator can attribute his feelings of insecurity, inadequacy, and hesitation in action to the fact that he lives in an environment in which physical danger is a realistic threat if he becomes too politically conspicuous. The politician can rationalize his psychological needs to domineer and completely control his subordinates and to be abject and servile to his superiors on the grounds that objectively he is constantly exposed to threatening circumstances. And so the realities of violence when combined with the feeling about the tenseness of politics seem to produce myths about violence which are congenial to the fantasies of the Burmese political class and which color their calculations of politics.

THE RHYTHM OF POLITICS

There is a disjointed quality about Burmese politics. The members of the political class do not envisage the possibility that developments can have their natural tempo and rhythm, that, for example, many at first apparently unrelated events may come together and, assuming a definite form, move toward a culmination or climax, after which there is a sense of completedness and relaxation before the next sequence begins to take form. In Burmese politics any given event is generally seen as having neither antecedents nor consequences and a major development as something which happens spontaneously—as a "break" without planning or warning and does not necessarily move to a climax or to a sense of completion. The non-Burmese observer who feels at some point that developments in Burmese politics have manifestly moved to a stage which calls for an act of resolution, is likely to be surprised to learn that the Burmese do not share his feeling and are no more impatient than usual. He finds that, largely because neither the participants nor the people expect clear and definite climaxes, there are few conclusive events in Burmese politics.

In part the Burmese politician seems so paradoxically relaxed in the face of apparent crisis situations because he believes that politics is in a constant state of tension. He assumes that there will be no change in its pitch or rhythm. This attitude seems to stem from the fact that the Burmese lack any feeling for tidiness in history; they do not see history in terms of stages or phases, and so they are not led to see one sequence rounded off before the next is begun. Unlike foreigners, for example, the Burmese seem to be unperturbed by the propensity of the Burmese government to announce casually in which year of which five-, four-, or three-year plan the country is supposedly engrossed.

The mass media of communication in Burma tend to confirm the sense of a lack of any continuity in Burmese politics. The newspapers give little space to expected developments or to following up major events; instead, they tend to treat all developments as sudden occurrences that have no histories.

The leading Rangoon newspaper in December 1958 gave only four stories front page treatment in two consecutive issues; in September 1959 only six stories received as much consideration, in February 1960 only four stories, and during none of those months did any story cover more than two days. (Comparable figures for the *New York Times* would be 48, 37, and 35, and one story made the front page for a period of 12 days.)

This type of reporting seems to encourage the expectation that major events can take place with relative ease and with a lack of forethought completely out of keeping with the seriousness of the consequences, and, conversely, that dramatic crises can disappear overnight leaving no traces. This is particularly true with respect to the behavior of government agencies, for the Burmese press tends to follow the practice of publishing all government announcements but not reporting on the record of performance; thus the impression is created that the government can suddenly arrive at plans without experiencing a process of planning.

Preference for Uncertainty and a Dislike of Determinism

A basic reason for the Burmese calculations about the tempo and rhythm of politics is that they would rather accept the concept of unpredictable change than the concept of deterministic unfolding of history. They seem to find comfort in the basic Buddhist doctrine that nothing is permanent, all is in flux, and change alone is constant; at the same time they seem to find extremely distasteful the equally fundamental Buddhist doctrine of the *kan* according to which the fate of each individual is rigidly determined by previous incarnations and the cumulative record of present behavior. Possibly determinism is too closely associated in their minds with the prospects of being personally punished to make it a congenial concept. This is particularly likely in political calculations since the Burmese readily turn to political participation in order to escape from the more morbid aspects of their religion. The hope is always that politics and power can give pleasure, and apparently the more deterministic aspects of Buddhism do not suggest such a prospect.

Another related basis for the Burmese reluctance to accept a more orderly sense of events appears to be their fundamental perspective on time, a matter we shall have to examine shortly in greater detail. We need only observe here that Burmese culture is oriented more to the present than to either the past or the future. Since people prefer to think about immediate events rather than look to the future, long-run planning runs into many pitfalls in Burmese politics, of which two in particular stand out. The first, related to the Burmese hope that the future can be filled with pleasant but unexpected surprises, is the attitude that the future is so unpredictable that long-run planning can at best be no different from short-run calculations. The second, related to the anxieties about a deterministic universe, is the concern that in thinking ahead for long-range planning the mind may very likely come across that most unpleasant of all possible subjects, one's own demise. Not only is death treated as an extremely unpleasant matter in Burmese culture, but more important, there seems to be very little in Burmese culture to sustain the individual in considering the possibility that material objects are likely to outlast his own physical existence. He is not encouraged to put faith in the possibility that works will count, and he prefers to believe that all that counts will end with himself.

It is significant that our respondents showed little enthusiasm for a point of view that Americans often feel reflects an optimistic outlook in life: "It is worth striving to improve life in our country, for even if I do not live long enough to see all the benefits, my children will have a better life." A majority of our respondents showed, in one way or another, slight resentment over the idea that others, including even (and in several cases especially) their children, might live to benefit from their toil. Those who had no children tended to laugh off the whole matter as being happily irrelevant in their cases. Members of the administrator class often indicated that they would be happy if their children could have essentially the same experiences they knew in their youth during the prewar period, but few showed any interest in dreaming of a better world to come after their lifetime.

Another indication of the dislike the Burmese political class has for the concept of a deterministic universe is to be seen in their hostility toward profits and the market mechanism of a competitive economy. In large measure, of course, this attitude toward the concept of profits stems from the feeling that Europeans, driven on by their thirst for profits, once exploited Burma, and that Indians and Chinese are probably still doing it. Profits are thus associated with the evil ways of foreigners. In addition, many of the Burmese leaders feel that profits are inherently unjust, indistinguishable from usury, and a sign of unscrupulous, crass, and vulgar motives.

But this is not the whole story. Behind the Burmese distrust there also seems to lie a genuine appreciation of precisely the function profits are expected to perform in guiding allocations and decisions in a free economy. Given the view common in the West that most of the leaders of the new countries do not understand the nature of a modern economic system, it was surprising to learn through our interviews that not only Burmese administrators but even politicians were knowledgeable about most of the elementary principles of economics. In particular, most of them seemed to know that the rationale of profits is to provide the most effective and sensitive mechanism known to man for allocating scarce resources so as to maximize the possibility that people will obtain what they really value. It was precisely this miracle of the market mechanism, which can inspire awe among Western students, that disturbed Burmese the most. For they saw in the theory the possibility of impersonal forces, an "invisible hand," making decisions which would control their own actions. By accepting the logic of profits, apparently powerful people would have to give in to the demands of the common public; thus instead of controlling the public and dominating events they would have to serve the public and respond to events. The Burmese preference is for a less impersonal and deterministic method for allocating resources, and hence they have generally favored political forms of decision making for guiding investments. The Burmese feeling that political decision making can be "humane," "considerate," and "accommodating to human values," while more impersonal decision making is likely to be "harsh," "thoughtless," and "efficient," is central to the Burmese feeling about law and controls, the subject we consider next.

THE COMPLEXITY OF POLITICS

Possibly the most striking characteristic of the calculations of Burmese politicians and administrators is their extreme sensitivity to the possibility of numberless complexities in any political situation. Every political relationship, event, or issue is seen as having so many dimensions and endless possibilities that only the sophisticated can fully appreciate them. There is thus a constant need to analyze, interpret, and reinterpret every shred of evidence in order to avoid being taken in by the obvious.

The sense that politics is infinitely complex operates not only when Burmese are responding passively to political events as they see them but also when the Burmese politician seeks an active and manipulative approach. No problem can be handled directly and in a straightforward fashion lest someone be offended. Moreover, it is assumed that if people understand what one really wants, they will naturally and automatically act to deny one's wishes. Thus every act calls for elaborate planning, much reflection, and a search for the most subtle and hence most skillful approach. The ability to find endless complications in what would seem the simplest of problems in other political cultures constantly leads the Burmese politician astray from the purpose for which he began his calculations. In particular there is a strong likelihood that, by the time he has elaborated in his own mind all that might or could be done with respect to a particular problem, he has become so sensitive to all the possibilities of offending and provoking others that he suffers a complete paralysis of effort, usually followed by a feeling that others with malicious intentions have been frustrating his desires and making his life difficult.

Their exaggerated sense of the complexity of politics leads the Burmese to place a great deal of reliance on intermediaries. They do not, however, follow the Chinese custom of using a middle man whom both parties explicitly recognize as performing a positive function in arranging an agreement. The Burmese rarely put all their trust in one middle man. If the matter is really important, the Burmese politician seeks out several possible intermediaries and requests the help of each with respect to some limited aspect of the total problem. Consequently, the process of arranging a solution is divided into so many parts that the problem invariably becomes more and more complicated; thus, in his effort to keep from appearing as though he were trying to control anyone, the Burmese politician is in constant danger of losing all control over the situation. He works himself into a position in which, unless things all fall into place at once to produce the desired solution, the failure of one part of the operation leads inevitably to a compounding of his difficulties.

The Easy Slip from Omnipotence to Incompetence

The Burmese politician thus frequently finds that instead of being on the verge of engineering an amazing array of relationships according to his will, he is entangled in a web of confusion. He is constantly learning that only a thin line separates his expectations of omnipotence and his sense of incompetence. As a consequence, in Burmese political calculations the belief that great things are about to be accomplished is always crowded by the feeling that nothing is really going to happen except more trouble. The two extremes of great success and complete failure are seen as close together and not separated by a broad range of near successes and partial failures.

Senior administrators may declare at one moment that dramatic changes are in the offing and exciting plans and programs about to be initiated, and then confess at the next moment that nothing can be expected for nothing is ever accomplished by government. The combination of resistance to a deterministic world and the capacity to see unlimited complexities in politics contributes to this sequence of feelings in which a sense of omnipotence can easily give way to one of incompetence. This is seen in Burmese officials' feelings about the need to make exceptions in the application of rules and laws. The distaste for rigid standards makes officials feel it appropriate and just to humanize or, as they like to say, "Burmanize" the law. Also, their feeling that they can see infinitely more complex ramifications in any particular case than does the impersonal code of law makes it easy for them to feel sincere in rationalizing the need for exceptions in the application of the law. At the same time the capacity to conceive of, and actually to make, exceptions easily becomes confused with the feeling that one can rise above mere laws and be omnipotent. Once the Pandora's box has been opened, however, and the exceptions pile up, the official finds that the calculus of favoritism must take over and that he has lost all control over the situation. In trying to be greater than impersonal laws, he easily falls under the tyranny of personal obligations and feelings of incompetence.

THE REWARDS OF POLITICS

It is probably not particularly significant that the members of the Burmese political class tend to picture politics as belonging to the elite of the society, and it is only a bit more noteworthy that they are also rather candid in admitting that they expect politics to be personally and materially rewarding. Their open concern with the benefits of office merely reflects the fact that the Burmese political culture was shaped in part by a phase of colonial administrative politics during which great value was placed on the relative perquisites of different positions. To this day there are considerable jealousies among politicians and administrators as to who gets car allowances and who gets what kind of housing.

Of much greater importance is the basic expectation that out of the very unpredictableness of politics can come the greatest rewards, from which it follows that in politics there is little connection between effort and reward. Here we see what appears to be a direct consequence of the Burmese experience of drastic and unexpected social and political change. If the process of cultural diffusion and social change has implanted profound feelings of insecurity in the Burmese political class and left them feeling that they must grope about in an unpredictably changing world, the same process of change has also unexpectedly thrown people up into positions of high influence and brought rewards completely out of line with degrees of effort or commitment.

One of the members of the civil service who came from a strongly Anglicized family background described his experiences in the following words:

My first years at school were uneventful. I thought at that time that I knew all the people I would ever have to know in my life. Within my own family, I had all the connections that seemed to be necessary. But since the war I have met the most extraordinary and important people, people I never knew of or even dreamed of meeting. I have met prime ministers and presidents and I have met people from Asia and from Europe and people from countries that I had never even heard of. I have shaken the hand of Tito. It has all been most puzzling, most extraordinary. Frankly, I'm not even sure today whether there really is a country of Yugoslavia, but it has all been most exciting. I would have had to work much harder before the war to hold an ordinary civil service job. Now without doing a thing I am at the top.

For the politicians, the sense of the unpredictability of life is possibly even more dramatic, for most of them had little prospect of achieving high status before the war and then suddenly, as a result of events over which they had no control, they were brought to the top to be national leaders and cabinet members. One politician, reflecting on how his life was unpredictably changed, commented:

I could not possibly tell you how it all happened. It came as such a surprise to me for in just one day it seemed I became an important official. Before that I had hardly had even dreams of being a great man. At school and at the university, we talked about independence and the need to create a Burmese government, but I never thought of myself as actually running a government. I never thought of myself at the head of any kind of organization. Then suddenly, it all happened and there we were. We really didn't have to do much, it just happened.

The extraordinary events in their own lives, combined with their basic lack of self-confidence about managing public affairs, seem to have weakened the sense of the plausible in many of the political elite. Indeed, their unsureness about both the limits of the possible and the difference between the likely and the implausible seems to leave both the administrator and politician vacillating constantly between naive enthusiasm and a stubborn determination to resist being taken in by anyone. These feelings appear in their ambivalent attitudes toward planning and toward the possibilities of predicting the future. Since all manner of extraordinary things have occurred in their lives without foresight or planning, there is a certain willingness to close their eyes to the future and hope for the best. At the same time, the very lack of any strong sense of the realm of the plausible encourages a rather excited interest in the prospects for planning. It is possible to dream of even more extraordinary occurrences.

Basic to these considerations is the powerful resistance of the Burmese politician to the idea that a close link might exist between the expenditure of purposeful effort and the realization of political returns. To try too hard and to suggest too obviously one's goals can only result in others automatically seeking to frustrate one's desires. A strong commitment to any goal means some loss of control over the total situation, for to push too hard is to be off balance and easily tripped up by others. This reluctance for positive measures is reinforced by the experience of having the best of personal rewards generally follow from the least predictable of developments.

As we have suggested, many of the features of the Burmese political culture, both in its spirit and its calculations, can be traced to the historical evolution of the contemporary system and to the structure of power in the society. With respect to Burma we explored features of this form of macroanalysis before presenting the outlines of the political culture. We may now turn to other sources of the political culture and examine the ways in which the members of the Burmese political class were inducted into Burmese culture and came in time to learn about the modern world of government and politics. To avoid clumsiness in exposition and the likelihood of tedious repetitions, we shall not attempt to point out possible connections between the political culture and specific aspects of the socialization process. Mere suggestion should be enough to make the links apparent.

PART IV

The Socialization Process

CHAPTER 13

A Note on the Burmese Family

Burmese politics are in part a distillation of certain fundamental qualities of Burmese culture and personality. In turning now to these sources of Burmese politics, it should be noted that there is considerable literature on the Burmese character and Burmese culture, both of which have had an intense fascination for many Western observers. Certainly the dominant mood of most of the early English descriptions of Burmese life was one of sympathy and warmth for a people whom the English seemed to enjoy both as subjects and as individuals. After their experiences in India, with its castes, its heat and dust, its poverty, and its masses of aggressive but subservient peoples, the British apparently came with enthusiasm to life in the tropical lushness and greenness of Burma and wanted to see only the best in the handsome people they found there.

The call of Burma—"Go ye back to Mandalay"—was to the land, "a neater, cleaner land" than even England, and to a people of striking charm and romance. India evoked in the Victorian Englishman a sense of duty, honor, a task to be done, a burden to be carried, hardships and grandeur; Burma, on the other hand, offered the suggestion of pleasures and gentleness, of the desirability of respecting the customs of others, of laissez faire. India could confirm an Englishman in his values and convince him of the need and the justice of spreading his version of progress and development. Burma challenged his values by subtly bringing them into question and casting doubts as to whether effort and progress are really significant goals for human life. The story is much the same today. India now suggests to Americans the urgency of five-year plans and the merits of modern industrial development, while Burma continues to evoke a question as to whether modern life is really the ultimate way.

Two themes emerge in nearly all the early Western attempts to describe Burmese character. The first relates to the quality we have placed at the center of contemporary Burmese political culture, the contradiction between gentleness and violence. Whether the point of view was friendly or critical or objectively neutral toward the Burmese, all observers agreed that there were many paradoxes in the Burmese character.

One side to the Burmese character was usually described with such words as: happy, carefree, tension-free, outgoing, easygoing, cheerful, spontaneous, laughing, without a thought for the morrow, loyal, noncompulsive, and childlike. To this day the Burmese themselves tend to use these same words in describing what they consider to be their better national characteristics. The other side of Burmese character was usually referred to by such words as: touchy, overly sensitive, cocky, aggressive, sullen, quick tempered, cruel, quick to take offense, shy, selfish, opportunistic, and other terms suggesting a potentiality toward anger and violence. Not surprisingly, in present-day Burma these same words are used to describe what are still considered to be national weaknesses and faults.

The second theme which emerges from a survey of the literature on Burma is that Burmese character has consistently been corrupted by government and politics no matter who the rulers have been. The persistent assumption has been that all the negative generalities of the Burmese are attributable to governmental policies, and that, therefore, if the government could only be changed—or better still, if all government could be completely eliminated—the positive and profoundly good qualities of the Burmese would readily emerge triumphant and uncompromised. Significantly, the Burmese of today have also taken over this theme and customarily attribute the negative qualities of their character to the evils of governments, either past or present.

When the English first came to Burma, they quickly came to believe that the positive qualities of Burmese character were the true ones. They attributed the negative features to corruption caused by enforced life under the manifest tyranny of the Burmese kings; with better government, a truly good people would emerge. Their desire to see only the brighter side of Burmese character is reflected in the quotation from Matthew Arnold which H. Fielding Hall, the most articulate spokesman for the Burmese, used to convey the theme of his book: "To see things in their beauty is to see them in their truth." Hall, whose affection and sympathy for the Burmese was so great that he too often slipped over the line into sentimentality, expressed the common feeling of the British for the Burmese in the titles of his two extremely popular books, *The Soul of a People* and *A People in School,* and in his theme that the Burmese were a good people with souls of virtue who would overcome their few defects by passing through a period of schooling.[1]

After the introduction of British rule it was impossible, of course, to continue to attribute the less likable qualities of the Burmese people to the evils of a system which no longer operated. Consequently the British writers began to wonder more and more whether the British rule itself, by destroying the customary norms of Burmese social intercourse, might not have created the negative side of Burmese personality. Different policies, possibly even a different rule, might bring out the better side.[2]

Contemporary anthropologists see many of the same qualities in Burmese culture, but they tend, as should be expected in this post-Freudian epoch, to link Burmese character more closely with the pattern of early childhood experiences. In seeking enlightenment on the Burmese family, we are primarily dependent upon the work of four social scientists. Hazel Hitson has produced a data-rich and penetrating report on the basis of a year of field work in a Burmese village.[3] A second recent

1. *The Soul of a People* was first published by Macmillan in 1898 and then went through four editions, the last of which had eight reprintings. *A People in School,* also published by Macmillan, first appeared in 1906 and was only slightly less popular.

2. The former British colonial official, J. S. Furnivall, became a leading spokesman for the view that most of the faults in Burmese character stemmed from British rule. (See especially his *Colonial Policy and Practice.*) Furnivall, acting in a spirit not uncommon among leading British colonial officials, tended to be highly critical of the distant policy makers at the Colonial Office and in the Secretariat who, he felt, had little understanding of reality in the countryside and no sympathy for the people themselves. In siding with "his people" in his district, Furnivall, like so many other British officials, developed a deep attachment to the Burmese.

The fascination of British officials with Burmese culture resulted in an extensive literature describing all phases of Burmese life. One of the most distinguished of these was Sir James G. Scott, who for reasons meaningful and compelling only to a Victorian mind, chose to write under the pseudonym of Shway Yoe, "Subject of the Great Queen." On the basis of his painstakingly meticulous and yet witty and insightful work, *The Burman: His Life and Notions* (London, Macmillan, 1882), Scott must be ranked as one of the outstanding members of that amazing band of 19th century Englishmen who fancied themselves as merely ordinary colonial officials but who in fact were the pioneers of anthropology.

3. Hazel Hitson, "Family Pattern and Paranoidal Personality Structure in Boston and Burma," dissertation, Radcliffe College, 1959. Hitson's thesis is that there is a relationship between the type of family culture, the socializing process, the way in which anger is handled, and the most likely form of mental illness in the culture. In particular, she advances the hypothesis that if the family culture deals with anger by turning it outward toward the environment there is likely to be a high incidence of violence and homicide, and if mental illness develops it is likely to take

study of Burmese national character was done by Lucien M. Hanks on the basis of field observations in Arakan at the end of World War II.[4] The third suggestive study of Burmese personality, an outstanding example of studying a culture from afar, was done by Geoffrey Gorer during World War II when field observations were impossible.[5] The fourth analyst of Burmese character, U Sein Tu, is possibly the most sensitive and certainly the most explicitly Freudian.[6]

---

the paranoidal form. Conversely, if the home environment results in turning anger inward there will be a greater incidence of suicide, and mental illness will take a depressive form. On the basis of her data, Hitson concludes that the high incidence of violence in Burmese culture is related to the pattern of directing hostility against others.

4. Lucien M. Hanks, "The Quest for Individual Autonomy in the Burmese Personality," *Psychiatry, 12,* no. 3, 285–300.

Hanks concludes that at the basis of the Burmese character is a compulsive quest for autonomy, a need to be freed from all restraints, particularly those of superiors, and to escape from the dangers and uncertainties of human relationships. Hanks relates their urge to be rid of all superiors to the childhood experiences of, first, extremely permissive early years, and then, the sudden introduction into the highly disciplined monastery schools.

5. Geoffrey Gorer, "Burmese Personality" (mimeographed; New York, Institute of Inter-Cultural Studies, 1943).

After perusing carefully all available literature on Burma and interviewing people with firsthand experiences in the country, Gorer hypothesized that the Burmese socialization process produces a high proportion of insecure males, who as children were indulged but whose treatment by parents was subject to extremes of mood, and more competent women who early in life were forced to assume responsibilities. Thus for Gorer the final Burmese paradox is that "the dominant women act as though they were subservient . . . and the hen-pecked passive men talk and strut and pose as though they were really in control, consulting their wives surreptitiously, but announcing the decisions as if they were their own. The Burmese character is doubly distorted; the broken male struts like a master; and the dominant woman smiles and gives way to him."

6. Sein Tu, "Ideology and Personality in Burmese Society" (mimeographed; Harvard University, 1955).

The heart of Sein Tu's analysis is the hypothesis that the Burmese family provides an intense oedipal situation which is homosexually resolved. The child is extremely close to the mother and feels small and helpless before the domineering and frightening father who offers no basis for the son to identify with him. The son resolves this situation by identifying even more closely with his mother and emulates her in psychologically submitting passively to the father. By linking himself in this way to his mother the boy is able to feel closer to her, reduce his fear of being forsaken by her, and at the same time by "identifying himself with the aggressor" he is able to view his father as a seductive rather than destructive threat.

To the extent that this pattern is psychologically valid in Burmese life, one is inclined to speculate that it may leave the Burmese peculiarly sensitive to any appeals to changing his identity—a sensitivity which certainly exists, as we shall be observing in our discussion of the acculturation process. This is to say that the complex of feelings that the child may have toward his father may later be re-

On the basis of these four interpretive analyses and other sources,[7] it is possible to outline the most significant features of the early socialization process within the family setting. Broadly speaking, the Burmese family resembles the type of family common to most of tropical Asia. The Burmese, however, have tended to make less of a formal ideological issue over the importance of family associations than many other Asians, such as the Chinese, Japanese, and even the Filipinos. They are less prone to employ explicitly such concepts as family honor and loyalty, and they have not surrounded the principles of filial piety with quasi-religious sanctions. In spite of these qualifications, it remains true that no other institution in Burmese society places a greater demand on the individual. The family provides the unmistakable focus for all Burmese social life.

The atmosphere of the Burmese family conveys the impression of an intimate, active, crowded, and noisy way of life. Whether the home is that of the rural peasant or the wealthier resident of Rangoon, it provides almost no possibility for developing a sense of privacy. As the physical size of dwellings expands, the number of people who are expected to live together increases in almost direct proportion; so the amount of space for the individual does not change greatly with income levels. Consequently the Burmese is brought up to feel that nearly all activities should normally occur in a group setting. This characteristic of the family situation may help explain why throughout life any urge toward privacy is more than counteracted by the comforts of being in the center of activities. Certainly a striking quality of the Burmese political class is that its members are never alone throughout their waking hours; they tend to surround themselves with at best an entourage and with at least a few cronies who never leave their sight. Just as in the family setting,

---

enacted in a psychological sense in his reactions to the modern world which he can perceive as threatening, demanding, but also attractive and seductive.

Thus while the child may long to be possessed by the father (feeling deep down a sense of competition with the mother), he also fears and repudiates his desires; hence he has the need to deny what he truly feels, and he may experience the transition from "I love him," through "I hate him," to "he hates me," which is the basis of a paranoid reaction. (O. Fenichel, *The Psychoanalytic Theory of Neuroses,* New York, Norton, 1945, pp. 427 ff.) As we shall be observing, the same pattern of transition seems to be basic to the reactions of many Burmese to the initially attractive but fundamentally threatening appeals of modern culture and of the West.

7. The most useful general description of upper-class Burmese family life which conveys some nostalgic sentiments for the prewar Burmese life, is Mi Mi Khaing, *Burmese Family* (Calcutta, Longmans, Green, 1946).

well-being is associated with a constant need to interact with others and not to experience any of the sensations of physical isolation.

Within the family context, children are generally treated with a very high degree of indulgence; in Western eyes Burmese children are constantly in danger of being "spoiled." They are warmly accepted as a source of happiness and amusement, and almost no demands are placed on them until they are ready for schooling. The Burmese mother displays a high degree of genuine happiness and affection toward her child. The nursing relationship is apparently a physically and psychologically satisfying one for the child; he is nursed whenever he cries so that feeding occurs frequently and under quite matter-of-fact circumstances. The child is the object of attention by all members of the family, who casually pass him around among themselves while freely fondling, cuddling, and playing with him. Nobody, however, except the mother has any sense of responsibility for the child; others, when bored with him or attracted to something else, will unexpectedly break off the affectionate relationship.

There is also substantial anthropological evidence that the mother herself tends to vacillate between extremes of warmth and affection and of disinterest and exasperation. She too can become unexpectedly cold, distant, and uninterested. Frequently she may tease the child, excite him, arouse him, and then, if her mood changes, suddenly stop and seem to put him out of her mind. The child is thus brought up to feel that he has no control over the ways in which he is treated by others. Whether he is the object of kindly affection or completely ignored has little relationship to his own behavior; it is not a question of reward and punishment but of the mood of his mother. Thus from the time of his earliest experiences the child exists in a world in which there is no rational relationship, no recognizable cause-and-effect connection between his powers of action and choice and the things he most desperately wants. From this beginning the Burmese child comes to feel unconsciously that the world is fickle, and that those who seem warmest and closest can become the primary source of one's isolation. The Burmese child thus learns the most profound lesson of his life: there is impermanence in life, a far more profound form of impermanence than that implied by Buddhist preaching about the transitory nature of physical things, for this is the impermanence of human relationships.

As the child grows older, the spirit of permissiveness continues but in an erratic fashion. He is expected to cause his parents less trouble and absolutely no anxieties. He is not, however, given a clear set of standards of performance, the achievement of which might yield predictable rewards. The parents make few demands for achievement; indeed, there appears to be very little in the Burmese socialization process which would produce what David McClelland has called a high sense of the need for achievement.[8] The world becomes increasingly demanding and dangerous, but the child is not taught in any firm fashion how to behave in order to reduce the element of danger and unpredictability in social relationships. He learns only that he should avoid as best he can becoming in any sense a nuisance. He thus tends to expect security from being subservient and yielding to all who are his superiors.

In addition, there is considerable evidence that the Burmese tend to rely heavily upon shame and ridicule in the socialization process, with the result that the child becomes extremely sensitive to the opinions of others. His sense of self-esteem is socially conditioned so that his sense of identity is determined to an unusual degree by the way in which others regard him. Fear of shame and need for praise and reassurance become all-important guides to behavior. Basically, however, the Burmese becomes dependent upon the opinions of others because the socialization process has left him with few internalized standards of behavior that are self-exacting and self-demanding.

Another feature of the early socialization process is the explicit use of fear. The child is apparently frequently controlled by being told that unless he submits to the will of his parents, he will be carried off by ogresses, bogies, or *nats* of the spirit world. The parents frighten him, but they themselves display no sense of fear. Thus in time fear becomes associated with loneliness, and conversely, loneliness and isolation become in themselves fearful; thus a Burmese can experience the sensations of fear when socially isolated, and it is possible and understandable for him to lose his head to fear when others about him are keeping theirs and appear relaxed.

The Burmese child is explicitly taught to think of his family as the center of his existence and as a shelter against all the dangers of the outside world. Loyalty and subservience to parents is the ultimate test of the character of the individual. From earliest childhood, the Burman is taught that he should always be infinitely careful not to bring any distress or unhappiness to his parents. Since the child is not trained to highly explicit standards of behavior, "good" conduct tends to become subservient and docile conduct. To yield to the wishes of the parents is to please them and to act in an exemplary fashion. Hence at a very early

8. David McClelland et al., *The Achievement Motive* (New York, Appleton-Century-Crofts, 1953).

stage in life the Burmese child is taught to be completely submissive before any form of authority and to expect that a passive and yielding attitude is most likely to please those with power.

It is significant that in the relatively loosely structured Burmese society almost the only cumulative and reinforcing patterns of social pressures are those prohibiting any explicit revolts against the family. Once the child has entered the age of reason he is not expected to demonstrate even the slightest sign of opposition to family control. We may speculate that in Burma, as in much of the rest of Asia, the continued denial to youth of any possibility to express legitimately any sense of revolt against parental authority has led young people to direct their spirit of rebellion to an inordinate degree against other and less sacredly protected forms of authority. Thus in these societies many modern forms of authority become the ready objects of attack of a youth who paradoxically wishes to rebel against the old authorities and to accept the new ones. The sentiments of family are still far too powerful to be directly challenged, and yet the necessity of yielding to an authority that is unable to give psychic satisfaction, especially in a changing world, produces an increasingly rebellious spirit.

From the anthropological evidence about the Burmese family we can draw some very tentative conclusions about the early stages of the Burmese socialization process which may throw light on some of the problems of nation building. Specifically, it is possible to identify within the family relationships practices that may contribute to the paradoxical sentiments so central to the Burmese political culture. In terms of the early years of life, the contradictions take the form of an odd combination of optimism and distrust, a combination which in varying degrees seems to be present in many transitional societies having difficulties in modernizing.[9]

Personality theory might suggest that the qualities of cheerfulness and optimism so frequently noted in descriptions of Burmese character may be related to the relaxed, generous, and even blissful pattern of infant nursing. The family setting and the sympathetic spirit of the Burmese mother are conducive to a powerful sense of omnipotence, for in the beginning the world belongs to the child, responding to his every demand and eliminating his every frustration. Every time he signals displeasure or

9. The tendency to vacillate between unfettered optimism and profound suspicion emerged as a dominant characteristic of Indian personality as analyzed by A. Morris Carstairs, *The Twice Born: A Study of a Community of High-Caste Hindus* (London, Hogarth Press, 1957).

tension his world reacts to bring him food and oral gratification. This may possibly provide the dynamic basis for the irrational and almost compulsive sense of optimism which is never lost in spite of all the tests of reality.

Yet right after this phase of infant bliss comes the "betrayal" by the mother, who turns out to be controlled more by her own unpredictable moods than by the wishes of her child. The relationship that has shown the potentiality of being the warmest and closest has turned out to be unreliable—a traumatic experience. Thereafter it may always be hard for the Burmese to push aside a basic distrust of any relationship that pretends to be constant, loving, and generously helpful. For him, there is true danger and uncertainty in all human relationships.

A comparable and hence reinforcing sequence of experiences occurs when the boy is suddenly confronted at about school age with the shock of responsibility. The early and highly permissive years are devoted to instilling in the child a diffuse but powerful sense of dependency upon his family. The open, cheerful, noisy, and active qualities of young Burmese children, and for that matter most young Asian children, may be closely associated with this permissive and undemanding period. The sharp increase in demands for conformity at school age may contribute to the more withdrawn, cautious, and even sullen and suspicious airs of the older children when confronted with the outside world.

The sum effect of these early experiences appears to be a peculiar blending of a perennial capacity for optimism with a diffuse, all-pervasive distrust and suspicion of others in any particular relationship. The need to suppress all protestations against the very one who has done the most to damage faith in human associations may be the origin of the violence and cruelty, the touchiness, the explosive tempers, and the readiness to take offense that many have observed to be one side of the Burmese character. These aggressive tendencies may spring from the child's denial of any legitimate way of expressing his aggressive and hurt feelings over his mother's having forsaken him. As in most traditional Asian cultures, he is forced to display unqualifiedly submissive respect to both his parents irrespective of how they may tease, ignore, love, or punish him. Any suggestion of hostility toward the parents is likely to be met on the manifest level with severe punishment, and on the latent level it is likely to appear as an attack on the mother, the one person with whom the child is seeking intimacy. Thus, deep down, the danger of offending the mother is that of courting isolation and loneliness. The child cannot strike back either directly or symbolically, but instead must show only greater respect and submissiveness. Aggressive feelings are thus dammed up, to explode later in other contexts where it is safer to drop the front of courtesy and deference.

These conflicting experiences within the family may possibly stand behind and give strength to the extraordinary resilience of the Burmese people, making it possible for them to believe constantly that the present is "the best of all possible Burmas," even while always acting on the basis of a profound distrust of those with power. Unable to resist the temptation of enjoying the pleasures of a superficial optimism, the Burmese at the same time seem equally unable to take a trusting view of the motives of others. On the one hand, the sense of optimism makes it possible for the Burmese people to go through crisis after crisis with remarkably little psychic damage; on the other hand, their fundamental feeling of distrust in human relationships, and particularly of the possibility for stable relationships, makes it extremely difficult for them to perform effectively in any organizational context. In terms of the requirements of nation building, it would seem that this peculiar combination of faith in the diffuse and suspicion of the particular is precisely the opposite of what is needed. A greater distrust of institutions and of forms of power and a greater faith in people would provide a far stronger basis for nation building. At least this would seem to be the case if we contrast these Burmese attitudes with those of people in more industrially developed societies. For example, the very basis of the American governmental system and its division of powers is a diffuse suspicion of institutions and of man's motives in general which, however, is coupled with an open and trusting approach toward particular relationships among individuals.

CHAPTER 14

A Sense for Order and the Idea
of Purposeful Action

Although an individual's basic personality may be largely formulated in
the early years of life, the experiences of becoming a full man and a complete member of a culture are of much longer duration. In transmitting
the more complex and sophisticated cultural values and attitudes, the
socialization process extends well into the years of schooling and early
adulthood. Indeed, it is during late adolescence that the maturing person,
by achieving a satisfactory balance between his unconscious and his conscious processes of development, gains a sense of his own identity as both
an individual and as a member of a community.

There is thus a need in the maturing person to bring together his accumulating experiences and to resolve what Erikson has called the individual's "identity crisis." In his words:

> I have called the major crisis of adolescence the *identity crisis;* it
> occurs in that period of the life cycle when each youth must forge for
> himself some central perspective and direction, some working unity,
> out of the effective remnants of his childhood and the hopes of the
> anticipated adulthood; he must detect some meaningful resemblance
> between what he has come to see in himself and what his sharpened
> awareness tells him others judge and expect him to be.[1]

In treating the later stages of the socialization process, the problems
of analysis become considerably more difficult because the process itself
becomes increasingly more diffuse, involving so many institutions and

1. Erikson, *Young Man Luther,* p. 14.

relationships that orderly classification becomes almost impossible. In contrast, the circumstances and relationships of infancy are infinitely more limited and determined, and therefore, if for no other reason, more amenable to classification and systematic analysis. The problem is somewhat analogous to that of analyzing chess games: because of the limited possibilities it is feasible to give standardized names to the opening moves and initial defenses, but the range of possibilities and combinations soon increases so rapidly that it becomes impossible to identify and standardize the strategies and moves of the middle game.

In our initial discussion of the theories for understanding the problems of nation building we noted that there are three levels to the socialization process: the learning of the technical skills and competencies, the acquiring of motivations, and the development of the capacity to work together in associations and organizations.[2] It is this last aspect of the socialization process which is of particular significance in our understanding of the basis of Burmese political culture.

There are, of course, a wide range of attitudes and values that may influence the tone and quality of interpersonal relationships in a society and determine the capacity of people to develop and maintain complex organizations. For our purpose in trying to relate basic attitudes to the problems of political development and nation building, it is possible to concentrate on those ways in which the socialization process encourages and discourages people to feel that their universe is orderly, predictable, and manipulatable.

In so focusing our attention we are proceeding on the assumption that the extent to which people believe that political action can be and generally is purposeful is directly related to their capacity to sense the possibility of an orderly and law-directed world. The basic rationale of a modern political system is that human effort can be purposefully directed to producing significant results because there is a minimum degree of predictability in human relationships. The ability to think in terms of systematic patterns of human relationships, and then to appreciate the full significance of such concepts as a "political system," an "economy," and a "social order," calls for a capacity to generalize about behavior and to sense the meaning of an orderly world. For people to build all types of organizations necessary for a modern society it is essential that they be able to identify themselves with larger collectivities, and to do this they must be able to envisage a systematic and predictable world.

With these considerations in mind we can now examine the Burmese

2. See above, Chap. 4.

socialization process in terms of certain themes that are critically pertinent in shaping the individual's sense of identity and in governing his feeling for order and meaning in human affairs. We shall be dealing with six themes which range from attitudes about the sacred and concepts of causality and prediction, to considerations about the nature of human feelings and the character of amity and enmity. We must make it clear that our data on the Burmese socialization process are inadequate to provide answers to all the questions suggested by each of the themes. Neither the existing literature on Burma nor our field investigation provides the necessary intensive data, and therefore our discussion will often have to take the form of hypotheses about Burmese practices based upon the fragmentary evidence at hand.

The Dimension of the Sacred and the Secular

In all societies religion provides a fundamental basis for the individual's sense of identity, but in transitional societies religion and race tend to be the dominant considerations. Religion also mainly provides transitional peoples with the most elaborate and systematic ways of thinking to which they are exposed, particularly during their early years.

Are the sacred and the secular seen as two separate and distinct spheres, each with its own laws and standards; and how far are the principles of the one supposed to guide behavior in the other? Are the two spheres mutually compatible or conflicting? Does concern with the sacred supposedly strengthen man in his relations with others, or does it make it possible for man to ignore the opinions of others in order to pursue higher goals? What are these higher goals?

It is appropriate to begin our discussion of the secondary stages of socialization in Burma with an examination of training about the sacred and secular, for in general both foreign observers and Burmese are likely to agree that religion is at the center of Burmese culture, pervading all aspects of daily life. Pagodas dominate the landscape and *pongyis* (monks) in their yellow robes and black begging bowls are never long out of sight. Religion seems to lie at the very basis of the Burman's sense of identity both as an individual and as a member of a community. In identifying himself and distinguishing himself from Indians, Chinese, Pakistanis, or members of the ethnic minorities, he will call himself a "Burmese Buddhist." Burmese generally take a fierce pride in their claim that their Therevada Buddhism is a purer version of Buddhism than that of the Mahayana school of China and Japan. Politically, many Burmese find it difficult to think of their state in secular terms, and many of the non-

Buddhist minority peoples doubt whether the Burmese are capable of rising above a partisan religious point of view.

The Burmese child is brought up in a world in which religious events are the high points not only of the yearly cycle of events but also of his own life. The excitements and thrills of his early years are mainly associated with the calendar of religious feasts and holidays: the Water Festival in April, the beginning of Buddhist Lent, the Light Festival in November. Every Burmese has to spend at least a few days as a monk within the monastery, obeying the vows of the order and living the daily rounds of the *pongyi*. By doing so he becomes a man and not a mere animal; he becomes something which no foreigner, no non-Buddhist, no woman can become: one who may realize Nirvana on passing from this world.

As in most traditional societies, many secular aspects of life in Burma are governed by religious considerations, while many religious activities are approached in what often appears to be a secular and profane spirit. There does not seem to be a clear line between the sacred and the secular in Burmese life. Consequently, there is considerable uncertainty and even confusion over the place religion should occupy in social and public affairs. Behind these more or less intellectual confusions over the appropriate place of religion, many Burmese also appear to have some genuinely ambivalent attitudes toward essential elements of their religion. This is to say that there appears to be confusion about the relationship of the sacred and the secular at two levels: first, that of social convention and conscious judgment, and second, at the deeper level of personal commitment and psychological anxieties over substantive aspects of the religion.

Historically, as we have noted, religion was the very basis of most of the Burmese social and political structure, and thus it should be expected that the process of modernization would create difficult issues about the place religion should continue to occupy in Burmese life. The old tradition that religion should pervade all spheres of life stands in direct contrast with the tradition established during British rule that new institutions, newly introduced from abroad, should have a purely secular quality. The basis of a functional division between the sacred and the secular was thus established by the very logic of colonial rule, but since independence the nationalist desire to "Burmanize" all institutions has raised as an issue the arbitrary distinctions between sacred and secular introduced by British rule. Should not all institutions reflect the Buddhistic traditions basic to Burmese culture?

Intellectually, this is an acute problem with which in varying forms nationalist leaders throughout the newly emerging countries are challenged. Significantly, the general pattern is very similar to the one we find in Burma: much public discussion of the desirability and of the absolute need to find the nation's identity in its religious traditions, but in practice a considerable hesitation and uneasiness over matters touching on religion. It would seem that members of the political class in particular have certain deep personal ambivalences toward religion that must have a psychological and not just an intellectual basis.

In our interviews with Burmese politicians and administrators the evidence of ambivalence emerged out of their responses to questions about the relative social status of the various professions in Burmese life. In a very striking fashion our respondents tended to rank *pongyis* or the Buddhist monks either near the top or the very bottom of the social hierarchy. It might seem that those who ranked the *pongyis* high might either be more religious or less touched by the process of social change, but further questioning revealed more agreement than differences among our respondents on this matter: those who placed the monks at the bottom could, on being further queried, easily reverse their decision and place them at the top; conversely, those who began with them at the top could be easily induced to reverse their judgment. This might be taken as a sign of the general nature of our respondents—who always found happiness in pleasing—except for the fact that they generally displayed considerable stubbornness in defending their initial ranking of all other professions.[3] Our respondents did not really disagree over the significance of monks, but they showed ambivalent and tension-laden feelings about them. In general, they felt that they ought to give a high place to the *pongyis,* but they seemed to derive real pleasure and satisfaction from ranking them below most others in their society.

In exploring further the attitudes of our respondents, it became apparent that no institution that had trained them about religion had in any significant form adapted itself to modern life. Thus they tended to identify religion both with tradition and with the issue of modernizing and changing their way of life. The socialization process has apparently left the Burmese with overtones of anxiety about religion while expecting to find security in it.

For most Burmese, instruction in Buddhism came largely from family, peers, and general social relations. As one of our respondents explained, "In Burma we just learn about religion automatically. People are always

3. The only significant exception was that of the politician who, to a slightly lesser degree, was ranked in much the same extreme ways as the monk.

using religious expressions, and the Burmese boy learns about religion in the same way as he learns to speak his language." Another respondent observed that "most Burmese don't study their religion, they just pick it up as they grow up. It is like learning about sex in a civilized society. We would never deny our children the pleasures and excitements of having mysteries."

In spite of this general and unstructured pattern of learning, most of the respondents said that they had either attended a monastery school or received formal instruction from a Buddhist monk or lay leader. Their picture of these experiences as they were and as the respondents felt they *ought* to have been provides us with the basis for hypothesizing about the sources of the ambivalent Burmese feeling about religion.

Although there is considerable evidence that, as Hanks has suggested, the Burmese monastery schools impose an unexpected and demanding regime of discipline on the boy, our respondents displayed a fundamental belief that the understanding of religion should rest at its very essence upon a warm and positive student-teacher relationship. Most of the respondents wanted to think of the relationship as the "purest," "most selfless," and the "safest" relationship possible among human beings. In their minds the teacher, the *pongyi,* should be a man without passion, without emotion, without the corrupting wisdom of the world, and with a concern only for ultimate (and hence inherently innocent) things. It is almost as though these Burmese would have liked to find in their associations with their religious teachers the kind of relationship our anthropological authorities suggest the Burmese infant wants to have with his mother: a secure, warm, unchanging, predictable, protecting, and completely asexual relationship.

It seems, however, that certain sexual overtones tend generally to color the relationship between student and teacher and create a basic feeling of dissatisfaction and a latent uneasiness about religion. The demand that the student abjectly and unqualifiedly accept the authority of monks who symbolize a denial of masculinity has apparently some comforting aspects. The relationship with the father was never so potentially safe and neutral. And yet the need to be utterly submissive and passive in both thought and action toward men who have rejected the complete male role is also profoundly disturbing. Above all, the experience of deeply wanting a relationship with such men, while at the same time sensing fear from being disciplined by them, appears to have unsettling consequences. The basic paradox for the Burmese boy is his need to recognize that only by acknowledging the complete superiority of men who appear to be rejecting manhood can he himself realize his manhood and his basic identity as a Buddhist, a male, a Burmese, and a possessor of a soul—as a man superior to all foreigners. There is thus at the very heart of the matter a discordant element which is enough to compromise the basic feeling for religion.

It seems that the Burmese feeling toward religion is essentially the same as what the anthropologists tell us is their feeling toward their families. Just as the Burman is taught to think of his family as an island of security in an otherwise dangerous and threatening world, although at the unconscious level his family has come to represent the greatest possible threat to his security, so at a later stage he is taught that his religion is the basis of his identity as a Burmese, even though at a deeper level his experience with religious instruction has threatened his identity as a male.

This basic pattern of induction into religious life appears to leave Burmese with the permanent feeling that their personal and cultural identity is firmly associated with their religion. Whenever challenged by foreign ideas and practices to the point of feeling uncomfortable and insecure, the impulse seems to be to seek reassurance by returning to and reasserting this religion-based sense of identity. Although to a degree religion represents an avenue of escape from unpleasant realities, it also provides a strong reinforcement to the Burmese personality, giving one a striking quality of composure, self-confidence, and poise when confronted with foreign pressures. This pattern of personal development also helps to explain the ability of Burmese to return from studying abroad and reimmerse themselves in their own traditional culture.

On the other hand, whenever the Burmese sense of identity is not being threatened by a manifestly foreign danger, the basic element of uncertainty, which was at the core of their early religious experiences, seems to encourage a latent impulse to escape the bonds and restraints of religion. In conversations the Burmese political class freely displays scorn for monks, referring to them as country people, poorly educated, of low social status, and not deserving of respect. University students spend much of their time in group discussions enumerating the stifling effects of Buddhism in Burmese national life and professing their desire for their country to become a more secular, more modern, and more economically developed society. They will declare emphatically that most of the ills of Burmese society can be traced back to the influences of religion. Yet at the next moment the same students will proclaim that Burma would achieve something far greater than mere economic development and material advancement if its leaders would only rally the people to a purer version of their traditional Buddhist faith. Even for the contemporary youth the search for secular goals can become very easily a sacred quest.

The diffuse and pervasive way in which Burmese are educated about the realm of the sacred seems to have particularly significant consequences for the Burmese political culture and the problem of nation building. It has made religion itself a delicate issue for all political leaders. Historically, Burmese politicians were relatively satisfied with the British colonial policy of separation of church and state, for as national spokesmen they could safely criticize the British for the division without having to come to grips with the substance of the problem. The significant fact is that, in spite of the central place religion is supposed to occupy in Burmese life, all Burmese politicians, until U Nu found himself in serious difficulties, have carefully skirted the realm of religion.

Even in the case of U Nu, who has openly espoused the idea of making Buddhism the state religion, there has been ambivalence, and he has been able to intervene in religious matters precisely because he has been able to preserve his status as a secular leader. Indeed, much of U Nu's popularity may stem from his ability to suggest the bold but comforting idea that the sacred can be dominated by a secular leader and not be threatened but actually strengthened. In the eyes of many Burmese, U Nu, the layman, has demonstrated his superiority over, and has also implied a certain contempt for, the monkhood by convening their synods, establishing their councils, and by professing to be practicing chastity while still married. He has managed to suggest to all that even without the benefit and support of vows and monastic life he is able to lead a life as good as, and hence really better than, the life of the *pongyis* themselves. By criticizing the monkhood but accepting the religious tradition, U Nu seems to appeal to the basic Burmese sense of ambivalence toward religion. He has also found the formula that makes it possible for the Burmese politician to touch upon the delicate subject of religion.

At a more fundamental level, the ambivalent feeling toward religion creates a serious obstacle to national development and planned social change. The Burmese sense of identity is so closely associated with his religious identity that he is likely to feel seriously threatened by the idea of abandoning his religion. Members of the political elite in particular are likely to find considerable reassurance and comfort from Buddhist religious teachings which tell them that they deserve their superior status as a reward for their conduct in a previous incarnation. Understandably, they are not enthusiastic about minimizing the significance of concepts that hold that their power is a natural right which merely reflects their moral superiority. At the same time, however, the element of insecurity about religion means that it is difficult for the Burman to find in his religion-based sense of identity the necessary security to become a creative and innovating political person. Thus the socialization process with respect to religion erects a double obstacle to modernizing and nation building by making it peculiarly hard for the individual to disengage himself from his traditional religion and yet not making him secure enough in that religion to accept and seek change.

The Nature of Causality and the Possibilities for Prediction

The second dimension of the socialization process covers the ways in which people are trained to think of the nature of causality. Are events governed by open, manifest forces, or by secret, latent ones? Are there predictable laws, or is life governed by chance and the whims of extra-human forces? And can these forces be influenced in any way, and if so how? The answers to such questions indicate the basic orientation of a people toward change and their expectations about what they or others can do to govern the flow of human affairs.

Two aspects of the socialization process are particularly significant in conditioning people's feelings about causality. The first relates to the early experience of the child in seeking to command and manipulate his environment through communications with his parents, and the second relates to the extent to which the subsequent cognitive, and usually religious, training encourages him to see his social and physical universes as orderly and manageable.

Young children in all cultures are introduced to a magical view of the universe through the apparent omnipotence of their parents. The child is at first helpless, but he soon learns that his whole world can suddenly be changed, as if by magic, from sadness to happiness. In time he may begin to recognize that through communications he has the power to affect these changes, and thus his world of magic begins to shrink and is replaced with one of causality. In some cultures he will come to believe that there is a powerful connection between his own behavior and how the world treats him, for he will be introduced to an elaborate scheme of predictable rewards and punishments, from which he learns that his own actions can govern his world. In other cultures the child's magical view of the universe may be destroyed by exposure to an unpredictable scheme of rewards and punishments which teach him that his actions have consequences but of an uncertain and unpredictable nature.

As we have observed, the Burmese child remains for a long time in a capricious world in which he is taught that there is only a minimal connection between his own behavior and the moods of his parents. At the same time that he learns of the unpredictable world of human relationships he is also being introduced to an equally unpredictable and equally real world of spirits. Long before he is given formal instruction in Buddhism, he has been warned and frightened by accounts of not only the quasi-canonical thirty-seven *nats* of Burma, but also countless numbers of haunting spirits also called *nats* that live in trees and rocks. To these are further added cannibalistic ogresses and ogres, hobgoblins and spectres, and evil spirits in human guise called *bilus* which devour men.[4]

Even as the child is being told about this fearful spirit world he is also being taught that the emotion of fear is dangerous and can easily be his undoing. For he is taught that his soul is like a butterfly which flits about whenever he is asleep and visits other worlds and other places. (Hence the importance of dreams which are the recollections of these journeys.) If he is frightened or startled when asleep, or overcome by fear when awake, his butterfly soul is certain to shrink. This should be the cause of alarm, and all efforts should be made to coax the butterfly back to normal size. Most respectable *sesaya* or medicine men claim that the probability that anything can be done is extremely low. The danger is that an under-sized butterfly can be easily blown away or caught and devoured in one mouthful by even the slowest moving ogress, and that will be the end of the person.[5]

Westerners usually find it difficult to appreciate how tangible the spirit world is for most Burmese and how seriously their notions about the workings of that world affect their views of the workings of social relations. For example, in his autobiography the first president of the Union of Burma treats his experiences with ghosts and *nats* and haunted areas in the same matter-of-fact manner as he reports his Cambridge education and his career in the law.[6]

For most Burmese, knowledge about the spirit world represents their first exposure to a world that is more complex than just that of family

---

4. An excellent introduction to the spirit world of the Burmese is to be found in Shway Yoe (Sir James G. Scott), *The Burman: His Life and Notions.*

5. Ibid, Chap. 40.

6. U Ba U, *My Burma,* especially pp. 6–13.

and village relationships. Knowledge of this world thus tends to color their expectations about the mechanics and dynamics of more impersonal human relationships. The Burmese child is thus inducted into a world where magic exists and where he can only marginally protect himself and fight back.[7] As in most cultures in which there is belief in malicious magic—and this covers most of the cultures of Southeast Asia—the basic expectation is always that one's enemies are likely to have easier and greater access to magic. The individual is left with the feeling that he is powerless in an unjust world in which his neighbor with the help of spirits is about to do to him what he can only impotently wish to do to his neighbor.[8]

For the sensitive young Burman the danger is compounded, for he is also taught that good moral behavior is no protection against evil spirits; quite the contrary, it is only bad and evil people, and also foreigners, who are safe from the clutches of spirits. The good man and the man of high social and economic status are in fact likely to attract the attention of spirits, while bad men and foreigners are so lowly and insignificant as to be outside the pale of the spirit world.

Aside from the obvious difficulties that such ideas and sentiments place in the way of modernizing Burmese society, it must also be noted that the successful diffusion of the world culture is further impeded by the belief that foreigners have no souls, and that foreigners can therefore be free and fearless in their conduct. It follows that since there is this basic difference in kind foreigners cannot be simply imitated by Burmese. It is not relevant to insist that what the one can do the other should also be able to do. Foreigners can do many amazing things, for example, but that is their nature, and therefore it does not suggest possibilities for Burmese. Foreigners are not to be envied for seeming to be less beset with frightening considerations, just as one does not envy animals for having less complicated problems than people.

7. In Sir Richard Temple's *The Thirty-Seven Nats* (London, W. Griggs, 1906), instructions are given for constructing apparatuses for black magic that will throw stones at an enemy, attack him with sticks, and even burn down his house.

8. The fact that the spirit world is fearful, threatening, and unpredictable has suggested to some that it represents to a high degree a projection onto the outside world of the inner insecurities and fears of the Burmese. Their accounts of the behavior of the spirits represent their fantasies about how other people are likely to behave toward them (which they are afraid consciously to formulate or articulate) and which in turn are based on their own feelings of aggression.

For a discussion of how "the belief in demons permits a persistent externalization of one's own unconscious thought and preconscious impulses of avarice and malice," see Erikson, *Young Man Luther*, pp. 60 ff.

The Burmese child's introduction into the spirit world is followed in a few years with instructions about the infinitely more deterministic world of Buddhism. He learns that his current lot in life was determined by his *kan* and the record of his behavior in a previous incarnation, and now he must do all he can to gain merits so as to strengthen his *kan* for his next existence. He is thus exposed to an essentially bookkeeping theory of the universe according to which all the pluses and minuses of his actions will eventually be totaled up, and his fate will be calculated in an almost mechanistic fashion. This Buddhistic view seems to encourage the Burmese to feel that every person must follow his own peculiar ways, and that what others do is somehow determined by their natures. Consequently one cannot really feel any strong responsibility for the behavior of others, nor is there a need to criticize them. (An apparently happy conclusion, given the basic fears and anxieties about others which seems to be a part of the Burmese modal personality.)

Clearly this orderly and deterministic universe of Buddhism is the direct opposite of the chaos of the spirit world. In various ways Burmese must seek to reconcile these two views of nature. In the main they seem to tend toward the practice of accepting the deterministic view when considering their own personal fates and toward the more unpredictable one when confronting relations with others. The result is to magnify the extent to which they feel that their own actions are, and must be, controlled and inhibited while the actions of others are completely free. This differentiated view not only profoundly affects social relationships but also colors Burmese expectations about the human potential to manipulate affairs and control the physical and social environment.

It is customarily argued that in pre-industrial societies people tend to feel that man cannot dominate or manipulate nature, but at best can seek harmony with it, and that only with modern scientific societies do people come to believe that they can dominate nature.[9] The Burmese evidence suggests almost the opposite conclusion: a people who lack the fundamental notion that nature is governed by unalterable and impersonal "law" can, as the Burmese seem to, conclude that there are no limits to the possibilities of manipulating nature, especially as it is done by others. Indeed, the feeling of personal impotence is very close to the feeling that others may have unlimited freedom to change and manipulate the world. Given these feelings, one's own limitations cannot be taken as a guide

9. For a criticism of this view see Marion J. Levy, "A Philosopher's Stone," *World Politics,* 5 (July 1953), 555–68.

to the potentialities of others; those in high places are likely to be seen as completely unfettered and thus capable of changing the world according to their whims.

These attitudes seem to lie at the bases of Burmese expectations about economic development. Beginning with a view of causality which does not accept an inexorable link between effort and reward, the popular Burmese expectation has been that their leaders, who seem to have unlimited power, should be able to change their country and give it a modern economy, *if they only wished to do it.* Thus the general expectation that the announcement of economic development programs was a sufficient basis for the creation of a new life for everyone in the country.

Similarly, the popular belief in the almost magical manipulative powers of others causes Burmese to doubt the ability and sincerity of any leader who asks for any form of sacrifice in order to achieve national goals. Real leaders can do all that is necessary themselves for they are supposed to be omnipotent. The suggestion that the common people should expend their energies is interpreted to mean that the leader is either a fraud or is conserving his power so as to exploit the common people. One Burmese politician expressed the dilemma of the leader in the following words:

> The people believe that just because I am important there is nothing that I can't do. If I don't do something for them they say that I am either mean to them or that I am a weak leader and they should find another. Our people have no idea at all of how hard it is to do anything. They believe what we tell them about how their country can be improved but they do not believe that they need do anything about improving it. If we admit that we can't do it alone they want to know what is wrong with us. They'll just look for other leaders.

Since these attitudes about the possibilities of changing society appear to rest upon very fundamental views about the universe, they can probably only be changed very slowly. The process of political development thus seems to involve a gradual learning about both the possibilities and the limits of human influence and political manipulation. Paradoxically, the process of acculturating to the modern world seems to be mainly one of learning about the limitations on political power. Just as the child must learn that his parents do not have magical powers, so the Burmese must learn that their leaders are not omnipotent. Largely because of the characteristics of the socialization process, the gradual realization of the limitations of their leaders has unfortunately not led the Burmese to a general and healthy form of skepticism about the extreme promises of politicians, but instead has been accompanied by a feeling of suspicion and distrust of the motives of their national leaders.

Objective and Subjective Reality

Closely related to cultural sentiments about causality and the possibilities of prediction and manipulation are the feelings of a people about the appropriate focus for the most important of human actions. Specifically, is it more important to try to relate one's actions to considerations about the objective social and physical worlds or to concentrate on improving one's inner well-being and spiritual life? Is action seen mainly in terms of its objective implications for relations with others, or is it primarily valued in terms of its intrinsic meaning to the self?

In all societies people are taught to think of some actions as essentially instrumental means to higher ends, thus having a sequential quality, while others are accepted as ends in themselves, thus having an autonomous quality. Some cultures, however, seem to stress more the likelihood that most phenomena are parts of larger designs and thus are to be viewed instrumentally, while other cultures encourage the feeling that most actions can stand alone. For example, in some societies children are told to eat so they can grow big and strong, and encouraged to play so they will learn skills and attitudes of value for later life. In other societies eating is satisfying and playing is fun and no more need be said. In some cultures children are taught to expect that all their behavior should fit into a larger pattern, and that therefore nothing they do can escape the possibility of being judged and evaluated according to some inexorable logic which relates instrumental means to higher ends. Such might be the basis of the scientific and moralistic outlook on life. At the other extreme are the children who are encouraged to accept each phenomenon on its own terms, to value the spontaneous act which contains its own rewards. Such may be the basis of the aesthetic outlook.

Thus the important question is not whether the socialization process encourages people to seek reality by looking outward toward the material and the objective or inward toward the spiritual and the subjective, but whether in looking in either direction they are taught to sense all phenomena as being probably related or essentially autonomous. To facilitate exposition we can suggest the four possible model types by the following table:

	OBJECTIVE	SUBJECTIVE
Instrumental causality	The scientific and/or moralistic view: the manager and the manipulator	The contemplative and self-exploratory view: the meditator and the monk
Autonomous ends	The passively accepting and the unreflecting view: the extrovert	The hedonistic view: the sensualist

Burmese generally insist that their socialization process leaves them more sensitive to spiritual than to materialistic considerations, and, with some reservations, foreign observers tend generally to agree. The significant consideration is not, however, the relative importance which Burmese attach to either spiritual or materialistic matters. It is, first, whether the Burmese tend to focus outward on the objective world or inward on their subjective world, and second, whether they tend to consider actions and feelings as generally instrumental to greater ends or as simply ends in themselves.

Throughout their socialization process the Burmese are constantly being taught to reject and distrust the objective and to seek comfort and security in the subjective. From their Buddhism they learn that the physical world is in constant flux; all is transitory, all is sham and illusion. They are also taught to think of the outside world as evil and dangerous. Their real world is within the self, and thus through the techniques of meditation and the forms of contemplation it is possible to find the only significant causal relationships in the universe which provide the path to enlightenment and self-realization.

Although most Burmese do not become skilled in the arts of meditation, they all learn that nothing is more important than developing a tender concern for subjective phenomena. It is appropriate that each person should go his own way, seeking his own inner well-being and ignoring external realities as much as possible. The danger is that most of the people who do not become adept in meditation will not develop a sense for the causal relationships in the subjective world and will thus tend to treat their feelings as ends in themselves. That is, according to our fourfold table the Burmese are constantly in danger of slipping from the upper right-hand corner to the lower right-hand one.

With respect to subsequent political behavior and the problems of nation building, the Burmese expectation that causal relationships are more likely to be found in the subjective than the objective universe means that the Burmese do not have a strong sense of the reality of social collectivities. It is customary to speak of the Burmese spirit of individualism because they display so much concern for self-realization and so little feeling of responsibility toward the larger community and society as a whole. The socialization process trains Burmese to perceive people as individuals and not as elements in an intelligible system of relationships. Specifically, little in the early development of the Burmese prepares them for the concept that there are collective realities which may assume the form of, say, an economy, a polity, a society, a nation. Instead of seeing reality in the relationships among people, the Burmese tends to see only the individual seeking his own self-fulfillment.

This bias in perspective means that Burmese tend to see each other as individuals seeking personal material advancement or personal political power rather than as members of economic and political systems. It is therefore a peculiarly foreign idea to the Burmese that people with extremely base motivations can still contribute to the collective good. Most of our respondents, regardless of the extent of their education, continue to think of economic activities as little more than the attempts of people with excessive self-interest to cheat and exploit others. At heart the idea of improving the national economy has little meaning beyond the idea of making it possible for Burmese rather than foreigners to cheat and exploit others.

The basic inability to recognize systematic relationships among objective phenomena is thus a serious and fundamental obstacle to national economic development. There exists no real feeling for the realities of an economic system, only a distrust for the systematic self-seeking motivations of individuals; the declaration that the economy or the nation should be improved has little meaning since it is only individuals who can improve themselves.

By encouraging the belief that the subjective world is more real, more manipulatable, and more predictable than the world of physical relationships, the Burmese socialization process warns the individual that surface appearances are to be distrusted and that all people have extraordinarily complex feelings to which they attach inestimable importance. Both the later conscious training of the Burmese and the earlier phases of their socialization encourage them to project to others their own unconscious feelings. Other people like themselves are seen as being largely influenced by subjective concerns. The Burmese child is taught that the manifest level of relationships may not accurately reflect the true feelings of others. The burden of his training in manners and etiquette is his constant need to display deference and subservience toward all who might in any respect be considered superiors. Social forms are thus a means of warning that others can be dangerous, and not a guarantee that one can find safe ground in social relations. It appears that even in traditional Burmese society when there were elaborate forms of etiquette the Burmese did not develop efficient and subtle forms of social communications; now as a consequence of social change and the weakening of old standards it is even more difficult for Burmese to be confident that they are either interpreting correctly the feelings of others or communicating fully their own intentions.

Time Perspective

A fifth dimension of the socialization process that is peculiarly important in influencing attitudes toward purposeful action relates to the perspective from which time is viewed. Does the socialization process encourage people to focus on the past, present, or future; and therefore, do people act as though they had their eyes on history, on the possibilities and dangers of tomorrow, or on the demands of the moment? How impatient are people with the rhythm and sequence of events? Are they made to feel that the longer one waits, the better the outcome will be? Is the expectation that the more painful the delay, the greater will be the reward, and that good things will always follow unpleasant periods? Or is the basic expectation that any request or demand for delay is bound to be followed by disappointment? That is, does the culture teach the individual that naturally and automatically time works with one's interest if one can only be patient, or is time essentially against one so that what one does not get today is probably lost forever?

It is customary to think of traditional societies as facing backward and looking mainly toward the past. In fact, however, it is the present that has always dominated most action and thinking in Burmese culture (and in all the major Southeast Asian cultures except the Vietnamese). Experience with life seems to leave the Burmese with very little sense of history, little curiosity about the past that lies behind the early years of the current generation; Europeans have done most of the historical research on the early periods of Burma, and the archeological wonders of Pagan are largely ignored by the Burmese themselves.

The Burmese preoccupation with the immediate can be related to Buddhist doctrines which emphasize that nothing material is lasting and all in life is transitory. The child is taught not to place great value on material possessions but to seek merit in acts, which have no lasting significance and are important only in the doing. Paradoxically, the effort to create in the Burmese child an awe of the infinite seems to give an exaggerated appreciation of the immediate.

At an earlier stage in life, through his warm associations with his mother, the Burmese child is given a strong sense of confidence about time since he can be fundamentally optimistic about the prospects of his needs being satisfied without any undue delay. At a slightly later age the notion of delay is related to the unstable moods of the mother and to fears of rejection. From then on, the child is not given any systematic training in how to cope with postponement. He is not, for example, taught that waiting and patience can be highly rewarding. The fact that he is not trained to see events as standing in sequential relationship to each other means that he does not come to picture one thing as leading to another with a climax expected at the end. Patience in Burmese culture is thus less an act of self-denial and self-control, than a denial of the predictability and manipulatability of events.

The stress on seeking order in subjective rather than objective relationships also seems to contribute to the Burmese orientation toward the present rather than the future. In believing that self-realization is the ultimate reality, the Burmese is made peculiarly sensitive to that generally disturbing problem of the ultimate destruction of the self. To look ahead means to look toward one's inevitable death. To look backward introspectively is also to contemplate the nonexistence of the self, to experience what has been called an "ego-chill, a shudder which comes from the sudden awareness that our nonexistence . . . is entirely possible." [10] Only when introspection concentrates on the present and on the control of the sensations of the moment is it possible to avoid the unpleasant thought of death.

Burmese culture offers little support to the individual in reflecting on ways of preserving his own identity beyond death. The new incarnation calls for a completely new identity, and the Burmese is discouraged from believing that he can put himself into things and thus leave any lasting memorial to his own identity. People build pagodas in search of merit for the next incarnation; they do not believe that there is any way in which an individual can strive to conquer death by leaving behind any lasting testament to his present existence.

In sum, then, the Burmese prefer not to think too far ahead. As we have already observed, they can even be disturbed by the idea that they should make sacrifices to leave the world a better place for their children, because it reminds them too strongly of their own inevitable death. But nation

10. Erikson, *Young Man Luther,* p. 111.

building calls for thinking past one's own death and believing that the state of affairs in the material world can be of unqualified importance even after one is gone.

Aspects of Amity and Enmity

Since so much of politics involves management of conflict and tests of loyalty, a crucial dimension of the socialization process relates to how people are trained to perceive and differentiate between friend and foe. What are the obligations of friendship and how should a person react to enemies? Are people taught to think in terms of a continuum extending from the poles of amity and enmity, or in terms of two categories? In classifying people, how important are such differences as those between neighbors and strangers, between those in high places and those with no status to lose? Are most people like "us" and can they therefore be trusted to act as we do; or are most people "theys" who are different and dangerous?

There is possibly no aspect of the socialization process to which Burmese parents give more attention than teaching their children about the differences between friends and potential enemies. Nothing is more important than instructing the child to have absolute faith and loyalty in his family and unrestrained suspicion of strangers. Hitson has observed that the Burmese child is taught in countless ways to feel that he is safe only among his family while all outsiders and especially strangers are sources of danger to be treated with caution and suspicion.[11] Thus, for example, when the young child cries he is fed, but if he cries as he grows older, he is frightened into silence by threats that ogresses, or strangers, or Indians will carry him off. The child begins to learn that his society has a vertical dimension, consisting of authority figures that extend on into the supernatural realm, and also a horizontal one consisting of the in-group of which the family is the center and all the out-groups which are to be feared. The child learns to look upward toward a social hierarchy in which all above are to be treated with complete deference; and he also learns to look outward from his immediate family to his relatives, his neighborhood, his village, on to distant strangers, and to feel that each concentric circle is increasingly an area of danger.

In teaching the child to think of the family as a relatively safe island in a dangerous world, the parents give him a picture that is realistic in many respects. Loyalty to family is strong, and one never consciously harms

11. Hitson, "Family Pattern and Paranoidal Personality Structure in Boston and Burma," pp. 73–76.

another member of one's immediate family. However, in a deeper psychological sense there seems to be a basic conflict between family and self in Burmese culture. The test of a good child is whether he is *lein-mah-deh*. A *lein-mah-deh* child is one who is always ready to deny and sacrifice himself for his parents. The concept is a somewhat secularized version of the Chinese concept of filial piety. Not only is the child supposed to show respect for his parents, he is expected to be cunning and crafty in helping them against all outsiders. Even the daughter is expected to continue after her marriage to make sacrifices for her own parents. (Thus the insecure Burmese male must accept the fact that his wife, just as his mother before, has a prior obligation and commitment to someone else.) A deep sense of conflict arises because the *lein-mah-deh* child is expected to forget himself for his family, but his parents may act in an unpredictable manner toward him. He is told that the family is the safest of all places, and yet it is precisely within the family that he has received his deepest psychological damage, which has left him insecure. All the sentiments that might make him want to turn his back on his family come into conflict with the demand of continual sacrifice for them. His desires to forget the family in his quest for security conflict with the ideological belief that the family is the only safe place.

This sharp distinction between the in-group and all outsiders teaches the Burmese to believe that very few relationships can be affectively neutral. Casual relationships are almost impossible, for others may turn out to be more dangerous than they appear. Ideally the commitment of loyalty within the circle of friends is a powerful and demonstrative emotion, while actually the absence of conspicuously warm feelings suggests that there is a need to be wary. Since there is little middle ground, most relationships call for strong emotional reactions of one kind or another.

The intensity of Burmese feelings of friendship is revealed in the extraordinarily tight cliques common to student life. The groups of friends that form at Rangoon University tend to become the central forces of nearly all the activities of the individual student. The group may determine not only his extracurricular interests but also the subjects he studies. Moreover, the bonds of association are expected to last throughout his life, and particularly among the political class they can become the most basic ties of the individual's life. The loyalty is not to the idea of fraternity but to a particular set of individuals. Within the AFPFL many of the most basic relationships could be traced back to these university associations.

In many respects the Burmese seem to ask too much of friendship, especially in the light of their feeling of inner unsureness about others. The basic pattern of much of Burmese social life, whether in the village, the university, or national politics, is one of an anxious search for friends leading to the formation of a small but demanding clique, which becomes increasingly more intimate and all-encompassing until the strain becomes unendurable, there is an explosive falling out, and the search for friends begins again.

The problem of enmity is peculiarly great because to Burmese the socialization process does not provide the individual with explicit rules for handling conflicts. The individual is only taught that violence and disagreement are bad and dangerous, and cooperation and unanimity are good. There is little recognition that honest differences can arise and that conflicts can be conducted in orderly and lawlike ways. Within the society or within its politics there is little room for the concept of the opponent who is still the friend, and of a loyal opposition.

PART V

Political Acculturation and
Reactions to Changes in Identity

CHAPTER 15

The Costs of Political Acculturation: The Administrator

We earlier observed that in well-established and stable societies it is possible to picture three more or less consecutive stages of involvement of the individual in his society and his polity: first, the process of socialization by which he is inducted into his culture; second, the process of political socialization out of which comes the understanding of citizenship and of membership in a polity; and finally, the stage of political recruitment when the few assume their active roles in public affairs. In transitional societies a sharp distinction does not exist between political socialization and political recruitment; for there is little sense of citizenship, only a division between observers and participants, and in place of a polity there is a realm of politics composed of principals and their followers. In a sense the process of political socialization in transitional societies takes the form of acculturation to the world culture. For, as we have noted, the political class usually represents the more acculturated elements of the society, and the process of learning about and relating to the modern world thus tends to become the essence of political socialization.

Of course, there need not logically be a political dimension to the acculturation process, and many people become members of the modern world without becoming sensitive to the realm of politics. Yet to an overwhelming degree acculturation has produced political responses. And certainly for members of the political class in societies seeking to build national institutions the experience of learning about the world culture has colored their understanding of the particular political roles to which they aspire.

We have already emphasized the fact that the complex reactions to the acculturation process provide the very dynamics of politics in most transitional societies. Here we turn to the genuine tragedy of that dynamics—that some degree of acculturation is necessary for a people to learn about the essentials of nation building, and yet the process of acculturation tends to produce psychological reactions which inhibit and frustrate the nation-building effort.

In the context of transitional politics this means that the more intense the acculturation the more will its influence be felt, until a point is reached at which there is a steep decline in political effectiveness even as the process of acculturation continues. And so in most transitional societies the more acculturated have tended to be replaced by the less, and this process has not stopped with the replacement of those trained by former colonial rulers. The more acculturated, even if they were nationalist leaders, have often lost out to those less in tune with the modern world.

The customary view of this phenomenon is that the leaders as they become more modernized lose touch with their people. This is the view that at bottom politics is an atavistic and unreasoning business in which the more civilized must always give way to the less. This is also the view that as people become more at home in the modern world they lose their capacity to communicate with their more tradition-bound compatriots. In essence, these views undoubtedly contain some elements of truth. However, there appears to be more to the process, for the decline in effectiveness appears even among those whose positions do not depend upon communicating with the general public. For example, in Burma British officials were surprised after independence to find that Burmese officials whom they knew well proved in time to be far less competent than they had once been. Similarly, some of the more modernized politicians seemed to be plagued with indecision, unsureness of commitment, and an inability to consummate political acts.

As we turn now to an examination of the recruitment of the Burmese political class, we shall be particularly concerned with how the process of acculturation may have tended to limit their full potentialities as creative and imaginative people and leaders. Treating first the experiences of the administrators and then those of the politicians, we shall observe how at different psychological levels they appear unable to conquer various forms of ambivalence that in their cumulative effect destroy the capacity for those forms of action necessary for nation building.

THE PERFORMANCE OF THE BURMESE ADMINISTRATIVE SERVICE

As in most other colonial countries, the passage to independence in Burma saw a decline in administrative politics and the emergence of popular politics. The future of the country, however, still depends upon the ability of the administrative class to perform effectively. As members of the bureaucracy they must manage the most significant structure in the political process, and their ability and skill are possibly the most crucial factors determining the pace of modernization and the course of nation building.

It would not serve our purpose to attempt to catalogue the various weaknesses in public administration in Burma; such a listing would have to cover practices commonly noted in most transitional political systems. We need only summarize them in terms of three general categories: first, ambivalence on the part of the administrators over the nature and forms of progress and modernization; second, profound confusion over the difference between ritual and rationality in bureaucratic operations; third, and most important of all, fundamental and all-pervasive lack of effective communication among officials.

Backward-looking Modernizers

At present the civil service occupies a strangely ambiguous position in Burmese society. No matter at what level it is viewed, it offers contradictory impressions, for it seems to be pointing in two directions at once: it is peculiarly attached to the past and to conserving established practices, and yet it is also commonly identified as the principal agent for modernizing the country. On balance, the Burmese civil service represents the most modernized, the best educated, and the most skilled people in the entire society. It seems to be designed to fulfill modern functions of government; its standards of performance and its ideals of action are all taken from the modern world. Yet in spite of this apparent attachment to change and progress, it is in fact in the grip of tradition, and a tradition that reaches back not only to British colonial rule but also in some respects to the old East India Company and to the ethos of government of the Burmese kings. Thus, paradoxically, the logical agents for change seem in many ways to be as changeless as any aspect of a transitional society can be. The very men who should be champions of innovation and initiators of action if the country is to develop are to an alarming degree the victims of immobilism.

This ambiguous quality of the civil service is to be noted even in physical appearances. The Secretariat building is one of the most imposing structures in the entire country, but it is a memorial to the past and more particularly to a period of British, not Burmese, greatness. In the districts every physical aspect of administrative authority communicates an identity which is more modern than most other aspects of the setting but also unmistakably tied to a colonial past. Within government offices one finds the same divided world. The forms, the procedures, the files—all suggest an outmoded version of once modern procedures.

Even when speaking about new programs, senior Burmese officials convey a certain sense of nostalgia and a feeling that their golden age may belong to the past. Repeatedly in the interviews older civil servants would inquire whether we had ever been to Burma before and, on receiving a negative reply, would indicate that it was a pity because in various ways Burma was once a better, more presentable land. When pressed for an explanation for what had happened, they generally said that before the war they—meaning the civil service class—used to run the country but that now the politicians have their hands in everything.

To a striking extent, the adminstrative class tends to picture itself in retrospect as a more powerful and influential community than it actually was during the colonial period. Men who have any form of official status are not prone to minimize their own significance, and sons tend to remember their fathers as powerful figures, even if they were no more than clerks. The Burmese administrative class is remarkably united in its belief that Burmese officials were important in helping to build up their country when it was under colonial rule. In actual fact much power did slip from the grasp of the limited numbers of Britishers, and the Burmese were not always outsmarted by the Indian officials in their land. Out in the districts, in particular, Burmese officials, even though of low status on the civil lists, still were important and authoritative people in their communities.

Regardless of the precise extent of Burmese influence and power before independence, senior officials now deeply resent the suggestion that they were insignificant before the war and that all credit for the orderly and efficient operations of government should go to foreigners, either British or Indian. Some have even expressed the opinion that the Burmese nationalist viewpoint that Burmese had no power in the colonial administration and that none were adequately trained was advanced by Burmese politicians in their efforts to discredit the entire administrative class. As one senior official has remarked:

> It is quite true that we began with a shortage of trained personnel, but we did have the cadres and orderly expansion was possible. It is not true, as our politicians and many foreigners have said, that we had no experienced people. The politicians were anxious to make

everyone believe that we had no people about trained for the jobs, for all they wanted to do was to put their friends and workers on the government rolls. By claiming that there were no trained Burmese they could put their untrained and incompetent people in all the high jobs they wanted.

At the same time, however, the senior members of the administrative class cannot openly and forcefully insist upon their own importance before the war because to do so would raise questions about the extent to which they may have been lacking in true patriotism, serving as the "handmaidens of the imperialists." This touches on a deeper problem of guilt and anxiety about personal identity for the administrators which we shall be examining in a moment; it is enough to point out here that those who set the tone for the Burmese administrative class would like to be able to look back with more pride and to receive more recognition for their abilities, but they are also disturbed that their finest period may have occurred when foreign rule still existed. Thus the past is constantly with them, and, even though they have modern education and skills, they cannot forget what they once were.

Rituals in Place of Rationality

The Burmese administrative class suffers also from confusion between ritual and rationality. In characterizing the period of administrative politics, we noted the spirit of legalism and the reverence for procedure characteristic of the acculturated Burmese. That attitude now takes the form of believing that government can be strong only if all the proper procedures are carefully followed. There is thus an almost magical potential to government which can be tapped by a cautious respect for the proper.

This concern for ritual lies at the basis of the peculiar mixture of almost uninhibited optimism and complete cynicism which is the hallmark of the Burmese administrator. We have noted that in the calculations of Burmese politics there tends to be a constant vacillation between a sense of omnipotence and one of incompetence. At one moment belief and faith in the potentialities of ritual suggest that much is about to be accomplished; at the next moment a feeling for the decline of the entire administrative class and a sense of personal unsureness produces a bitter mood of cynicism about the government's ability to accomplish anything at all.

To a large extent Burmese anxieties about the importance of the rituals of administration can be traced to their experiences under colonial rule. The British sought to create a machinery of administration which could effectively preserve law and order, and thus appear as a stable and unchanging institution in a stable society—not as a force for change and innovation. Similarly, the British did not intend to imbue the individual Burmese recruited to the government service with initiative and a drive for change. Anxious to develop the most economical system of administration possible under existing conditions, they relied heavily on the initiative and talents of a few highly trained British officials while depending for the maintenance of routine operations upon large numbers of Burmese and Indian subordinates. The British thus erected an extraordinary mechanism, indeed a mammoth machine, which operated impersonally and with easily interchangeable parts.

The Burmese were trained to see the machine as a completely impersonal structure within which communication must follow formal channels and set procedures. Their concepts of impartiality and justice became confused with the belief that security and wisdom—to say nothing of prudence—called for an inflexible adherence to rituals. In sum, the Burmese were trained in the spirit of the clerk while believing that they were being trained to take part in the decision-making process.

Formalism and Imperfect Communication

Under the British a gap existed between the formal and informal patterns of British administrative organization which was most conspicuous when viewed in terms of the flow of communication. Formal communications involved the activities of the Burmese and Indian clerks and had to follow set lines, while informal communications conformed to patterns of personal association among British officials. A British official could usually facilitate the communication process by dealing directly with other officials; then, informal commitments or decisions having been made, clerks could be instructed to draft the appropriate requests and the formal machinery could be called into play.

At present probably the main weakness of the Burmese administrative structure is that it rigidly adheres to formal procedures and does not utilize informal and interpersonal channels of communication. Indeed, the problem of the Burmese bureaucracy is almost exactly the opposite of what the student of prerational legal social systems might expect. The Burmese, instead of being unduly influenced by personal relationships in their administrative procedures, have gone to the other extreme. They have tried to operate their administrative machinery without the benefit of reinforcing and functionally compatible informal patterns of communication and association. They have assumed, as they were trained as clerks to believe, that all problems can be solved by finding a relevant regulation in an appropriate rule book.

As a consequence of this attitude, the machinery of administration has little capacity to discriminate among problems. Major problems are treated in the same manner as minor ones, and all tend to be moved up the hierarchy. The Burmese cabinet is called upon to resolve a hopeless array of issues. The operations of all aspects of the government seem to be excessively rigid and grossly overcentralized. The task of the administrative service becomes that of maintaining procedures, not solving problems and making decisions.

It is only at the point when the formal procedures are so overloaded as to produce paralysis that informal considerations enter into Burmese administrative behavior. At this stage, however, the informal considerations no longer reinforce the purpose and spirit of the formal procedures but become counterlegal in nature. For example, when the processing of applications or the granting of licenses overpowers the formal machinery, the question of whose application is to receive attention requires some personal act of persuasion, some means of attracting attention, which was not included in the formal procedures. There is no wonder that so many people seem to suspect the civil service of petty forms of corruption and graft.

Most of the difficulties of the Burmese civil service—its inflexibility, its passive rather than active posture, its overcentralization, its excessive reliance on the skills of clerks rather than the knowledge of specialists— can be traced back to the fact that the formal structure is not built upon and reinforced by informal patterns of communication. However, the crucial problem of communication involves far more than merely the formal training which the Burmese administrators had as clerks under colonial rule. It is also a manifestation of their deeper psychological reactions to the experiences of acculturation, reactions which have made them unsure of themselves and of each other and which take the form of distrust and suspicion which further reduce effective communication throughout the bureaucracy.

THE BACKGROUND OF ADMINISTRATORS

Of those we interviewed who had had administrative experience before the war, the vast majority came from families in which the father at least was already to some degree acculturated to the modern world of his day. Of those who first became administrators after the war nearly two-thirds had the same kind of family background. These considerations may explain the extent to which the members of the administrative class tend to feel that they are confronted with an issue of collective rather than individual identity with respect to the entire problem of acculturation. They readily use "we" and "us" when speaking of the challenges they have felt to their own positions in Burmese society.

Two general experiences colored most of the attitudes of the prewar trained administrators, who still set the tone of the Burmese civil service, toward their political and social roles. The first was the formal education they received in a Western-styled school, and the second was their initial experience of informal apprenticeship within the service when they came under the direction of a senior British official.

Formal Education: Source of Social Status and Cause of Insecurity

In almost all Asian cultures there is a profound faith in education and knowledge, in the Mandarin and the *Swami,* the sage and the Enlightened One. The mystique of knowledge and knowledgeability has in all Asian cultures been closely associated both with religion and with self-fulfillment. Education is thus a value in itself.

In Burma the elite status of the educated man is the cardinal article of faith of the Burmese administrative class. From low echelon clerks to senior secretaries, all seem acutely aware that their claim to superiority over the masses of their people can be justified most convincingly by their years of formal education. Many of our respondents indicated that their parents had impressed upon them from a very early age the relationship between schooling and getting ahead in life. Those who came from Anglicized families would naturally have been expected to go on to school, but significantly, even those who had extremely traditionalist parents said that their fathers wanted them to get a modern form of education because of its potential economic and social value.

The high value which the Burmese administrators tend to place on their years of formal schooling is not, however, combined with an equally high regard for either the skills of the specialist or the role of the intellectual. On the contrary, most of them still reflect the attitudes of their former British mentors, who, in the tradition of the British ruling class, had a well-articulated distrust of both specialized knowledge and any form of intellectual pretension. Some of our informants, for example, in discussing their experiences in England spoke of how hard it had been for them to learn the proper British custom of always appearing to be slightly less intelligent and less informed than one really is.

A Burmese judge remarked:

> I was very anxious to tell the guests [at a dinner party] all I knew
> about Buddhism in Burma and Ceylon, but I knew I shouldn't say
> anything on that subject because I had been told that English gentle-
> men discuss with animation only matters of common knowledge
> and of little import.

A university instructor said:

> Our Burmese students were often trying to display their intelligence.
> It didn't go down well with their classmates [in a British university].

However, the Burmese urge to display intellectual achievement is too
powerful to have been checked by an awe of British forms alone. There
seems to be a more basic inhibition reflecting the underlying doubt many
officials have about their own intellectual abilities. School was for most
of them the most intensely competitive experience of their lives, and the
test of modern educational standards raised in the minds of many Burmese
officials the question of whether they might not in fact be somehow
inferior. Thus, although their modern education distinguished them from
the great masses of their countrymen and justified their superior position,
it also left them with a more precise awareness of their own deficiencies
and inadequacies.

Hence, their extremely mixed feelings toward intellectual matters. On
the one hand, the Burmese administrators have an endless need to extol
the virtues and the inherent superiority of those who have passed the
various stages of formal schooling and possess the appropriate degrees.
In their thinking most of them divide all people between the educated
and the uneducated; in the common vocabulary of the class, the usual
way of attacking, denouncing, or belittling individuals or groups is to
suggest that they are deficient in formal schooling. For example, in the
interviews they made such remarks as these:

> They think they should run the district, but they haven't even been
> to a proper school.

> He is a minister, but he has never been to the university. Uneducated
> like all our politicians. What hope is there for us?

> The times have changed and even people without educations hold
> office and get rich.

On the other hand, the same people generally find it painfully difficult
to discuss the details of their own experiences in school. They generally

220   POLITICAL ACCULTURATION: A CHANGE IN IDENTITY

prefer to have it assumed that their credentials are in good order, that they belong, and that the rest can be left unsaid. Although some were among the best in their school classes, and all had to meet the minimum standards, most tend to display varying forms of hostility toward the idea of intellectuals and specialists. Those who came to the administrative class before the war easily direct this hostility against the new generation of Burmese—the "state scholars"—who have just been educated abroad at government expense and are expected to serve within the government on their return. In turn, most of these young men are quick to claim that the older generation fears their new and more specialized knowledge and thus seeks to neutralize their influence and impede their advancement. True to the traditions of the administrative class, the state scholars have expected that their formal education should be enough to place them within the circle of the inner elite. Yet at the same time their schooling experiences have left them feeling peculiarly vulnerable and defensive in their own country. The test of education has brought to them the same awareness of their own personal limitations as troubled the senior officials in their day.

In a sense, then, the state scholars find themselves confronted with precisely the same conflicts as their predecessors who are now their "obstructing" superiors. For both groups the easiest course has been to accept the status their education has given them but to minimize the content of the modern knowledge they supposedly have received. The need to cling to elite status, the risks of disappearing into the great anonymous mass of the nonelite, and the sense of personal inadequacies are all too great to permit ability in the application of knowledge to become the criterion of status.

Hence the paradox that is the common tragedy for so many underdeveloped countries: those who have been exposed to modern forms of knowledge are often precisely the ones who are most anxious to obstruct the continued diffusion of the effects of that knowledge; they desperately need to hold on to what they have and avoid all risks. The lasting consequence of their formal education has thus been an inflexible and conservative cast of mind. Modernization has bred opposition to change.

Apprenticeship in Loyalty: The Warmth of Charisma and the Pleasures of Stolen Authority

While formal schooling provided the generalized preparation for administrative roles for most members of the service, the more formal and intensive preparation came from a period of on-the-job training. As in nearly all former colonial countries, the young Burmese aspirant to official roles was inducted into the realm of authority by a fairly rigorous period of apprenticeship in which he came to learn all the practices and conventions, the forms and procedures, the language and style, the traditions and ethos of his administrative service. The period of apprenticeship provided him with more than just a sense of morale and enthusiasm; it gave him his true sense of identity as one who could legitimately wield power and authority.

Much of the apprenticeship had to be spent in the districts dealing with country people and tradition-bound villagers, a circumstance which helps to explain an apparently unrealistic belief common to the Burmese administrative class, namely, that they have a peculiarly intimate knowledge of what goes on in the minds of the peasants. For the Westerner, the gap between the outlook of the Westernized official and the peasant masses is often the most conspicuous feature of a transitional political system. The eagerness with which officials seek posts at the capital and their displeasure with service in the rural areas are easily documented and seem to reflect a politically unhealthy situation. But in Burma, even the less Westernized and less educated party politicians who would appear to have genuine roots in the districts acknowledge the administrators' understanding of the peasant. The origin of the belief is easily traced to the apprenticeship period and to the paternalistic role of officials in the rural setting. Because of this background the administrative class, the most modernized segment of society, is at times characterized as being more effectively oriented toward traditional ways than to the modern world. For example, Prime Minister Nu felt it appropriate in berating the senior administrators to challenge their capacity to deal not with the peasantry but with modern urban problems. He said:

> The question to be asked is, "Will the Civil Service, which has its training among the peasantry in lonely districts at least for the earlier years, and which claims to have acted as kindly fathers of the poor, rise to the occasion and throw up men capable of guiding and inspiring the New Burma?" [1]

This widespread belief makes it difficult for Burmese officials to take seriously the recommendation that they should seek to bridge more effectively the gap between the peasant and the modern world. Instead, they feel that they should concentrate on adapting themselves to the styles and mannerisms of urban society. Some of the junior officials trained

1. U Nu, *From Peace to Stability,* pp. 34–35.

after the war now claim that the British policies of bringing young Burmese officials to the districts was another diabolical tactic to keep Burma backward, for it encouraged Burmese officials to think in terms of the peasant world and not the modern one.

Thus one of the lasting consequences of the apprenticeship period seems to have been rather the opposite of that intended. Officials appear to have come through the experience with a stronger sense of their own elite position, an exaggerated sense of understanding all aspects of peasant life, and the conviction that thereafter they need only concern themselves with intrabureaucratic problems.

The other major aspect of the apprenticeship period during the prewar years was the close association which most of the young Burmese had with British officials and which now colors their feeling about their new profession. When the older Burmese administrators describe their relations with their British superiors, they reveal in various ways the intensely personal nature of the apprenticeship experience. Most of them dwell on their relationships with individual British officials, speaking their names with a certain awe and affectionate respect, very much as American enlisted men talk about the commanding officers under whom they have served and whose personal mannerisms and habits of authority are still matters of continuing importance to them. The traditions of the Burmese civil service were clearly built upon the personal qualities of its great and honored members.

The relationship between Burman and British was that of disciple to mentor, and hence it was a charismatic relationship. The association provided a basis for pride, dignity, and excitement. To some extent, no doubt, the relationship was exhilarating because the subordinate Burmese shared the prestige and honor of his superior and he could find some glory in the impression he created. Some senior officials now speak of the much greater respect which the "Burmese people in the districts used to have for all government officials." Other officials will now talk of how some of their fellow officers cynically exploited their superior's power in their districts in order to achieve personal benefits. As we have noted, the British officials did not monopolize all power, especially not in the lonely districts, and there were no doubt substantial opportunities for even most junior Burmese officials to establish claims of superiority over their fellow countrymen.

His early period of apprenticeship, besides being exciting, taught the young Burmese official that becoming a modern person and associating with the representatives of the world culture could be a friendly experience. Basic to the entire experience was his feeling that he was being accepted and trusted, and over the years he appears to have been increasingly compelled to believe that he was trusted on a highly personal basis. For it was his belief that trust existed which brought legitimacy not only to the entire relationship but also to what he was doing in following foreign ways.

Fundamental to the Burmese feeling that he was trusted was a deeper sentiment: "I was deserving of trust; hence I must have been acting in a completely honorable fashion." This personalized relationship thus offered proof of one's worth, and whatever doubts and anxieties the young Burmese may have had about attempting to follow the ways of a foreign culture could be suppressed by this knowledge.

Acculturation and the Issues of Loyalty and Identity

The experiences of our respondents suggest that the early years of their careers were generally pleasant ones. They had been able to resolve in their own minds any doubts about working for a foreign master by reflecting on their own personal superiorities. As juniors in the service they accepted as natural and just the social distance between themselves and their superiors. They emphasize the extent to which they were personally accepted by their British superiors and cite examples of personal kindness and occasions when they were singled out for special treatment.

Apparently, profound personal issues did not trouble the prewar administrators until after their first promotions when they began to become significant and hence more conspicuous individuals within the governmental structure. At this stage they first realized that they were at home neither with their own people nor with the British. But in speaking of this, our respondents stressed how gradually they became aware that the British would never fully accept them and that, no matter how well they did their job, there would always be that margin of difference in treatment which signaled that they were being unjustly discriminated against. Strong feelings of resentment did not take form until a significantly later stage. (It must be remembered that Burma, like most colonial countries, was a communal society in which each ethnic group had its place, its advantages and disadvantages, its occupations and special preserves; only after life in general had become increasingly politicized was there much questioning of the justice of the existing divisions of labor according to ethnic lines.) [2]

2. Interestingly, other Burmese, including some of our politician respondents, say that at about the same time as our prewar administrators began to be aware

From this gradual beginning the prewar administrators seem to have soon found themselves torn in many directions as they tried to ask themselves what they really represented; with the gradual rise of the politician class, they found themselves increasingly being charged with "being on the side of the British." As a group of people who had some deep and disturbing questions about what they really wanted to be, the administrators were peculiarly vulnerable when confronted with that most evil and threatening of all political accusations, the charge of being a traitor. Each of them had to ask himself, could it be that I liked the British too well? Did I in fact sell my soul to the foreigner when I decided to value his ways? In helping to rule my own people, did I in fact turn against them?

In being forced to raise such questions in their minds, the administrators were also forced to turn against the British. All of them knew what the answers were, for they had not the slightest doubt that the British had never accepted them and that therefore they could never have really been on the side of the British and against their own people. With surprising ease, and with not surprising anger, our respondents frequently spoke at length of the injustice of the British for not really accepting them and for making it appear as though the Burmese administrator was working against his people. However, at a deeper level the anger of the administrators against the British seems to stem from the suppressed thought that they might have become traitors had it not been for the British refusal to accept them. Possibly the most humiliating thought a man can have is that he was perhaps saved from being a traitor to his people by the arrogance and the racial discrimination of others and not by his own will and his own convictions.

---

of the limitations on their career prospects, they were becoming aware of the extent to which the Burmese in the civil service were working with the British and against their own people. In fact, the general but confidential view of our politician respondents was that the Burmese civil servants were "worse" than the British, acting as "little kings," and "finding pleasure in doing the dirty work for the British."

These two apparently contradictory views are probably both correct; here we have a case where the logic of politics is not subtle enough to capture a basic psychological truth. In all probability what happened was that, as the Burmese officials sensed their exclusion from the real realm of modern life and from full association with the British, they tended to express their frustration, their sense of denial, by unconsciously turning upon their own people and treating them in increasingly harsh ways. Denied a full place in the elite world, they needed to reassure themselves that they were the superior ones in their society.

This pattern of behavior so common to colonial administrators has been well discussed by John Plamenatz in *Alien Rule and Self-Government*, pp. 78–79.

The fact that many of the administrators had fervently wished to be accepted by the British, had wished that no racial bar had existed, takes on a new psychological meaning in the light of these considerations. They make the wish to be accepted equivalent to a wish to be a traitor. There is the thought that if in fact they had their way they would probably have committed the most serious of sins against their identities; there is the equally shocking idea that the foreigner in behaving at his worst had performed the necessary acts to keep the self from doing a far worse thing.

These are the kinds of thoughts that unconsciously seem to have profoundly demoralized the older generations of the Burmese administrator class. They are only now able to put into words their conviction that they had never been traitors, that they had never been accepted by the British, and that they had finally been abandoned by the British. This last sentiment is now expressed in many ways by the senior Burmese administrator but appears most strongly in the charge that in the end even the British believed that those who had worked with them to build a Burmese state were not the true Burmese nationalists. It was bad enough to be charged with being a traitor by one's "illiterate," "half-educated" countrymen, but it was the final blow to be told by precisely those who had been training one that one could no longer be considered a real nationalist because one had responded to their training. Some of our respondents spoke quite movingly of the shock they received when they discovered that, in spite of all the apparent value the British placed on intelligence, rationality, justice, science, law, and other aspects of the world culture, the British in the end respected less those Burmese who also prized these values than they did the Burmese who opposed them. The disciples who had tried to follow the inspiration of their mentors were now being told that their efforts rightly made them in the eyes of their mentors second class citizens in their own country, and that those who had been the common foes of progress and good government were the rightful heirs.

It would be almost impossible to overestimate the extent to which many individual Burmese administrators feel that they were cruelly abandoned by the West for no other crime than that of trying to the best of their abilities to bring the benefits of Western civilization to their country. We can best convey their feelings by quoting a senior administrator's seething criticism of a distinguished former English official who always wanted to do the best for Burma:

I knew all kinds of Englishmen. Many of them very very bad men: they swore, they drank too much, they abused us Burmese and they showed no respect for our religion. But these were the kind of bad people you find in every country, and they never really hurt us. They just had bad manners and were not gentlemen. The Englishman who hurt me more than anyone else in my life was Mr. ——. I will never get over the shock and the anger I felt one night when Mr. —— told a group of us at his house that we were not the real Burmese because we had studied abroad or at the University. He told us we ought to accept the AFPFL politicians as the real Burmese leaders. In all the years we had known Mr. —— he had always encouraged us to study and he had said many times that Burma needed trained people. Now he was saying that it didn't matter, that he admired more the Burmese who had opposed him than those who had listened to him. You can have all your "liberal," "progressive," "friends of Burma," types. I know now that they are not to be trusted, that they will leave you whenever it suits their interests. Mr. —— started talking all about the need to accept Burmese nationalism, but all he wanted was to get on good terms with the new politicians.[3]

Our respondents indicated in many ways the strains they have felt. Significantly, however, most of them reflected a strong need to hold up a positive picture of their very first relationship with the service. Whatever

3. The sequence of first finding satisfaction in the warm initial dependency relationship with their British superiors, then learning the anxieties of being discriminated against, and finally coming to the resentment for being abandoned which we observed in the career patterns of the Burmese officials is very much the same pattern that O. Mannoni observed among the Westernized Malagasies of Madagascar.
Mannoni presents a psychologically sensitive picture of the Malagasies, first accepting and valuing the warm dependency relationship they knew in colonialism. This was possible because a people close to tradition tend to seek total commitment in any relationship. More specifically, the tendency toward functionally diffuse relationships in traditional societies means that if people accept dependency in one sphere, they tend to feel that it is appropriate to be dependent in all relationships. As the Malagasy became more Westernized, however, the remaining differences between himself and the European became increasingly intolerable as his psychology of dependence was replaced by a psychology of inferiority. In the end the Malagasy reacted strongly against the European for "abandoning" him before making him an equal. The charge now is not that the European imposed his civilization on another people, but rather that the European withheld some of his civilization. See O. Mannoni, *Prospero and Caliban: A Study of the Psychology of Colonialism* (New York, Frederick Praeger, 1956).

else may have happened they needed above all to believe that they had been *deserving of trust*. By insisting upon the integrity of that first relationship they could present themselves as blameless against all subsequent charges. They could also look back to the happiest, least tormented and conflicting phase of their careers with the belief that the pleasures they had known derived from acting in the most honorable of ways.

THE TRAINING OF NEW RECRUITS

We have stressed the psychological experiences of the generation of prewar trained administrators because it is their attitudes and sentiments that still set the mood and tone of the Burmese civil service. New recruits have poured into the service since the war, and many of the contemporary high officials never knew the inside of colonial government. The traditions of the service, however, still stress the personal instruction of the new cadet officer as he serves under his more experienced superior. Thus the new generation of administrators is being strongly influenced by the reactions of its mentors to their earlier experiences.

From Subordinate to Superior: From Trust to Loneliness

Our younger respondents were proud to claim the same traditions as those held by their superiors, insisting that not only the practices but also the standards of training were precisely the same as before the war. A few even held it against history that they had come along too late to have been able to become members of the famed Indian Civil Service, but they took comfort in the idea that they were "just as good as the members of the I.C.S."

Those who knew the prewar service, however, to a man insist that all is different now and that the new generation is no match to theirs. To some extent this is simply the usual posture of an older generation, but there is something more here, for the specific complaint about the new people is that they do not have the same "capacity for loyalty toward their superiors as we had toward our superiors." The old elite characterizes the new breed of civil servants as a group of young, cynical aspirants for power and office who without conscience would usurp from their superiors the power that their superiors have rightfully derived from having once been worthy subordinates. The older men also recognize that the glow of official office has lost lustre in the eyes of all, and that as high officials they do not radiate the same charisma as high administrators once did.

Above all, the older men insist that because of the lack of loyalty of the young officials they cannot and should not trust their own subordinates as their British superiors once trusted them. Troubled by doubts about the propriety of their allegiance to the British-directed service and about their own competence, they must make much over the fact that they had once been loyal subordinates and hence at present are worthy of being superiors. They partially resolve their doubts by saying that anyone who does not have absolute loyalty for his superior is not deserving of trust.

The urge to withhold confidence in subordinates permeates almost all hierarchical relationships within the present-day Burmese bureaucracy. Thus barriers are established to casual, relaxed, and informal relationships, creating a situation especially disturbing to men who initially learned that government service could and should offer warm, close, and exciting personal associations. Now all relationships seem to be cold and indifferent. There is an increased need to emphasize status considerations in order to insure one's security in the hierarchy. The result is an enveloping sense of isolation and loneliness. In addition to feeling that they have been under constant attack from politicians on the outside, the senior administrators feel themselves about to be waylaid and criticized by people within their establishments.

The feelings of isolation and insecurity of course breed further distrust and the belief that discipline should be more strongly enforced, which, when combined with the basic Burmese desire for status but fear of decision and choice, tend to choke off the flow of communication within the administrative service. Superiors cannot share their problems with subordinates, and subordinates feel it necessary to adhere rigidly to correct form and procedure in all their dealings with their superiors. There is thus a profound psychological reason why it is impossible to hold staff meetings within the Burmese bureaucracy, and why superiors and subordinates cannot explore operational problems together. Trial and error and free discussion might only prove that superiors are fallible. And here we find the basic psychological reason why the Burmese administrative class clings so tenaciously to formal procedure. Confronted with a pervasive sense of insecurity, everyone must fall back on the safest course of action; everyone must adhere strictly to form, to procedure, to ritual. It is all they have left from the days of the old service.

The younger people in the service often profess to understand the basic weaknesses of their organizations, but they claim they must act as they do because of the feelings of their superiors. They must withdraw and not press their opinions and views. So both groups in their different ways feel the need to withhold all passion from government and to insist only upon the maintenance of the old forms.

The Costs of Acculturation: a Fear of Innovation

We may summarize the attitudes of the administrative class by observing that the recruitment process was not really training for highly specialized roles but diffuse experience in acculturation. It might be supposed that their induction into the modern world would have left them open-minded and eager for change. In fact, however, the manner in which the administrators were acculturated has left them primarily sensitive to questions of personal conduct and not to matters of public policy.

The Burmese administrative class has given a public dimension to their own private conduct, for they have believed that by behaving as modernized Asians they have been bringing progress to their country. Without fully realizing it, many of them have reasoned that if the elite of a country becomes modern, the country must also become modern. Modernization has thus been related less to public policy matters than to personal and private standards of conduct.

Given this point of view, Burmese administrators have been able to feel that they are performing as modernizers even though they do little or nothing to bring about change through public policy. Since the realm of individual conduct is the all-important one, their attention and energies are absorbed to an extraordinary degree by small, private, and even petty matters. As people who have gone through the experience of rather profound social change, they have emerged with an almost compulsive need to seek security and reassurance in their command over small details.

A final obstacle to efficient action for many of the senior administrators has come from learning that in paying a high psychic cost for being acculturated they may not have "bought" the best and most modern ways of the world. Firmly believing that if they could only behave like Englishmen they would be able to remove the stigma of backwardness from their country, it never occurred to them that there might be any distinction among "Anglicized," "Westernized," and "modernized" ways. With the war came the rude shock of learning that there were "modern," "progressive," and even "Western" and "European" standards and forms quite different from those they had learned from the British. Now they wonder whether they were cheated.

One British-university-trained official remarked:

When the AFPFL politicians began to say that we would throw out all the old-fashioned British practices and adopt more advanced and progressive ones, I was dumbfounded. It was as though someone had tried to argue seriously that it is dark in the day and light at night. We all knew that the British procedures were the best.

Another earnest official said:

The most difficult time I had with Mr.—— [an American adviser] was when he attacked the ways we had been taught to do things. I had always been proud of all I had learned. I would go home feeling angry and tired whenever he told us we ought to learn new and better methods.

Another administrator said:

I suspect that if the Americans are more advanced than the British, then the Russians are ahead of both.

And a British-trained professor said:

You can no longer tell what are the best ways. It doesn't seem to matter any more. Everyone claims he has the answers but who can say that it might not have been best if we had just stuck with our prewar ways of running the country.

In losing faith in themselves and in bringing into question their identity with British culture, the senior Burmese officials seem to have become increasingly indecisive in their own actions and less and less capable of giving clear guidance to the younger generation of officials. Unable to separate the technical practices of administration from the diffuse commitment they made to the culture of British Burma, the leaders of the administrative class can still profess to favor change and national development, but they no longer seem capable of so channeling their emotions. They seem to understand that a real effort at change would call for another attempt at changing their personal identities, and it is both too late and too costly for them to commit themselves to such an effort.

CHAPTER 16

Profiles of Administrators:
Sketches in Acculturation

In discussing the experience of the Burmese administrators, we have been able to dwell only on the dominant themes and general patterns in the development of an entire social class. It would, however, be incorrect to leave the impression that the modal patterns we have elaborated describe all members of the administrative class, and it is not enough merely to protest our awareness of the rich variety of individual differences among our respondents. We shall have to present some of them as individuals. They will be well disguised, however, for the country is a small one, and we gave a promise of privacy to those who would discuss their lives and beliefs.

In focusing our attention on the respondents as individuals, one general point stands out: even transitional people in a society without a well-defined community of modernizers may experience confusion and uncertainty in their relations with others, they still seem to have remarkably consistent and inflexible inner themes to their lives. Indeed, it would appear that people undergoing the experiences of acculturation develop reaction mechanisms which have the inner "logic" of economizing the individual psychic effort and leaving him with some very clear-cut habits. Thus there is something of the stereotype about most transitional people who have to live in psychic isolation without the benefits of belonging to a creative community; in presenting in brief outline the lives of a few Burmese we are not doing as great violence to their total life histories as it might appear.

U Po Thant: The Sensitive Anticolonialist

U Po Thant freely admitted his pride in knowing that "all the people who count know that I come from one of the first families of Burma." He also derived considerable satisfaction from the fact that "those who don't count haven't an inkling." [1] U Po Thant's grandfather had been a high official in the court of the last Burmese king, and before that his ancestors were "all leading members of the government who always directed the affairs of state." Apparently, like the grandfather of former President Ba U, U Po Thant's grandfather ran afoul of the intrigues of court politics and found it expedient to flee Mandalay and seek his fortunes in British Burma.[2] There he threw in his lot with the British, and, without any apparent sense of conflict with his identity as a member of the Burmese aristocracy, insisted that his son be given "the best possible English education."

U Po Thant's father thus went to school, first in Burma and then in England, and became one of the first Burmese members of the Indian Civil Service. U Po Thant talked of having had a "very happy childhood in which I met all the most important people wherever we were stationed." His father, he insisted, "wanted me to have a life just like his; he did all he could for me, and I received the best education possible." This involved several years in England during which he experienced the range of emotions common to schoolboys from exhilarating elation to homesickness. Formal schooling may have improved his capacity for abstraction and generalization; it did not wipe out, indeed it may have contributed to, the extraordinary assortment of notions, mostly about race, religion, and culture, which were the mainstays of his small talk, and possibly even of his great thoughts:

> Wouldn't you say that people who are weak and can't hold liquor are inclined to make temperance and abstinence into religions? This explains the strength of Islam and Buddhism and Hinduism in Asia, and why none of these religions are popular in Europe.

1. In Burmese culture there is nothing in the name to indicate family identity; surnames are not used. In a highly particularistic culture, one just "knows" who is related to whom and who "belongs" and who doesn't.

2. U Ba U's father used to say to him, "Do you know, son, our people were big people. They came from Upper Burma. Your grandfather and his elder brother had to run away to Lower Burma though, because of bad times." U Ba U, *My Burma*, p. 1.

We Burmese, like Europeans, are fair-skinned and hence find it difficult to work hard in the tropics. We are not like Indians and Africans who don't mind the heat. We really belong to the temperate zone; when Burma was great, the climate was probably different.

The trouble with Burmese is that they can't control their religion. The European boy is always taught to hold his liquor and to hold his religion.

The Burmese are too sentimental and that is why we can't compete with the rest of the world. We must wait until the rest of the world becomes more civilized and less ambitious, and then we shall be more truly appreciated.

He did not, however, apply any racial generalizations to his own experiences in school: "I was just the same as all the others; sometimes I got good marks, and other times I enjoyed myself and I was mischievous and lazy. Boys are all the same the world around." Indeed, throughout his life he apparently coupled an acute awareness of cultural differences with a dogmatic insistence that, as far as his own life went, no differences existed between himself and others. Empirically, he could not look out upon his world without spotting endless differences which he attributed to race and culture; theoretically, however, he was wedded to the ideological view that no differences could exist.

As far as his own life was concerned, this contradiction was resolved by what he treated as the most important single fact in his entire existence: he had obtained a respectable English university degree. The degree, of course, admitted him to the ranks of the elite. But far more important, it was the great equalizer, for in his mind all who held degrees were exactly the same. Differences in marks and standing, in relative performance, and in ability were all wiped out by the fact that all received the same degree.

U Po Thant spoke of returning to Burma and beginning with enthusiasm his career in government. "I knew that I was to become all that my father wanted me to be. Everything was in order, and I just needed a little time. I came from a leading family and I had the best education." Belonging thus to a double aristocracy—that of family and of degree, of both Burmese and English traditions—he felt secure in the belief that all those who thus "belonged" should and would take care of each other. He no longer need have any further cause for worry. And initially he had no complaints.

In a few years, however, he began to find flaws in the service which, he learned to his distress, had never caused his father any discomforts. He had expected to be accepted by British and Burman alike on an "old boy" basis, but this was not to be. Increasingly he felt that he was being slighted, ignored, and above all not fully accepted by British colleagues in the service. At about the time that he was becoming sensitive over being treated as inferior, his entire world collapsed about him. On top of his frustration with the service came a sudden awareness of the rising influence of the Burmese political agitators. These were no longer the old Burmese politicians he had scorned; they were more dangerous, and they were people with whom he had little in common except for the fact of his race. Before he could adjust to these developments, he was engulfed in the complete confusion of the war and the Japanese occupation.

He survived the war as a government official, but he emerged from it with the feeling that he was challenged and threatened from all sides. In the first place, the British had denied him the place he had fully expected in their world. He developed a diffuse sense of bitterness toward the British:

The British just used Burma for their own purposes.
We had to build up whatever we could in spite of them.

The British neglected us.

The British should have protected us from the Japanese.
It was their obligation to maintain law and order and give us peace and security. They failed.

The British deserted us; they abandoned us after the war.

The British to this day don't really care what happens to Burma.

The British never established democracy in Burma. They didn't even back up the people they trained; they failed to protect and advance democracy.

But his anticolonial sentiments had firmer and deeper foundations than mere political issues. His feelings toward the British were colored by his conviction that they had violated their trust to him as an individual and as a person who could think and act and respond according to their system of logic, their patterns of emotions. He had been maltreated in the deepest way a man can be maltreated: he had been outwitted, provoked to self-sacrifice, and then abandoned. Finally, by leaving Burma the British shattered his orderly world and made it impossible for him to achieve the particular career goals his father had set for him. In particular, his father had told him from earliest childhood that he was destined to become the senior Burmese official in a world of British officialdom in which gentlemen dealt with gentlemen on an easy and aristocratic basis. The British departure meant that he would have to violate his father's image of him; the British had forced him to break his trust with his father. Or so U Po Thant wanted to reason.

He also felt directly threatened by the emergence of the AFPFL government. They were not his type of people; he could not recognize his dream for Burma in them:

> We didn't know who most of the members of parliament were. We had never heard of them and we knew nothing about their families. They probably don't have any families. They are all just opportunists.

> The country has been ruined by an ignorant group of people. If you want to know the truth about Burmese politics, you have to know that none of the leading politicians has any education; not one of them has a *degree*.

As a present-day administrator, U Po Thant still has contemptuous feelings toward the AFPFL and the Burmese politician class, feelings which are linked to his bitterness toward the British:

> When the British realized they could no longer rule, they lost their reason and their nerve, and handed everything over to troublemakers.

He is convinced that the entire history of postindependence Burma justifies his view.

In assuming a defensive posture toward the world, he has come to believe that he represents the real Burma. He clearly resents the claims of the politicians that they are the champions of Burmese nationalism, and he scornfully points to the concessions they have made to the various minority ethnic groups in the country. In his mind he has defined uncompromisingly the real Burma as a combination of the elite of traditional Burmese aristocracy and the elite of the Anglicized Burmese, those with college degrees. Thus his class symbolizes for him both his country and his own political identity.

In order to get his bearing in any social or political situation, he tends to ask a single question: Is the other person pro- or anti-Burmese? For he divides the world between the two, and even Burmese may fall into the latter category. His definition of pro-Burmese begins at the general level of simply being friendly and sympathetic to Burmese, but in the ultimate test "Burmese" is defined according to his vision of his own political self.

In clinging to this method of distinguishing people, he is frequently forced to accept distasteful positions, for he often finds that those whom on this basis he must classify as "good" are in every other respect unworthy of being on his side. He accepts such "friends of Burma" as the costs he must pay for his patriotism. However, he is deeply disturbed, as only a man who places great store on propriety, form, and a sense of class can be, by the fact that he often admires those he must accept as enemies and feels embarrassed about his "friends." No longer can he face the world or even tackle particular problems with straightforward and uncompromised emotions.

At present, U Po Thant still holds a high and significant government post; but, since almost all of his attention and energies are concentrated on distinguishing between potential friends and foes of Burma, he is not an effective administrator. He has few dealings with others, he shows little initiative, and his basic posture is that of waiting for trouble to come to his desk. Although it might appear that he has reached a station in life that would match his initial ambitions, he still feels cheated because he no longer has the world which gave meaning to those ambitions. Unable to achieve the particular goals his father set for him, he experiences a sense of failure. In a guarded fashion, he can now talk about his initial commitment to his father's ambitions for him. He does not respond or show any emotion when asked whether his father's ambitions for him should still be seen as praiseworthy and honorable. Could it be that U Po Thant's present ineffectualness stems in large measure from an inner awareness that both he and his father were fooled by history into becoming the tools of aliens?

U Min Gyi: The Hard Driving (but Indifferent) Official

U Min Gyi's story is very similar to that of U Po Thant except that he came from slightly less esteemed origins and is a few years younger. U Min Gyi's father was a schoolteacher, and before that his ancestors were "probably *myosas*," literally "town eaters," that is, officials who received all the revenues from a particular town. He was sent to an Indian university for three years and spent two years reading at the law. Otherwise, the entire scope of his life seems to have been bounded by the administrative service. He is now thought of as one of the old professional administrators, one of the best of the British-trained, and one of the handful of men who have held the country together.

U Min Gyi's manner is cold and brusque; he conveys a sense of action and efficiency. He is completely at home in the Secretariat. The *peons* (messenger boys) always step a bit faster when going in and out of his office even if their mission is no more than delivering a cup of tea. His aides are always close at hand and respond instantly to his every call.

A stranger in his office generally finds that he gives an impression of being extremely impatient to learn the cause of the visit. He answers whatever questions are put to him with quick dispatch, in an official and proper manner, and without revealing much information. Whenever appropriate, he likes to pepper his answers with figures, either statistical data or the numbers that identify parliamentary bills and administrative orders. He speaks with clipped accent and absolute authority. His actions convey an appreciation of style and effect.

On closer acquaintance, it becomes evident that he protects himself in all human relationships with a shield of manner and formalities. He tries hard to maintain considerable social distance in all his personal associations, and he can do this in what appears to be a relatively relaxed fashion. He is clearly more at home, more articulate, more decisive when the setting is formal or well defined. Out of his office and in an informal situation, he seems to shrink considerably in size and his commanding presence vanishes.

U Min Gyi does not readily reminisce, but once he does talk about his early training, he becomes quite enthusiastic. His remarks tend to center about a particular British official who clearly remains his model of both the good official and the great man:

> Mr. C— was really a most extraordinary chap. He made us all toe the mark and he got good work out of us. But he didn't mind it when we played little tricks on him. Oh, of course, he had to pretend to be most angry, but we could tell that he rather liked it all . . . Mr. C— was really a good teacher, for everything he did, he did clearly and strongly and without any nonsense . . . If only we had more men in the service now who could act like Mr. C— used to.

He also seems to have learned very early that every person and every thing has its place, and that if everyone stays in his place the world can become wonderfully easy. Behind his shield of manners is a faith in the efficacy of ordered relationships. One may have to be a subordinate, but there is a respectable way of conducting oneself in that role.

In U Min Gyi's political calculus, all people can be divided between those who oppose, threaten, and weaken order in human affairs and those who strengthen, maintain, or just cooperate with such order. He states emphatically: "I don't understand why everyone shouldn't be a lot happier by just going along with the way they should behave and not causing a lot of difficulties."

The strongest emotion he displays on any subject appears during his frequent and vigorous attacks against people who willfully disrupt proper human relationships. The very intensity of his emotions on this subject suggests that deep within his own personality he may have some impulses toward disorder. Possibly he is not entirely sure of his ability to control his latent feelings of hostility and aggression, and maybe he desperately needs the hierarchy, the omnipresent mechanism of control, and the clearly-defined ordering of relationships of the administrative service to help him control himself. In a very real sense, the Burmese bureaucracy seems to have become a vital part of his very personality, for in giving unqualified support to the principles of order and control which are basic to the administrative service he seems to have found an answer to the search for order and control in his own personality.

He has no resentment toward history or toward any of the principal movers of events with whom he has had to deal. He can speak without malice, even with warmth, about the British period. At the same time, if the conversation shifts to the present he can employ, without emotion and essentially as formulae, the conventional anti-British criticisms. His discussions of the contemporary Burmese politicians have the same quality: he can speak well of them or poorly of them depending upon what the fashion was at the time to which his remarks are directed. The only distinction is that the most positive period is always the present one. He has been able to work with all manner of politicians and has learned how to maintain the full confidence of his current master without at the same time making too strong a commitment to him.

Since he conveys such a strong impression of leadership, it is surprising that U Min Gyi has almost no set views on either foreign affairs or domestic issues. He is simply indifferent to most of the world outside the civil service. He denies holding any strong opinions on matters of foreign policy; these are matters for the cabinet and the foreign office. Similarly, he refuses to express himself on domestic problems because they are not within his province of responsibilities. Indeed, it almost seems as though his mode of thinking does not recognize an outside world with autonomous problems; only one logic, one reality prevails, that of the Burmese civil administration which in its various divisions deals with all conceivable problems and in which he is completely at home.

In the last analysis, in spite of his appearance of authority and command, U Min Gyi is the spirit of the clerk blown large. It is disturbing to realize this, for he is the kind of Burmese official who seems capable of action and who is being called upon to build a new nation. His personal commitment to the proper ordering of things is so strong that he cannot be expected to be an innovator. It is true that he has accepted and willingly administered various new projects proposed by the new government of Burma. He is able to speak enthusiastically of the five-year plan. But in his own thinking there has been and there can be little change. No note of cynicism appears in his voice when he observes:

> The Army officers are now most anxious to say all the things they are going to do for the people. The AFPFL leaders did the same thing, and it was exactly the same before the war. I suppose that politicians must talk that way. Actually there is nothing new about good administration, and that is what people really appreciate the most.

U Min Gyi has thus adapted himself to the modern world without building up manifest resentments and hostilities. He is completely at home in the role of the modern, and even the modernizing, administrator. On the other hand, he cannot endure change and he must struggle against all who would alter fundamentally the structure and performance of the Burmese government.

U Maung Galay: The State Scholar

U Maung Galay is a product of modern, postwar Burma. Although he received his early education during the British period, he had no adult experiences with colonialism. He comes from a rural district where his father was a petty merchant until he became a politician and the local leader of the AFPFL. This political connection may have helped pave the way for U Maung Galay's selection as a state scholar to study abroad, but there is no question of his abilities. He is unmistakably an alert, intelligent, quick-minded, and ambitious young man.

A guiding principle of his conduct is that people should be rewarded solely on the basis of individual merit. He insists that family and class, race and nationality are all irrelevant considerations. At times this view causes him temporary confusion, for he cannot always quickly settle upon what should be the appropriate measure of merit. Invariably, however, he finally arrives at a judgment which seems to him to have been determined by the application of some standard of individual merit or worth; then he emphatically denies the validity of all other standards. He wants desperately to believe in a world in which everyone holds his place on the basis of achievement. He has learned well, and he will not let others forget that the test of a modern society is that people have to achieve their stations and that it is old-fashioned to permit ascriptive considerations to determine one's position in society. Since he harps on the view that it is backward, unjust, undemocratic, and "typically Burmese" to overlook the central importance of individual merit, he is generally thought to be a nuisance and a bore, especially by his superiors.

As a state scholar U Maung Galay spent several years studying in New York. These were, he claims, extremely exciting years. He apparently was very popular with his classmates and was welcomed into the community. He was asked to give numerous talks to both student and adult groups during which he described with enthusiasm the wonderful future in store for Burma and the evils and injustices of the colonial period. In a sense, he became a "Mr. Burma," and all his hopes and dreams became those of his country. In America he began to believe that all his values and judgments, his preferences and prejudices, were identical with those of his government. He had a sense of identity, he had recognition, he had sympathy, he was able to prove himself. It was an exhilarating experience but essentially political; it is significant that at the personal level he did not build up any friendships. He can no longer remember even the names of his college associates.

His return to Burma was a traumatic experience. The natural letdown from no longer holding the center of the stage was accompanied by the shock of seeing that his country had not changed during his absence in all the wonderful ways he had been telling Americans it had:

> I could see right off that everything I had been telling people about what was happening in Burma was untrue. It was all a pack of lies. All the wonderful schemes were just on paper.

Soon after his return, he had a second shock: he was assigned to a job which he felt was beneath him and which did not fully utilize his American training. His frustration turned to resentment and a personal hostility toward the leaders of the Burmese government.

> I could see that they were all selfish and really weren't interested in developing the country. I came to hate the politicians for they had made me seem like a liar; they had encouraged me to say all the false things I had told about Burma when I was in America.

He had a double grievance against his government; it deceived him about the future of both his country and his own career. He learned that there was no basis in reality for the most exciting and rewarding experiences of his life. He was angry that he had been led to fool others, but even more seriously, he was angry because he had fooled himself.

It is hard for us to judge objectively whether U Maung Galay was in fact assigned to an inappropriate job. On the face of it, the post would appear to have been a more responsible one than an American who has just received his bachelor's degree would reasonably expect to obtain; however an American degree might be expected to go much further in a transitional society like Burma in which so few have any advanced training. There is no doubt, on the other hand, that the lack of clear-cut career channels in transitional societies is a major cause for uncertainty, and hence frustration and resentment. Certainly in Burma, as in the rest of Southeast Asia, people like U Maung Galay have no difficulty in getting jobs. The big question is where the jobs are likely to lead, and since there is uncertainty on this score and no firm predictions can be made, people cannot derive satisfaction out of their present positions.

Because his aspirations were too high, U Maung Galay now feels that his society has let him down. He can find endless ways of applying his theme about lack of recognition for merit and ability in backward countries. Oddly enough, there are moments when he can still become extremely enthusiastic in describing the new Burma of tomorrow. In doing so, he seems to be recapturing the thrills of his earlier experiences in America. His mood, however, can change suddenly, and he will become sharply critical of all things Burmese, proclaiming that he can see no future for himself or his country.

His political criticism is diffuse and erratic. As a corollary of his basic charge that merit is not recognized in Burma, he is forced to suggest that behind all events and occurrences there must be some form of scheming and skulduggery and that therefore nothing can conform to any rational pattern. There is no particular logic behind his version of elite corruption; he characterizes it simply as a darkly malevolent influence. He thus has no method or theory for even crudely predicting development; he can only decry events after the fact and call them typical.

He is just as vague when he is asked to give positive suggestions for his country's improvement. Beyond saying that "they ought to make everything work better, and be more efficient," he does not have any ready alternatives. It is evident that he believes that all power resides at the pinnacle and that those who are not at the top can be of little consequence. He is exceedingly scornful of the suggestion that possibly experience and seniority are not incompatible with the principle of rewarding according to merit. He immediately denies completely the relevance of experience and claims that it is only a vague concept used by the powerful to intimidate the weak:

> People who have the top jobs always stress the importance of experience, but they can never tell you what experience really is. This is because there is nothing to it. The British used to use the argument of "experience" to keep Burma from getting its independence. They said we didn't have enough experience to run our country. Now the top Burmese are using exactly the same argument to keep those of us who have the real ability from getting any good jobs. It is exactly the same as it was under the British, and that is why the country remains so backward.

It is not unlikely that he clings to his belief that only the top people can be effective largely because of his relations with his superior, whom he clearly despises and to whom he refers in private as "quite stupid and unintelligent." He cannot effectively influence or even cope with his superior; he collapses in all of his relations with this person of power whom he says he despises. In fact, aside from some aimless sniping and grumbling, it appears that he is a docile and compliant worker in his office. For all his training, he brings little that is new to his job.

At present U Maung Galay is not completely discouraged, for he continues to keep alive the hope that someday Burma will become a fully modern society in which merit will be respected. He thus looks forward to the time when his dreams and the dreams of his country will again be identical. In the meantime, believing that only those with absolute power count, he does little to help bring about the realization of those dreams.

U Tin Lay: The Enthusiastic Technician

In contrast to the other administrative officials we have just introduced, who were not specialists, U Tin Lay is an engineer, living in a district far from Rangoon. His responsibilities are water conservation and the building and maintenance of irrigation systems; out of this concern he has built a little principality, if not an empire, which he commands with unbounded enthusiasm.

U Tin Lay received his training in the old Indian Army as a noncommissioned officer and engineer. He spent nearly a dozen years with his regiment on the Northwest Frontier. There is still a great deal of the soldier in U Tin Lay. He prizes brusqueness, quickness, neatness, and, especially, a spirit of camaraderie. He stoutly maintains that civilian clubs are no substitute for the old regimental mess. He genuinely prefers the out-of-doors to office work, the district to the Secretariat. At the same time, he is a gregarious person who is anxious to entertain all the significant people who may visit his district. He takes an intense pride in describing to such visitors not only his current operations but also his dreams for the future. He admits that progress has been much slower than he would like it to be, and he vigorously catalogues all the problems, ending each analysis with a chuckle.

Just as at one time his entire world was has regiment, so now it is his irrigation projects. The outside world he divides between those who can assist him or at least appreciate his efforts and those who are obstacles and sources of frustration. This calculus gives him a blunt and pragmatic approach. He will, for example, straightforwardly ask the individual American why America which is so rich cannot spare some money and assistance for his projects. When it is suggested that such matters are usually the concern of governments, and that the Burmese government had insisted on the discontinuation of American aid, he explodes:

> That damnable Secretariat! Always mucking up everything. We could jolly well get along better without a government for all the help they are. Those people in Rangoon can't understand the simplest things. It's best not to pay any attention to them.

Indeed, it seems that U Tin Lay pays little attention to Rangoon and that Rangoon unfortunately seems to reciprocate. Consequently he is able to preserve his island of hopeful enterprise, but he does not seem to be able to find the backing he needs to expand it. He sees in himself the hope of a new Burma, but largely on the ground that he is so successful in isolating and divorcing himself from the mainstream of Burmese government and politics. Thus, although U Tin Lay speaks constantly of his ambitions for change, in fact he is a mainstay in helping to preserve and maintin essentially routine functions which have been passed down from the British period.

CHAPTER 17

The Politicians' Search for Identity

In democratic societies the channels for recruiting and training politicians are far less well defined than those for administrators. The myth about the spontaneity of popular leadership is, as we have noted, a powerful component of most versions of democracy; the representatives of the people should be of the people, and not too conspicuously under the influence of specialized knowledge. Leaders "arise," "emerge," "appear"; they are not trained, educated or produced.

The democratic ideal that a country should be led by men infused with a spirit of amateurism serves some useful purposes; it inhibits, for example, the growth of a class that might be excessively preoccupied with the pleasures of controlling men and events. It helps to remind all that the ultimate function of the politician is to weigh questions of values in making choices, that after the technicians and administrators have outlined the alternatives, there must still be those who can be trusted to make the appropriate selections. Also, of course, the notion of the amateur makes it considerably easier for the professional politician to maintain his position and reduce "unhealthy competition." For if the channels of access to the political arena are too clearly marked out, and if the recruitment process is too well defined, it can be expected that excessive numbers of aspirants for power will clog up the process.

This last also suggests that for those who have become politicians there must have been a somewhat difficult, possibly slightly obscure, but still fairly standardized channel of recruitment. It is thus important for the observer to note that, although a society may deny explicitly the existence of formal procedures for the recruitment and training of politicians, there invariably exist some implicit and informal channels of recruitment through which most of the potential politicians must pass if they are to gain access to the arena of politics.

This truth applies directly in our examination of the political culture of Burma, for in transitional societies those implicit channels of access are generally determined by the turn of historical events, and thus there is usually little continuity or stability in either the source of recruitment or the method of training. We have already observed the dramatic changes in the scope and focus of the political process in Burma as the country moved from a form of administrative politics under colonial rule to agitational politics during the period of the nationalist movement and to popular politics after independence, each shift bringing a change in the avenues of admission to the political process and hence in the backgrounds and experiences of those admitted to active participation.

Moreover, under such conditions, once events have moved on, those who come later may find that the previous channels have disappeared and that they cannot follow in the footsteps of the older generation of leaders. When this happens, as it has happened in all former colonial countries in which the national leadership was mobilized during a conspiratorial or agitational phase of limited duration, the new generation may feel that it is being denied legitimate opportunities. Such is the case in Burma. Many of the younger aspirants to political power in Burma are becoming frustrated and even suspicious of those who are now the major holders of power. They see the present leaders as men claiming status on the basis of the accidents of history, not as men who gained their positions by the exercise of skill. The result is an acute conflict between political generations. The Burmese who came to power immediately after independence were remarkably young. With few exceptions, the first cabinet ministers were all in their thirties, and now the men of that generation are inclined to see their careers going on indefinitely into the future, with ever increasing recognition and honors. Meanwhile, men in their twenties who have been taught that it is appropriate for men in their thirties to hold down cabinet posts feel that their way is being unjustly blocked.

Thus in treating the recruitment of the Burmese political class, we must distinguish between those who emerged during the last phases of colonial rule and the Japanese occupation, and who therefore had to oppose an alien authority to achieve their status, and those who have emerged since independence and who feel that they must oppose a restrictive Burmese elite. In the main, this is a distinction between the high echelon and the low, between an older and an only slightly younger generation.

Social Origins

In their social origins the Burmese politicians are far less homogeneous than the administrators. Our politician respondents represented a far wider geographic distribution, with only a few of them coming originally from the large urban centers. On first view they seemed to be far more mobile, both physically and socially, than the administrators, who tended to come from the more established families. On closer analysis, however, even those from the rural areas and the villages appeared to have some interests which they needed to preserve and which inhibited to some extent their political flexibility.

Thus, although politics clearly provided them with an excellent channel for social advancement, most of the politicians remained to some degree caught up in a web of personal ties and had to balance their ambitions for advancement against a need to preserve elements of their communal relationships.

In describing the conflict between administrator and politician, we noted that there was a class dimension to this struggle which had contributed to a kind of national paralysis. On closer examination it is apparent that there is a division within the politician class which has aggravated that paralysis.

One group of politicians, who are more typical of the main national leadership, consists of men who were exposed to university education but usually failed to obtain degrees. They generally have come from quasi-middle-class families well off enough to have allowed them to go on to school for several years. Some have come from fairly wealthy merchant families. It is the mood of this group that is important, for these men represent a somewhat rootless class of people actively seeking to become a part of the modern world and anxious to participate in exciting and active events.

The other group comes from the districts and represents a considerably more stable element in the existing social order. It would convey too many inappropriate meanings from a European context to call such men potential rural aristocracy, but generally they do represent the more influential families at the top of a peasant-based community. Many of them are the leading landowners; even more of them have been able to expand their holdings rapidly as a result of the postwar elimination of the class of Indian moneylenders, the Chettyars. Others such as the rice brokers, the owners of small retail stores, and the like are associated with local economic interests. Thus, although they do not come from the best or longest established families in the district, they have considerable interest in maintaining the existing structure of economic and social relationships. Most important, they tend to control the distribution of the favors and rewards which a government that professes to be concerned with socialism is capable of giving to its citizens. They are, therefore, intensely interested in maximizing the belief that all is going well in the country while at the same time minimizing any likelihood that substantial changes will occur that might undermine their influence in essentially peasant communities.

Since independence these two types of politicians have formed the strange alliance that has governed Burma. As a consequence, Burma has been spared the problems that follow from the existence of an excessively sharp gulf between a Westernized, intellectually oriented elite and a rural-based elite. The bringing together of an urban group generally less acculturated to the modern world than the most Westernized elements in the cities and a rural group more modernized than most in the rural areas has provided a powerful force for stability. At the same time, however, the alliance of the two types of politicians has served to freeze most efforts at social change. Indeed the need of the urban, intellectual Burmese politician for rural associates helps to explain why transitional societies such as Burma can produce the appearances of a social revolutionary movement with few of its consequences.

This does not mean that the Burmese politician is not concerned with or involved in social change. On the contrary, both groups of politicians share the characteristic of being composed of people individually involved in a process of acculturation to the modern world. As individuals they confirm the fact that behind the immobilism of Burmese society there is a ferment of subtle but profound change in personal attitudes and sentiments. But this is the very kind of change that often leaves people incapable of effective and consistent collective action.

The Attempt to Define Their Profession

From the inception of their political experience the Burmese administrators could mold and adapt their behavior according to the concrete examples of individual British officials. The Burmese politicians, not so fortunate, had to learn their roles by relying upon abstract and only distantly perceived models of a modern and modernizing politician in a democracy, a condition which has denied realism to their understanding of their profession. A fascinating feature of political development in most transitional societies can be uncovered by trying to trace the ways in which the emerging democratic politicians have tried to find out the nature of their profession. How should an aspiring politician spend his day? What should he be doing with his time? How should he support himself? How can he convince others that he is a politician when the country doesn't have a stable political process? Who tells him what qualities he should affect, what skills he should learn, and how he should go about doing the routine business of his profession?

In the following words of various leading Burmese politicians, we can see something of their confusion of mind as they sought to define their roles:

> My ideas about what a politician should be came mainly from reading in European history. I liked the history of Rome the best, and Julius Caesar has been my hero ever since.

> I feel that Burmese politicians should follow the examples of Abraham Lincoln, William Pitt, and Lenin. These were men who could think on big affairs and never had to worry about little details or personalities. Unfortunately, it seems that in Burma we always have to trouble ourselves with matters of organization and we must be sensitive to human feelings. That is why we cannot be great politicians.

> In thinking about becoming a politician, I used to think of how wonderful it would be to help build up my country and to go around in the districts and lecture to the ignorant people on how they ought to behave. I am sorry to say that it has not worked out that way. We have all been much too busy in our offices, and we just do not have the time to tell people how they can improve themselves.

The ideals of leadership which our respondents claimed were guiding their conduct seem to be grossly inappropriate for the workday processes of a democratic system, to say nothing of politics in a transitional society. They tended to think in terms of heroic figures who appeared to rise above any concern with the details of life. Regardless of the historic figures they chose for examples, most of them seemed to share a common expectation that somehow the good politician was one who could divorce himself from personal considerations and precisely by ignoring all ties of friendship could become a popular, honored, and even revered man.

One can understand why, when the Burmese politician finds that he is constantly being called upon to make compromises and is rarely able to avoid being the object of conflicting and heated demands, he is readily convinced that something is wrong, that he is not living up to his ideals. His problem, moreover, is considerably more complicated than that of a person who feels that he has compromised his standards. For the Burmese politician, in idealizing the role of the politician, tends to assume that his image of the role is widely shared among the Burmese people. Hence when he fails to realize his own expectations, he is also convinced that everyone is aware of his failings.

Through this sequence of reactions the fuzzy and ambiguous image of the politician's role seems to have become a source of suspicion between politician and citizen. The politician, knowing that he has not become the person he thinks he should be, becomes extremely sensitive to the possibility that others may be criticizing him as a person. He must in the end defend himself by claiming that the fault lies entirely with the "backward state of the country," "the ignorance of the people," and the fact that the "Burmese don't understand democracy." In this way he becomes suspicious that his society has kept him from achieving his idealized sense of identity, that the people are against him. Here we come to a clue which helps explain the ability of the Burmese politician to vacillate between being the extreme nationalist and being the bitter critic of the ways of his people.

The feeling of having failed to achieve the ideal of the democratic politician's role and to win the praise and acceptance of the people has caused many Burmese politicians to become bitter, even cynical, and extraordinarily thin-skinned for men of politics. On finding that their initial and highly idealized version of the democratic politician's role was unworkable, some of the older politicians rejected democracy as unsuited to Burmese conditions:

> We cannot make democracy work in a country that doesn't let its political leaders carry on in the right fashion.

> It will be a long time before we can really hope to have a real democracy. The people are still too backward.

The Need to Be Popular

The majority of the Burmese politicians have not gone quite so far. They have sought instead to redefine the role of the politician by accepting a divorce from their ideals and by seeking only to gain acceptance among the people. As a consequence, they have become almost hypersensitive to many forms of popular criticism and even to demands for policy decisions. They need to feel accepted by the people more than they need to—or feel that they are able to—meet their own standards of performance as leaders.

This complex pattern of attitudes is extremely important in understanding an otherwise puzzling mode of behavior characteristic both of Burmese politicians and of those in most of the newly independent countries. These leaders appear to be relatively far removed from the masses of their people. Lacking the mechanism of interest groups and other channels for sensitive communication with their publics, they direct most of their actions toward devising strategies and tactics against other members of the elite world. As politicians go, they appear to be relatively free to carry out programs and policies according to their private notions. But at the same time they constantly protest that they are unable to introduce or carry out policies that are manifestly desirable from a national or developmental point of view because they are restrained by democratic forms and by the popular will.

Clearly in many instances they rationalize their own unwillingness to advance the necessary policies and, like democratic politicians the world around, find it convenient to plead that their hands are tied by public opinion. However, their basic reaction seems to stem from their urgent need to be closer to the people; hence, even though they may not have—or rather, precisely because they do not have—accurate information on the state of public opinion, they feel they cannot do anything which in their own minds would appear to be unpopular or unfriendly to the people. Thus their own insecurities make it impossible for them to champion programs that might in any way be seen as unpleasant, hard, or demanding. And thus we find men whose leadership is unchallenged, at least from popular sources, fearful of taking the lead and insisting that they are powerless in the face of public opinion.

We might note here that this set of attitudes lies behind the nearly complete collapse of the tax structure in Burma and in many of the other newly independent lands. It also inhibits politicians from calling for programs requiring the mobilization of resources for economic development. It has been argued that the democratic approach is inherently inadequate for the task of organizing and directing urgent national efforts at rapid economic development; but in actual fact the weakness is not in the machinery of democracy, it is in leadership which feels itself powerless to act because of insecurities arising from faulty concepts of the role of the popular politician.

This particular problem is further compounded for many Burmese politicians by the feeling that they are suspended in isolation, not just between their ideals and the sentiments of the people, but also between the modern and the traditional worlds. They sense that they are less Westernized than their opposite numbers in the administrative class, and at the same time they know that they are far more modernized than the mass of the population. Some of them are able to describe this feeling quite specifically:

> I don't care much for being with Burmese who have studied abroad or even with those who have graduated from Rangoon University. When I listen to them I find I have little to say and I begin to wish that I were back with the village type of Burman. I must also confess that when I am with villagers, I can feel just as left out.

> It is a little better now, but I still don't feel really at home at the —— Club [whose members include the most Westernized Burmese]. I am much happier being with other political workers.

The contradictory nature of their position causes some Burmese politicians to vacillate between opposite images of themselves. At times they think of themselves as legitimate members of the modern or Westernized community, and at other times they see themselves as "pure Burmese." To the extent that they are able to shift readily from one to the other, they probably provide a genuine degree of stability to the entire society, for in so doing they bridge the gap between the society of the urban moderns and that of the rural traditionals.

A few will confess that they derive some satisfaction from the tactic of claiming that they belong to the opposite world from the one they happen to be in at the moment. One AFPFL leader confided:

> Whenever I am with a group of Europeans or Indians or Anglicized Burmese, I always make a point of stressing my Burmese nature. It is also true that when I am among villagers it aways helps if they have the idea that I usually busy myself with national and international matters.

Another AFPFL party worker said in describing an election campaign:

> In conducting our political campaigns, we always keep in mind that city Burmese can be easily embarrassed about taking on foreign ways while the Burmese country folk look up to those who understand European practices.

It is significant, however, that in spite of the objective advantages, subjectively most of the Burmese politicians appear to experience genuine discomfort from their capacity for psychic mobility, and they are not easily convinced that their ability to adapt to two worlds is a positive contribution to their nation's well-being.

In part, their difficulty seems to stem from their own self-doubts and fears. We have already noted the complex feelings and anxieties of the Burmese about power, and that the cultural concepts of *ah-nah-deh* and *awza* converge to produce a high degree of suspicion of those who seem too openly to seek power. The Burmese press constantly informs the Burmese politician that there are "bad" politicians who are invariably "self-seeking opportunists." Being self-conscious of their capacity to shift between two worlds seems to raise in the minds of some Burmese politicians the question whether they may not be personally guilty of the great sin of opportunism:

> The way things are in this country, you have to jump about trying to please the people in Rangoon and then those in the district. I wonder how we can ever hope to be principled politicians.

> Politicians in America can follow their set courses, but unfortunately, we are not so lucky. I try my best, but it is exceedingly hard not to change your viewpoint all the time. It's something about Burma. I can't understand it.

Psychologically the lack of a stable self-image seems to raise feelings of anxiety and guilt in Burmese politicians, feelings that tend to become particularly strong whenever they have to face the realities of life. As might be expected, many of them respond to this predicament by being tensely assertive and ceaselessly self-righteous whenever the question of their self-image is raised. At the core of this confused sense of profession lie deeper self-doubts and an endemic fear of failure. Unable to define their role clearly in their own minds, they cannot be sure that they have not been failures. Whenever events force upon them an awareness of the failings of their country as a whole, they are likely to be highly sensitive to the suggestion that they as a class of people may be the prime cause of difficulties.

The Fantasy of an Omnipotent Government

The self-doubt of the Burmese politicians, rooted in part in ambiguities about the nature of their role, also stems from a more general uncertainty about the entire mechanism and function of government and politics. Unsure of precisely what should be expected of government, the Burmese politicians have not had a realistic basis for judging their own performance.

By the time Burma gained independence, the operations of government were essentially a matter of routine for members of the administrative class. Not so for the politicians. They had seen government only from afar and as an enemy, for government had meant to them alien rule. Consequently, they had little skill in distinguishing between what was possible and impossible for government to do. Even more serious consequences followed from their practice of confusing possible with probable events. In their minds what seemed possible easily became certain, and they tended to discount the need for effort and work to achieve anything within the sphere of government. The upshot was a tendency to exaggerate grotesquely the powers of government.

Through their opposition to British rule, the aspiring Burmese politicians came to see the British in more than life-size terms. Government was the ultimate symbol of all that the British and the modern world stood for in their minds; government was omnipotent. Also some of the politicians felt a need to make the British all-powerful, for the more powerful the colonial administration the more heroic was their victorious struggle for independence. In contrast to the anxious efforts of the Burmese administrators to minimize the significance of the struggle for independence, most of our politician respondents spoke readily and compulsively of their heroic efforts.

In picturing government as being so powerful, they also pictured the task of rulers as effortless. There was a period of complacency immediately after the Burmese politicians came to power, a feeling that there should be no need for exertion, which, when combined with traditional sentiments of *ah-nah-deh* and *awza* and with a latent fear of decision and suspicion of administrators, provided the psychological basis for political immobilism. Some of the politicians seem to have reassured themselves that if the British were omnipotent when they had government, then the Burmese, once they were in power, must be equally omnipotent to prove themselves the equals of their mentors. The proof of their omnipotence, in turn, depended on their demonstrating that they were relieved of any necessity for further strenuous efforts. Therefore, to suggest the need for effort and sacrifice after independence was to call into question one's own omnipotence; and the effect of this logic was to create a powerful subconscious need to proclaim a wish world but not to work strenuously for its realization. At the more conscious level, this mood was strengthened by the fact that, being ignorant of the mechanisms and levers of governmental power, the politicians were uncertain as to what they could or should do even if they were willing to exert themselves.

In reflecting on the immediate postwar period, some of the politicians now say that they were made complacent by the mood of the times and the common belief that they and their country were on the side of history. This was how they could explain the fact that they had been able to overcome the presumably omnipotent British. Everything should now be easy because the tide of history was running strong.

As it became steadily more difficult to expect wishes to turn into realities, it also became more difficult to push out of mind the fear of possible failure. A significant reaction to this fear was the feeling that the British had tricked them, that the British in some malicious fashion had taken the charm and magic out of government, and in doing so had left the Burmese weakened.

The feeling of having been tricked seems to have made the Burmese political class even more suspicious of all those who might be knowledgeable about the operations of government. They are suspicious of the British for having somehow removed the keys to the easy manipulation of government; they are suspicious of the administrators who seem too at home in the offices and who they believe must be subverting the effective operations of government; they are suspicious of other politicians who may know the tricks of running a government but are not willing to help. Suspicion of their own abilities has been diverted into suspicion of the intentions of others.[1]

Partly in response to this feeling of suspicion, and partly in an attempt to recapture the excitement of a faith in omnipotent government, older members of the Burmese political class return periodically to the theme of the evils of colonialism and the virtues of the anticolonial struggle. The younger aspiring politicians interpret such reversions as efforts of the old generation to monopolize power and cling to its arbitrary and essentially ascriptive claims to status.

1. This pattern of reaction to colonial rulers suggests that psychologically it may be easier for an emerging leadership to be realistic and vigorous if the retiring colonial rulers manifestly demonstrate some hostility to the new government. In such cases, an objective basis for suspicion exists and it even takes on a healthy form, causing the new elite to determine resolutely to prove itself. When the former colonial power acts only in an exemplary fashion and obviously seems to be sympathetic to the new government, then the new leaders lack the basis for being suspicious of their former masters; they can only be suspicious of their own abilities which will in turn tend to reduce their effectiveness and hence provide further grounds for doubting their own abilities.

The Question of Personal Identity

The intensity of the Burmese politician's need to be popular and the grip that fantasies of omnipotent government have on his mind can be attributed only in part to the uncertainty about the precise nature of his profession. These problems seem to be compounded by deeper uncertainties about what they represent as individuals, not just as politicians. The fact that they are expected to deal with power, to lead their country, and to speak for their people seems to have intensified many problems of acculturation for the politicians.

Much of the most penetrating work to date on personal problems of transitional people has focused on the Asian and African intellectual who feels that he is caught between two cultures, marginal to both, and isolated and rootless in his own existence. The drama of the conflict in values is also to be found in the lives of less intellectually and aesthetically sensitive peoples of transitional societies; and the overtones of these well-known problems are to be found in the behavior of the Burmese politicians. The basic problem of personal identity, however, seems to take on some distinctive forms for men who as they undergo acculturation are also engrossed in the particular range of activities basic to the politician's profession. For example, the need to calculate constantly in terms of power and influence and the effort to articulate representative and collectively appealing sentiments seem to create some peculiarly intense personal issues.

If we probe deeper, we find considerable evidence that the Burmese politicians' exaggeration of the power of the British arose from more than just the logic of their struggle. They are fundamentally still reacting to the fact that their crises in identity came out of the hold that British ways once had on their minds and emotions. They were citizens of a captive land, but their minds had been captivated without any effort on the part of the rulers and masters. The issue of identity under such conditions hinges upon questions about the meaning of falling under the influence of others, of being controlled by others. The power of others is thus absolute for it is the power of making one willing to change oneself into their image. There is possibly no other circumstance in which people can sense more fully the human meanings of power and attraction than at the heart of the acculturation process, for this is the point at which people are giving up the most precious thing they have, their own integrity, in order to take a part of the identity of others who are foreign, with all that that word can mean.

The sensing of power is also basic to the acculturation process because it seems that whenever there is uncertainty about the limits of the self the sentiment of omnipotence easily mixes with feelings of insignificance. The possibility of changing, of being everything, is close to the possibility of being nothing. Thus the vacillation between the elations and fears of omnipotence and impotence.

The Burmese politicians seem to have sensed in the acculturation process some of the deeper realities of power which they cannot fully articulate. They will say that the British exploited them and took from them what was rightfully theirs, but they can see that the objective record does not bear them out; they are capable of recognizing that the protest of righteous indignation which they wish to make sounds too much like the self-pity of impotent men. They cannot express easily the deeper problem of experiencing a loss of satisfaction with the self.

In order to explore these sentiments which the issue of identity has produced for our politician respondents, it is helpful to begin with their first feelings about the desirability to change themselves.

The Need to be Different

As our respondents spoke of their childhood and adolescent experiences, a dominant theme that emerged was the remarkably early and strong commitments they had made to the idea of being different from their parents and from most of their elders. Their need to be different seems also to have involved a need both to be superior to their peers and to be a part of the modern, urban, world culture.

> As long ago as I can remember I had always wanted to go to Rangoon. I didn't really dislike my village; I was very popular there and people thought well of me, but it was pretty boring. I knew that Rangoon would be exciting for it is one of the biggest cities in the entire world.

> The man I admired most as a boy was my uncle who had traveled to India. He spoke some English and he had many interesting stories to tell. His stories were not about olden days and childish myths; they were about what people actually can do. He used to tell me that some day I might be able to visit England. This would excite me very much and I would worry about doing the wrong things and embarrassing myself.

My father was just a typical Burman. He had no real ambitions. He had no interest in affairs, and politics was much too new a thing for him.

In large measure our respondents were only giving expression to the obvious fact that in comparison to their peers they were probably more ambitious, more interested in getting ahead, more desirous of power and leadership. If it were not for the dynamics of the acculturation process, their life stories could be largely told in these terms, which would make their experiences essentially similar to those of aspiring politicians in stable societies. Given the circumstances, however, their spirit of ambition meant also that they were accepting the idea that the modern culture was superior to the old world of their parents. Ambition in their cases had to carry with it the rejection of family traditions.

It is extremely significant that although both the politicians and the administrators had early ambitions to modernize their lives, they were faced with quite different problems, particularly with respect to their relations with their parents. For most members of the administrative class, becoming adult meant simply following in the footsteps of parents who had already made the initial commitment to an Anglicized culture; for most of the politicians, the commitment involved a definite break from the pattern of their parents. For the administrator, traditional Burmese ways were already slightly alien to his immediate family; for the politician, tradition was associated directly with the practices of his own parents. Thus inescapably the politicians were faced with far more complex problems than were the administrators. The family dimension of the problem made the idea of a modern life more exciting, more dramatic, more forbidden, and more dangerous to the politician. For him, modernizing meant rebelling against his family, while for the administrator it meant conforming to family demands.

This question of breaking with the family may help explain the subsequent paradoxical behavior of many of the politicians who have enthusiastically attacked the old verbally but have been unable to act forcefully to destroy the basis of tradition in the country. They are willing to speak against tradition, but they feel compelled to hold back from actually striking against things which they associate so closely with their parents. This consideration has only modified but not altered the basic fact that in the early years of their personal development the politicians wanted to be different and were excited by the idea of the modern world.

The Shock in Choosing a National Identity

In making their initial decision to be different from their families and to seek a place in the more modern world, the Burmese politicians had in some respects to turn their backs on their own culture and accept, possibly more unconsciously than consciously, the Westerner's opinion that there were undesirable qualities in traditional Burmese life. To this day there is hardly a foreign criticism of Burmese characteristics which Burmese politicians will not repeat in private and in unguarded moments, picturing their fellow countrymen in the very same unfavorable terms as those once employed by the British.

It appears that at first this negative view of their own culture raised no problems for their personal development. Later, however, judging from the words of our respondents, most of them experienced a moment of truth where with dramatic suddenness they saw what it meant to debase Burmese ways and yet at the same time accept their identity as Burmese. In very moving fashion, some of the Burmese politicians told of their shock of awareness of what it meant to be a Burmese. One said:

I had never given any thought to what it meant to be a Burmese. I must have filled in countless forms in which I called myself a "Burmese Buddhist," but it didn't have much meaning. I grew up in Rangoon and there were always Indians, and Karens, and Ara-kanese, and all kinds of people around; so it didn't seem strange that people were different from each other.

In my second year at the university, I met this young Englishman who was very keen on learning all about Burma. He had read more about Burmese history than I had, and he knew much more than I did about the old days of the Burmese kings. I remember telling some of my friends at the university some of the things he had taught me about Burmese history, and they all said that it was foolish to think about such things, for we should be looking to the future and to a modern Burma which would be much better. My English friend was most interested in learning about Burmese customs. He was always asking me questions about why the Burmese do all the things they do. Sometimes I didn't know, sometimes I just couldn't explain it to him.

Then one day, I still remember very clearly, he got quite angry with me when I could not answer his questions and could only laugh at the customs he wanted to know more about. He said, "Don't you know anything about your own beliefs; what kind of a Burmese are you?" The question really bothered me. You can't imagine how awful it was.

For another the shock came from an article by a noted Englishman who, by describing sympathetically traditional Burmese practices, left the young man with the haunting question, "Should I really be proud and not ashamed of things which I do not really respect?"

In many different ways the basic issue of whether one should be proud of one's culture was forced upon the consciences of the young politicians-to-be. Two incidents of historical significance caused this shock of awareness for several of our respondents. Specifically, the Saya San rebellion and the students' strike at Rangoon University seem to have had the peculiar capacity to provoke, in a disturbing fashion, the basic question of what one should be proud of in being a Burmese.

The Saya San rebellion which broke out in 1930 conformed to the traditional Burmese political and religious pattern of revolts which sought to establish a new monarchy.[2] Guided by soothsayers and supported by magicians, tattooers, and the sellers of protective medicines, amulets, and charms, the army raised by Saya San placed him upon a throne under the White Umbrella which symbolized royalty in old Burma and convinced themselves that they were invulnerable to mere modern guns and weapons. The movement clearly thrived on ignorance, superstition, and readiness to accept a mystical and magical view of the universe, to live on unreasoning and emotional expectations of political success—all the qualities the emerging Burmese politicians who wanted to be modern sought to reject. However, to their profound shock, Europeans, both those considered pro-Burmese and those considered hostile to Burma, pointed to the Saya San rebellion as a manifestation of Burmese nationalism. This movement, which Burmese who aspired to a more modern way of life considered repulsive, degrading, and the work of ignoramuses was identified as a grand example of the very Burmese spirit of nationalism with which they knew they should want to be identified. They could not say, and no one would want them to say, that they were not a part of Burmese nationalism.

2. For details of the rebellion, see Cady, *A History of Modern Burma*, pp. 309–21. Discussion of similar abortive, tradition-based revolts are to be found in Maurice Collis, *Into Hidden Burma* (London, Faber and Faber, 1953); and by the same author, *Trials in Burma* (London, Faber and Faber, 1938).

For the next generation of Burmese politicians, the incident that caused the shock of awareness was the 1936 Rangoon University student strike. The incidents that sparked the strike were so trivial that the participants are now generally embarrassed at their mention. The strike itself was an exhilaratingly irresponsible experience, an incident which the participants knew was little more than an act of boyish excitement. Yet, like the Saya San rebellion, it was hailed by foreigners as a demonstration of Burmese nationalism. Some of our respondents indicated that they were disturbed by this development which had made Burmese nationalism seem more like a childish outburst than a responsible movement. It was somehow too easy to be a national hero; national greatness should involve more than the particular chain of events associated with student action.

Whatever the nature of the particular incident which caused the shock of awareness about the question of Burmese values, the aspiring politicians were uniformly victimized by the assumption that the sentiments of nationalism are more truly reflected in atavistic feelings and destructive emotions than in reasoned efforts at improving oneself and one's country. Just as some of the administrators, when faced with the irrationalities of the nationalist politicians, came to wonder whether they might be lacking in nationalistic ardor, so early in their lives many of the politicians had found it necessary to accept behavior they could not admire as being truly Burmese. The individual politician was thus caught in a conflict between the attraction of the world culture with its stress on rationality and the demand of a brand of nationalism which became under the circumstances peculiarly antirationalistic.

Many of the respondents mentioned that in response to this conflict they had felt a need to be more assertive, more emotionally demanding, more willing to act on impulse; they tried to convince themselves that restraint, reason, and modern ways were alien qualities inappropriate in a Burman.[3] It was the combination of becoming more assertive while striving to become more identified with traditional Burmese ways which several of the politicians identified as the motivation behind their decision to affect the title of *Thakin* or "master" as used in addressing Europeans.

At the same time it appears that the politicians generally remained unshaken in their initial psychological commitment to being different and to becoming more modernized. Now they can generally speak quite freely of this conflict in values between the old and the new. We need here note only two aspects of this conflict.

3. Apparently some nonpoliticians had similar reactions to the Saya San rebellion, according to Mi Mi Khaing, *Burmese Family,* p. 94.

First, it appears that an awareness of even marginal participation in two cultures tended to make our respondents particularly sensitive to the possibility that others might be similarly torn and that therefore their behavior might be highly unreliable. Thus the Burmese politician will complain that his colleagues are constantly shifting back and forth between advocating modern ways and upholding traditional practices. There is a valid reason for this view of others: the Burmese politician has in a sense such a wide range of choice of generally acceptable bases for defining his position at any particular moment that at one time he can strike the posture of a progressive modernizer and at the next he can extoll the virtues of reverence for Burmese ways. The result, nevertheless, is that when one politician exploits such possibilities others inevitably tend to charge him with being an opportunist, a man without fixed convictions who seeks only to gain momentary advantage. It follows that there is a significant element of uncertainty in Burmese politics, and that, as we have noted, there is a high concern about opportunism.

A second significant consequence of the Burmese politician's inner conflict in values is that it gives him an exaggerated and quite false sense of the degree to which he is free to choose among alternative models for the future of his country. He tends to believe that it is possible to select the best ways from both the old and the new and in this fashion ensure that the "Burmese way" will remain the best way. This approach to the future is comforting since it implies that omnipotence is possible after all, and that a time will be reached when the country will have picked all that is good and eliminated all that is bad. But the result is a kind of reformism in which there are no forces of evil to be anxiously destroyed; there is only the pleasant task of choosing from the various acknowledged candidates for the best. Unfortunately in recent years it has become increasingly difficult for the Burmese politicians to feel satisfied that they have been achieving the best, and hence another source of suspicion of the motives of others has been introduced into Burmese politics.

The Feeling of Vulnerability

The Burmese politicians who can talk easily of their personal conflict in values find it somewhat more difficult to analyze how they might differ from their fellow countrymen. They are generally capable of appreciating that they have broader horizons than the less acculturated rural Burmese, but, significantly, they are almost unanimous in interpreting this greater breadth of vision as a weakness and not an advantage. This judgment seems to arise from their acute awareness that in becoming different they had been influenced by foreign ways. Although as a group the Burmese politicians are generally not slow in seeing the best in themselves and their country, it is important that on this subject they tend not to see their ability to learn new ways as proof of their superior abilities—as it probably is—but rather as evidence of inherent weakness.

This feeling that the self may be unduly vulnerable to outside influences seems to determine to a marked degree the relative ability of the Burmese politicians to work successfully with people who represent the different stages of the acculturation process. Specifically the Burmese politician has conspicuously greater difficulties with the people who stand at the two extremes of the acculturation process, the peasant and the Westerner.

In speaking about the peasant our politician respondents revealed extremely mixed feelings. At one moment they would characterize their fellow countrymen who were least touched by urban civilization as extraordinarily solid, capable, and firm people with the strength of character to resist the temptations of foreign ways. The next moment they would speak of the peasant as backward and contemptible. The peasants are somehow both the glory and the shame of the country.

The uneasiness of the politician toward the peasant does not stem in any way from a lack of intellectual understanding of rural customs and ways. The problem is purely psychological, and it arises from the anxiety of knowing that in spite of an apparent monopoly of power and prestige one is powerless in influencing the behavior of those who appear to be the weakest in the society. There is thus something hollow, something missing in one's own pretenses of strength, while there is something fundamentally stronger and firmer behind the peasant's façade of weakness and ignorance.

Some of our politician respondents, employing in essence a continuum extending from the traditional to the modern cosmopolitan man, pictured the Burmese peasant's relationship to themselves as being the same as their own relationship to Westerners. They were now seeking to influence the peasants, to change their ways, just as they had once been influenced. The way in which this form of thinking intensifies their anxieties about the vulnerability of their identities sheds considerable light on one of the most fundamental features of Burmese politicians' behavior, namely their readiness to exhort the peasants but not to act decisively to help them change their ways.

The genuine element of enthusiasm behind these exhortations comes in part from the politicians' tapping the excitement of their initial commitment to self-change. Also on these occasions the politicians seem to be exhilarated by the evidence that they can influence the emotions of others. Yet in the last analysis they shy away from any complete test of their abilities to manipulate and change the peasant. The prospect of such a test seems to arouse in them anxieties about being more change-able and hence weaker in character than the peasant they really despise.

The Burmese politician is equally ill at ease and unsure of him-self in dealing with Westerners, who in a sense represent the other ex-treme of the acculturation continuum and who like the peasant have not had to change their identities. In these relations the Burmese politi-cian is decidedly more effective when the circumstances cast the foreigner in the unambiguous role of an opponent whose every intention and de-sign must be vigorously resisted. Such situations offer the politician proof that he is true to his Burmese identity and that he can resist the attraction of the foreign. Most particularly the Burmese politician seems to derive satisfaction from those confrontations in which he is able to criticize the West on the basis of Western values, for these provide him with the opportunity to prove that he is acculturated to the modern world while at the same time he is true to his separate identity as a Burman. He can feel that in changing his standards of judgment he has not lost his sense of loyalty.

In spite of the conscious and unconscious efforts of the politician to formulate all his relations with foreigners along such lines, the cir-cumstances usually prevent such sharp and reassuring confrontations. Instead the politicians seem to find that most dealings with those who represent the modern world tend to take forms which bring into question the issues of personal identity and the vulnerability of the self. For example, skill in criticizing the West according to its standards seems to lead in time to the tendency to criticize Burmese practices according to these standards, a practice which in turn results in considerable dis-enchantment with this particular skill. One of the leading party politi-cians seemed to be describing this sequence when he remarked:

> I enjoyed very much my visit to England, for I spent most of my time in London talking to people about the various problems the British government would have to solve if the country was to become a real welfare state. That was right after the war, and of course, the British still had many unsolved problems. But so do we. I guess I have learned that it doesn't really matter much. Every people has its own ways and customs. Maybe we ought to just accept differences, and not try to say anything about them.

The clearest evidence of the Burmese politician's anxieties about the vulnerability of his identity appears in his behavior with the friendly and sympathetic foreigners who want to help change and modernize Burma. Gestures of kindness can be more disturbing than the open actions of an acknowledged opponent, for they bring into question the ability of the self to resist the appeals of others and the temptations to follow the ways of foreigners.

It is precisely when the West appears as a disinterested but sympathetic friend that the Burmese politicians' suspicions are most aroused. Their reaction is to defend themselves aggressively against the appeals of friendship which touch upon their own feeling of being too easily influenced by foreigners. The efforts of the West to be appealing are seen by the Burmese politicians as being essentially tests of their own character. The West would tempt them with all the attractions of the modern world to reveal their own weaknesses of character, their own lack of stable identities. Most Burmese politicians find it awkward and embarrassing to put into words their underlying sense of danger about friendship with the cosmopolitan world. Politically, the Burmese politician knows that it is difficult to make a realistic and convincing case that his country is in danger of losing its independence to the West. Nevertheless, he is appallingly aware that as an individual he is in fact in constant danger of losing his personal independence by yielding to the appeals of the modern world.

Thus it is that the Burmese politician, feeling the vulnerability of his own sense of identity, finds it impossible to suppress a diffuse and pervasive sense of suspicion. He is extraordinarily sensitive to the need to be on guard against any seductive attempts to influence him. He cannot relax in his relations with Westerners, and yet his greatest ambition is to be at home in the councils of the most powerful.

It is worth noting that these unconscious sources of suspicion of the West are not helped by the inability of the West and particularly of America to explain unambiguously the motives behind its efforts to help the underdeveloped areas. Many of our respondents in coping with our questions repeatedly tried to turn the discussion to questions of American motives and intentions. In particular they were deeply curious as to why the United States should seem hurt or offended by the Burmese decision to stop accepting her aid. The strange mixture of sentiments motivating Western aid seems to offer just enough basis in reality for Burmese suspicions to feed the fantasies of danger.

In between the two extremes of the peasant and the Westerner are the acculturating people with whom the Burmese politicians are most at home. It is significant for the problems of nation building that the politicians are most effective in their dealings with each other; the interplay of elite political relationships easily comes to dominate the attention and energies of the politicians, leaving them with room for little else.

The Spirit of Ambivalence

By way of summarizing the complex reaction of the Burmese politicians to the process of acculturation, we may refer again to the deep feelings of ambivalence at the core of their personal feelings of identity, which are touched most harshly by any issue relating to the modernization and development of their country. At one moment, for example, the Burmese politician must be the aggressive and sensitive defender of all features of traditional Burmese culture, attacking the British for having isolated and destroyed the old Burmese society. At the next moment he must be the equally heated critic of the British for not having changed Burmese images, for not having transformed the country completely into a modern society. Indeed, in an odd but psychologically understandable fashion, the Burmese politician will suggest that if the British had only done more to change the country it would be possible for more Burmese to find their true selves. Although in not quite the same personal terms as the administrators, the Burmese politicians in this way also give expression to the feeling that the British abandoned them. The British had made it seem exciting to want to be a part of the modern world, but they had also made it impossible to work fully and uninhibitedly for this objective. The concern of the Burmese politician for his own identity reveals an awareness that there is something wrong in wanting to become like the former colonial master.

The basic paralysis of will of the Burmese politician arises from his need to deny in countless ways the true nature of his feelings. He is so caught by his ambivalence that he constantly finds he must deny his feelings of the moment. He will declare that the British exploited and crushed his country, and yet at the next moment he is prepared to recognize that the sin of the British was that they made their ways too attractive. The Burmese politician has learned that the need to hold back, to distrust his own feelings, is greatest whenever he is confronted with action relating to changing and modernizing his society. The concepts of democracy and economic development provoke in the Burmese politician the feeling that restraint and caution are necessary. The concepts of democracy and economic development are thus closely associated in his mind with a sense of compromise and a need to be slightly artificial and unnatural. Thus the Burmese politician tends to be most inhibited and least capable of vigorous action on precisely those matters most basic to nation building.

The Burmese politicians' feelings of ambivalence are not aggravated by the refusal of others to accept their tentative assertions of identity. On the contrary, they have been far more affected by the all too easy willingness of others to accept them even when they felt that their credentials were not in order. We have noted how at the time of the student strike and in the process of achieving independence many of our respondents found that it was too easy to become national heroes. These identities were therefore never really satisfying, and in recent years the various leaders have had to continue their search for new identities. In this quest, U Nu and some of the others have turned in the direction of Buddhism and of the traditional Burma. Others who sought to find their own position in socialism also learned that it was all too easy to be accepted for more than one felt one was worth. Some of our respondents told of their sense of shame and disgust when they found that they were being treated as internationally significant socialists when they were aware that their knowledge of socialism was only a veneer. The quest had been honest, but it soon became vulgarized because people accepted them so readily, and in doing so the people had turned them into frauds. The inevitable reaction of the Burmese politician has been a feeling of contempt for precisely those who have accepted them as great men.

CHAPTER 18

Profiles of Politicians:
Further Sketches in Acculturation

In presenting an overview of the administrators and politicians as the two crucial groups in the Burmese political scene, we stressed the general point that the politicians have had less formal education than the administrators and come from families of lower economic and social status. As a group they would appear to be less affected by the Western impact; for example, the majority of the senior administrators speak English, while most of the leading politicians are not at home in any foreign language. However, in turning now to a more intimate view of five Burmese politicians who in their different ways represent different modal types, we find that the acculturative process was as crucial an element in their personal lives as it was in the lives of the administrators. It seems, in fact, that the issue of modernization and the question of identity have assumed more subtle forms and become more profound problems for the Burmese politician than for the administrator. In the profiles that follow, reaction to change seems to be the central theme; we shall be seeing how each of these individuals sought to achieve his own peculiar identity as an individual and as a spokesman for larger matters in the society.

U Ba Nyunt: The Old Guard Politician

As one of the early, prewar politicians, U Ba Nyunt lost influence rapidly after the rise of the nationalist movement and the coming to power of the AFPFL politicians. His period of influence was thus limited to a time when the colonial framework was still the crucial factor. Nevertheless, he set the style for many features of Burmese politics, and younger politicians still conform to some of the patterns of behavior that he and his group established. As an active leader his day has passed, but as a man who can judge political currents and who is considered to be a master at the inner game of Burmese politics, he is not forgotten.

Many aspects of U Ba Nyunt's early background seem to be essentially similar to those of the civil servants of his generation. He received a Westernized education, and he went on to study in the law. On the surface, it might appear that he was one with the group of early Burmese enthusiasts for a modern culture. Two features of his early life, however, stand out and may suggest why he did not follow the less dramatic path and become a government official. The first relates to his lack of family connections and the second is a reflection of his aggressive personality.

He came from a relatively humble family and had no relations within the fold of the administrative class. Thus, although he was intelligent and although his family was able to obtain the necessary funds to educate him, he did not have standing within the community of Anglicized Burmese. Ever since early childhood he has known the uncomfortable feeling of having to "crash" closed groups and demand a place among people who felt that he did not belong:

> My school days were the same as those of most Burmese boys. Our family was not very well off, but I was sent to school for my parents wanted to make sure that I got the best education possible. The students in my class all came from much richer families. They did not play with me very much, but I was better than they in my school work and they had to pay attention to me. My teachers knew that I worked hard and they respected me. I was also very popular with my classmates, for I made them laugh and I often played tricks.

In suggesting that he was smarter than most of the other students, he was making an accurate appraisal of his own abilities. He is still extremely quick-witted and remarkably articulate in both English and Burmese. The speedy retort and the clever remark have been his main weapons in social intercourse. He constantly seeks to win favor by destroying others, and he tends to see in every situation enemies who must be verbally attacked and a potential audience who must be won over. Although basically anxious to seek approval from all quarters, he has been willing to settle for the possibility of gaining the support of the many by attacking the conspicuous few.

Apparently at a very early stage in his school career, he came to confuse the sense of elation he received from showing up all who pretended to be his social and intellectual betters with the elation that might come from being a leader of the weak and downtrodden. His successes in scoring points against his classmates, and then later against the members of the administrative class and the British official hierarchy, tended to convince him that he was a popular leader of the common man. Without any organizational or other means of establishing relations with the broad masses of the Burmese population, he still became convinced that he was a part of the people and was acting according to their wishes whenever he strove to strengthen his own position within the elite hierarchy of prewar Burma:

> Our present-day politicians only have time for their clever ideological statements and their worries about becoming ministers. The real secret of politics is to understand what the common people who have no power and no friends really want. When I was active this was all I had time to think about.

The ease with which he achieved his verbal skills and the difficulties he had in being accepted by the Westernized Burmese made him contemptuous of all who pretended to represent the modern course of Burmese developments. He was able to see through these people with their pathetically limited understanding of Western civilization and derides the claims of the earlier AFPFL politicians to being the champions of a new Burma. He has learned to employ the most biting terms in striking the most sensitive vulnerabilities of both the earlier administrators and the young generation of nationalist politicians. He shows equal contempt for the tradition-bound Burmese. He has relatively little respect for Buddhism as a religion, and he feels that Burmese politicians who have attempted to identify themselves with Buddhism can only be cheap opportunists.

> The AFPFL people really don't know what they are talking about. They are like children. What do they know about the modern world of science, technology, of the arts and the law? They pretend that they know the Burmese people, but they don't really. All they know how to do is to hide behind the skirts of Buddhism and socialism. What fools they really are.

As a shrewd social critic of Burmese ways, U Ba Nyunt is as critical of both the traditional and the modernizing Burman as any Westerner might be. As a result he has a cynical attitude toward all suggestions about change and all proposals for grand developments. He discounts the possibilities of significant improvements in Burmese social life. He is equally pessimistic about the prospect of preserving the old order. Above all, he prides himself on being a realist, one who understands the forces in his society, but he does not see these forces moving in any consistent direction.

In discounting the possibilities of significant social and economic developments, he glorifies the significance of the personal political relationship. In his view, all change, maneuver, and manipulation in human affairs is limited to the interplay of personalities, the struggle of individuals. He is a past master of the personal game of politics primarily because he considers it the only realm of significant relationships. He sees those who are concerned with policies and programs of a more abstract nature as pretentious and not a little bit foolish. He is prepared to accept the fact that in a transitional society such as Burma great things cannot be done. He denies with a smile the suggestion, commonly advanced by Burmese nationalist politicians of a later generation, that in the prewar era Burmese politics was "merely a game of personal politics." His retort is that in his day people were more honest with themselves and each other and that while very little else is changed, the Burmese politicians have only become more self-righteous in their idle talk about founding socialism and initiating economic development. He knows, in short, that personality considerations still determine much of Burmese politics.

There is a familiar ring about most of his expressions and judgments which is at first perplexing until one suddenly realizes that they are, of all things, those of the typical British colonialist who was able to see the weaknesses of both the traditional and the modernizing Burmese but really had no feeling for the direction in which the potentialities of the country might lie. He is a violent critic of British rule—just as many British were—and would resent deeply any suggestion that his outlook coincides in any way with that common to the colonial mind. Yet the very basis of his present political isolation and ineffectualness is that he has indeed taken over on his own, and still keeps alive in his country, the British colonial attitudes and judgments about Burmese life. What is more surprising is that his reputation among Burmese is that of a wise man who truly understands Burmese affairs and is probably completely correct in his judgments of Burmese strength and weaknesses. The feeling is that he has chosen to be correct rather than sympathetic and thus no longer has the charm of leadership. Very few of his critics will point to his cynicism as a liability, for they seem to have as much difficulty as he does in distinguishing between realism and cynicism. Instead, the reaction seems to be that maybe in time it will be necessary to accept the views of U Ba Nyunt, but as yet things have not reached such a desperate state. Thus in an odd fashion this skeptic who doubts all the possibilities for change and development is seen as a last hope, to be heeded only when all others have failed in their efforts to improve the country.

U Moe Gyaw: The Model Nationalist Leader

U Moe Gyaw's life story is that of a model leader of a nationalist movement. He began his political activities while still a student at the Rangoon University, he participated in the 1936 students' strike, and he was an early member of the *"Thakin"* movement. During the war period he worked within the government the Japanese established; and after the war he was brought into the highest councils of the AFPFL. Since independence he has held several cabinet positions.

U Moe Gyaw belongs to the political generation that succeeded U Ba Nyunt's. His view of politics was mainly shaped by the need to organize activities, to appeal to the sentiments of national independence, and to create the impression of unqualified popular commitment to all political goals.

> The most important thing that a politician has to do is to keep the people interested in politics. It is politicians who make the people patriotic and interested in their country. To do these things the politician has to organize the people and have mass rallies. When we don't, the people begin to forget about us and they become less patriotic.

On the other hand, his early life was not very different from that of U Ba Nyunt and the earlier generations of politicians. He too came from a relatively humble background but obtained a Westernized education. Paradoxically, in spite of his having eventually adopted a far more radical political program, during his school days he had much more success than U Ba Nyunt in becoming an accepted and conforming member of a popular student group. While at Rangoon University he became associated with a small and intimate clique of friends who became the center of his entire existence at the time. As a group they were contemptuous of both those who were more serious students than themselves and those who came from the better Burmese families. Thus, while U

Ba Nyunt had had to struggle as an individual to assert his superiority over his classmates, U Moe Gyaw was a secure and satisfied member of a group which as a whole claimed leadership in student activities. His membership within the clique gave him a degree of self-assurance and self-confidence in his dealings with the outside world, and he shared with the others the feeling that they were linking arms and bravely challenging all who would suppress their assertions of leadership.

Academically he did not have a particularly distinguished career. The experience of university life, however, did influence him intellectually, and although he came away from the university without a degree, he developed a strong taste for and a curiosity about abstract ideas. He also became a rather extensive but undiscriminating reader of Western literature: he claims that he finds equally interesting Marxian writings, the *Reader's Digest,* the writings of Abraham Lincoln, and *Punch* magazine.

His two prime experiences at the university, membership in an intimate group of his own peers and introduction into the realm of abstract ideas, were never really integrated. He insists that he and his friends rarely discussed philosophical questions or even major issues about Burmese society. They felt that such talk belonged more to the scholars and to those they looked down upon; they preferred to picture themselves as men of action who might play an important part in the history of their country. Thus, U Moe Gyaw's interest in ideas was a lonely pursuit and not tied in any sense to his identity with the group.

> We were very active in organizing the students and we never had any time to talk about issues except for the arguments we used to get people to support us. I was the only one in the group who had any interest in reading. It was just my habit.

He has never been able to do more than marginally relate the ideas derived from his intellectual pursuits to his activities as a party leader. In fact, his interest in ideas has given him a sense of distance and even detachment in his political associations. Moreover, he seems to have fallen into the practice of retreating from one sphere into the other whenever confronted with excessive pressures in either. For example, when discussions about his political philosophy are carried to the point at which he begins to feel uncomfortable and unsure of himself, he shifts over and adopts an openly anti-intellectual point of view, claiming that he is really only a practicing politician. Conversely, whenever he becomes embarrassed by his identity as a politician, he tends to revert to the pose of one concerned mainly with general philosophical and political notions.

It would seem that he has on the one hand a deep need for the security and sense of identity that can come from being accepted by a group of people who look up to him and yet receive him as one of their own, and on the other hand an equally strong need to be identified with and to be effective in the realm of modern ideas. As a man interested in political action, he has been unable to find a single integrated approach that might satisfy these two needs. Unable to break away from the bonds of his personal ties and associations, most of which extend back to his university days, he finds his freedom of action, and especially his choice of associates, greatly limited. At the same time, his appreciation of ideas has made it difficult for him not to seem slightly contemptuous of and patronizing toward his colleagues; thus both he and they have gradually become aware that he is not completely a part of their world.

As another consequence of these two conflicting demands, he often appears to be acting in a most erratic fashion. A champion of ideology at one moment, at the next moment he suddenly denounces the need for an ideology and asserts that his identity is defined in full by his associations with his fellow politicians who are clearly not his intellectual peers. Similarly, at one moment he stoutly insists that Burma must change and become a modern society, but at the next moment he says that the country has moved too fast, that the pace must be slowed down and much of the past preserved. In short, he seems to have been unable to reconcile his intellectualized feelings about modernization with his emotional needs to belong to a small and powerful group within his community.

Although U Moe Gyaw may appear to be more the politician of principle and ideology than U Ba Nyunt, he may in fact be even more dependent upon personal relationships than his political predecessor. His commitment to his clique represents such a deep emotional involvement that he reacts to any threat to these ties as though his very personality were being threatened. In contrast, he has been able over the years to accept without great stress considerable changes in his intellectual position. It would seem that he has never been able to find any substitute for the security of the personal assocations built up during his university days. Whereas U Ba Nyunt utilizes personal relations because they are the only units of political calculation which he understands and trusts, U Moe Gyaw seems to have placed personal relations at the center of his political behavior because of deeply felt psychological needs. He clearly has many anxieties about being socially isolated, about being left out in a new world.

He says that he and his associates first learned that they needed each other when, at the university, they suddenly realized that there were relatively few career openings for them in the Burmese society of that time. They knew that the better scholars were likely to get the choice jobs that required superior ability and intellectual skill, and that at best they might become only minor clerks in government offices or private business establishments. They hoped that by sticking together they might become a political element of some significance. When in fact they did become rulers of a new country, they had an even greater need to stick together.

The dependence of U Moe Gyaw upon his politician friends means that, although at times he talks like an enthusiastic advocate of modernization, he is fundamentally an extremely conservative leader who hesitates to adopt original positions. Thus, although he has frequently been identified as a progressive member of the Burmese political class, he is not prepared to push hard for change except as it is acceptable to his group of peers.

Bo Min Ko: The Warrior Politician

The drama of the independence movement and the excitement of the Japanese occupation were the high points in Bo Min Ko's life. His position as a politician is derived almost entirely from his status as a veteran of the struggle for independence and he still clings to the title of "Bo," the traditional designation for a military leader, although all of his fellow comrades with a respectable amount of formal education have dropped the use of "Bo" or "Thakin" and accepted the more general honorific designation of "U." It is true that since Bo Min Ko never attended the university it would appear presumptuous if he were to adopt "U," but the real reason for his clinging to his old title seems to be that he would feel his own identity and his status in society threatened if he were to lose the designation which still identifies him with the excitement of those early days of independence.

Bo Min Ko came from a village and until the Japanese occupation had never been to a city. His father was the headman of their village, but otherwise his life was hardly distinguishable from that of most of the peasants within his immediate world. His only schooling was a few years in the village monastery school, and he is still self-conscious about not having ever attended a modern school. He claims not to speak

English although over the years he has picked up many phrases and probably can understand more English than he will admit.

In his village environment, he apparently had a relatively happy youth. He denies that it ever occurred to him to worry about his future career plans; there is every indication that he was quite content to be one of the leading youths in his village, his highest ambition being only to succeed his father eventually as village headman and thus become a member of the traditional rural elite.

The Japanese occupation jarred him out of his isolated world. At first the news of the war created only a minor ripple in his village, but the subsequent breakdown in communications created serious economic problems at the village level. His father was worried over the safety of the family. It was a time when throughout the country relatives were seeking each other out and drawing together. Jobs and food were scarce in the cities, and the countryside seemed to have an infinite ability to absorb people. In six months, however, people were faced with the shocking fact that their village economy was no longer able to support the influx. Among the refugees crowding the village was an uncle of Bo Min Ko who had been living for several years in Rangoon. At a family council it was decided that the uncle should return to Rangoon and take Bo Min Ko with him. This was his first introduction to the urban world, and even wartime Rangoon seemed like a dream world to the eighteen-year-old youth. Through personal contacts his uncle was able to obtain for Bo Min Ko a minor job in the post office, and this opened the way to acquaintanceships with clerks and young people.

It was through these friendships that he first learned about politics. His first lessons were largely international, trying to figure out who was on whose side in the war and what were the objectives of the various parties.

> We decided that it might be good for Burma if Japan should conquer all Asia. We learned that both the Chinese and the Indians were fighting against the Japanese, and therefore we decided that we ought to be with the Japanese.

In being introduced to political calculation, he was taught to think not as a principal but as one who hoped to extract some benefits from the acts of others. In fact, he had come to Rangoon without ever encountering the view that Burma might gain its independence through the efforts of the Burmese. Nevertheless, he responded to the idea with enthusiasm and when the Burmese Army was established, he became one of its first recruits from civilian life. Although he lacked the formal education to become an officer, a fact he still seems to resent, he rose quickly within the ranks to become a noncommissioned officer, for the army gave him the opportunity to demonstrate for the first time his innate leadership abilities.

As he now describes those days, the thrill of military life was at first more important to him than political issues; but after the Burmese Army turned against the Japanese, he became a full-fledged political worker. He joined the AFPFL and immediately after the Japanese surrender was sent back into the countryside to organize the peasants. Having prestige both as a military man and as a son of a former village headman, he was received in his district both as an official in the nationalist movement and as one who had been to the city and participated in important events. He was perceived by others as a new modern man, and he began to think of himself as belonging to the new and heroic generation. In truth, his acculturation to the modern world had been almost entirely in the atmosphere of a military establishment, and his notions of the modern world were heavily colored with the sentiments of soldiering. In the rural areas, however, he was accepted as one knowledgeable about all aspects of the outside world, especially the new world of independent Burma.

In the first election he was put up as a member of parliament from his district and had relatively little difficulty winning a seat. He began to lead what was in essence a double life. While in Rangoon he was easily intimidated and overawed by the more urbanized members of the AFPFL and was a docile worker who conformed to all the demands expected of a party member. When he returned to his district, however, he became a leader, an assertive and domineering figure in the villages. Thus while he was in one sense intimidated by the process of acculturation, his power in the countryside in fact rested upon his involvement in that process.

So Bo Min Ko has lived two sharply contrasting roles and as a result has been plagued by so many problems of identity that he seems not to have strong commitments to any position on public issues. He likes to have the AFPFL appear as a force for modernization and national development because his status in the district depends upon his apparent connections with the capital and the center of new developments. On the other hand, he has not been anxious to see many modern programs pushed into his rural areas, for his own position depends upon the lack of both competition and real change; therefore he has treated all increases in government activities within his constituency as a threat to himself. Since his own control depends upon there being only a very slow and modest rate of progress in the rural areas, it is not surprising that he can speak with great vigor about how the peasants do not want to lose the essential qualities of their way of life. By constantly making sure of his command over all agencies of government established in his district, he has established himself as a kind of local potentate with his own private realm. He resents deeply the charges that U Nu has made about the "bad hat" politicians in the districts, for he feels that the national leaders do not appreciate the problems of politics among what he calls the more "unruly rural folk."

> It is not easy to keep law and order among people who don't understand affairs. If you are not careful everyone will try to take your job away from you. U Nu doesn't understand how we have to work to stay on top. He is lucky because everyone accepts him as the right leader.

The split in the AFPFL in the spring of 1958 came as a great shock to Bo Min Ko. Suddenly his entire position was threatened. He found it impossible to accept either the idea that another politician might enter his domain or the idea that he might no longer have a place among the ruling elite in Rangoon.

In his own mind he is convinced that Burma has progressed and that the country is considerably more modern than it was before the war. He points to the undeniable fact that his own position in his district is more complex and demanding than the one his father had as village headman. He has had to deal with both the city and the country, and in doing so he has had to work out for himself a far broader view of his society than that which his father had. On the other hand, he has not been, and is probably incapable of becoming, an active champion of any programmatic approach toward modernizing his country. Indeed, in spite of his many likable qualities, Bo Min Ko is likely to strike the outsider as one who is probably retarding the process of nation building in Burma.

U Shwe Myint: The Sensitive Nationalist

U Shwe Myint is a powerfully built and extremely articulate man who is quick to take offense at any slur on Burma and the Burmese people. He is constantly on the alert for implied criticism and quick to single out in any remark the words that might be interpreted as belittling his people.

U Shwe Myint's youth seems to have been generally typical of that of most members of the administrative class. He learned English early; he attended a private school and then Rangoon University. As he now describes his early days, it becomes apparent that he does not feel that he had a typical childhood but believes that there was always something wrong, some blemish, so that he did not receive the best. For example, in the early years he received a Westernized education, but the school he went to was considered slightly inferior to the other schools in Rangoon. As a consequence he has always felt slightly defensive about his alma mater. When he went to the university, he belonged to no particular group, being accepted neither by the scholars nor by the future politicians. Throughout his adult career he has been in constant association with the group of politicians who first met each other at the university, but he knows that he is not really one of them. He was not a member of the *"Thakins"* although he was aware of their existence and in later years has even posed as a former member of the movement.

There is the unmistakable quality of the marginal man about U Shwe Myint. He seems always to have been in but not of, to be willing to start many things but complete few. At the university he proved to be a more serious student than most of the future politicians of Burma. On the other hand, he was not fully committed to the scholarly life; he could not accept the normal patterns of the Burmese administrative class, and he did not look ahead with any enthusiasm to a career in law. His interests in his schoolwork were strong enough to keep him out of the student political circles; yet his failure to become a serious scholar kept him from being accepted for government service upon graduation.

He now likes to think that he gave up the opportunity for a prosperous career as a lawyer in order to become a worker for Burmese independence and an active politician.

> It is not fair to say that we did not struggle for our independence. It is true that we may not have had to fight the British, but you must recognize that we had to make great personal sacrifices just the same. Some people had to make greater sacrifices than others. I could have probably made a sizable fortune if I had not turned to politics. Even U Nu had to make a sacrifice; he had to give up a promising career as a schoolteacher.

There is no record of his involvement in Burmese politics before independence. With independence, however, he became a member of the AFPFL, and he was sent abroad in one of the first delegations to represent the new government. His trip to Europe and to America seems to have marked an important turning point in his thinking. In an unguarded moment he once remarked:

> I always thought of Rangoon as the most modern of cities. I found the European and American cities quite interesting—not quite what I had expected. But, of course, all cities are the same.

Once again he discovered that what he had assumed as ranking with the best—such as his high school—was not so considered by those whose judgments he respected. And again he had to fall back upon denying the relevance of distinctions.

Now most of his energies are directed to denying differences in standards of quality in almost every sphere of life. He insists, for example, that there were no significant differences in the contributions that various individuals made to the cause of Burmese independence. He says, "It was the nation as a whole which united to create its independence." He also tends to deny any significant difference between Burmese politics and institutions and those found in the Western world. In his view, all politicians and government officials are the same.

The only difference he will acknowledge is that between exploited and exploiting countries. Whatever weaknesses Burma has can be attributed solely to colonialism—and, except for Burmese officials who must constantly deal with foreigners, he has more to say about colonialism than most Burmese politicians. Since he has few personal recollections of British rule, and he had no contacts with the government of Burma before independence, becoming politically involved only during the postcolonial period, his ideas about colonialism are theoretical rather than related to any practices he ever observed. At any rate, he never finds it necessary to relate his views of colonialism explicitly to any particular events in his own life.

It would be quite wrong, however, to suggest that he has aggressive feelings only toward foreigners as he tries to defend Burmese practices. He is equally aggressive in his relations with Burmese officials and with all who have had a better education or who may have a more secure claim to status in the modern world. The one class of people with whom he seems to be able to work well is the rural and less acculturated Burmese. Among such people he is looked up to as an exemplary model of a national leader, and he reciprocates by extolling not only the virtues of the Burmese common folk but also the virtues of the Burmese politicians, and especially himself, for being able to understand and appreciate the Burmese common man.

> It is you foreigners who are always talking about a gap between the leaders and the villagers. This just isn't true for I know the Burmese villagers well. It is you who don't understand them. There are no better people than the rural people of Burma.

He is now an active champion of the ancient Burmese medical practices.

> Western doctors will in time have to study our best medicines. When they do they will find that our village doctors will have a lot to teach them.

In a similar vein, he argues that ancient Buddhist practices of meditation are superior to Western methods of seeking relief from tensions and mental stress.

Though he himself takes seriously the Burmese of the village and most aspects of traditional Burmese culture, he is not prepared to accept the foreigner's agreement with him that there may be much of universal value in Burmese culture. He suspects the foreigner's sincerity, for it seems that deep down U Shwe Myint cannot believe that anyone who is really a part of the modern world can have any genuine respect for traditional Burma.

U Tin Win: A Man Divided between Private Feelings and Public Posture

The paradox in U Tin Win's life is that he learned as much about British culture as any Burmese but was never accepted into the Anglicized community of Burmese which presumably based itself upon knowledgeability of British ways. More fundamentally, the process of acculturation for U Tin Win was relatively painless because he was befriended by an English family and treated as an intimate, but it did not bring the one reward he expected of it, a higher social status, because his own family lacked status among the Westernized Burmese.

His father was a government worker of relatively low rank, and he probably would not have had much schooling had it not been for his family's personal friendship with a British family in Moulmein. His grandfather had become a personal friend of an Englishman who had settled in the Moulmein district, his father grew up as a friend of the

Englishman's son, and U Tin Win represented the third generation of this friendship. It was apparently a relatively relaxed relationship, and U Tin Win and his family felt that they were on rather intimate terms with the Europeans. Also it seems that the English family thought highly enough of U Tin Win to help support him in his schooling. Consequently he was sent to a far better school than his family might otherwise have been able to afford.

It was while he was away at school that he began to sense his own inferiority within Burmese society. His classmates came from some of the better families in the country and were proud of their command of the Anglo-Burmese culture. U Tin Win felt that he spoke better English than his classmates did, that he knew more than they about British ways, and that he was in most ways superior; and yet he belonged to no particular group and was still considered an outsider. As a result, his school days passed without his establishing the close and enduring personal bonds which are common with most Burmese schoolboys.

After high school he went to Rangoon University. Soon he was happily mixing with the students who were championing the nationalist cause and professing hatred of the British. In his vacations he went back to Moulmein and to the close associations with the English family of his childhood. One might expect him to have been torn by a sense of conflict at that time, but he says that he was happy to have the close and satisfying personal associations at both places. In Rangoon University he had found the first group of intimate Burmese friends he had ever known in his life, and he did not want to risk these friendships by questioning their hostile feelings about the British. At the same time, he was not prepared to sever or in any way mar his lifelong friendship with the English family in Moulmein.

> There was no point in trying to tell them about my activities at the University. They wouldn't have understood, and they might have been disturbed that I was saying anti-British things. And there was equally no point in trying to tell my schoolmates about how kind the C— had been to me, because they preferred to believe that all Englishmen were just terrible to all Burmese. I just had to accept things the way they were.

In many respects the clash between his need to belong to a Burmese group that was anti-British and his need to associate with his English friends came to color his entire outlook upon what constituted appropriate behavior; he now tends to make a sharp distinction between his private feelings and his public postures and actions, treating them as though they belonged to independent spheres of his life. In public situations he frequently says things that conflict with the views he expresses in private conversations without seeming to sense contradictions. In both spheres he is very articulate and susceptible to intense emotions.

Although he carries many of his contradictions lightly, he shows at times a deep resentment over a fate that has made it impossible for him to have consistent and reinforcing private and political views. Paradoxically, it seems as though his life would have been easier if instead of being befriended by the English family, he had known maltreatment by the English. Since his relations with the English family have made it impossible for him to identify himself completely with the political creeds which he has felt it so necessary to expound, they were in effect a greater threat to his self-respect than acts of unkindness and hostility would have been. The result is that the process of acculturation has given him two identities which are incompatible with each other. Although it has been necessary for him to accuse the British of exploiting his people, he has to admit to himself that his major opportunities in life all came from his associations with the British. In trying to live with himself, he has been desperately anxious to find different ways of explaining how, in spite of all appearances, he really has been mistreated by the modern world. This is why so often his anticolonialist remarks seem to become expressions of self-pity rather than honest appeals for justice.

U Tin Win's inability to bridge the gap between his private and his political worlds has apparently compromised his effectiveness as a political actor. In accepting a striking degree of inconsistency between his two worlds, he seems to be admitting to himself that political sentiments contain an element of fantasy which does not have any basis in the realities of human life. Perhaps, deep under his feelings about his friendship with the English family, he senses that somehow there was something unnatural about it all and that even that most humanly warm and sympathetic experience constituted some kind of basic violation of his personality since, in yielding to it, he had to compromise the purity of his Burmese identity in order to become a marginal citizen of the modern world. In any case, his political ideology can in no way express the complexity of his personal feelings, and, conversely, he has never been able to give his private feelings any public forms. He has had to settle for two separate worlds, neither of which he can fully believe in.

PART VI

Epilogue

CHAPTER 19

The Prospects for Nation Building

In approaching the problem of nation building by way of the dynamics of a political culture we have had to follow an intricate and twisting course. We took our initial orientation from a broadly defined analysis of the problems of political development, but the only way we could capture the subtle nuances and complex interrelationships of sentiment and judgment which are the essence of a political culture was to explore in some depth a particular political system. Our search for the structural sources of this particular political culture took us back into the general social and political history of the country, while our efforts to understand the spirit and calculations of the political culture forced us to look into the life histories of those who now set the tone and style of that system. In a sense we have been concerned with the intersections of life histories and a national history, which poses the complex problem of trying to bring together macroanalysis and microanalysis.

Our findings may well appear to support a gloomy view of the prospects of nation building. Whether we were looking at public developments or into the recesses of private lives, we were continually uncovering disturbing obstacles to rapid and satisfying progress in national development and modernization. Are we now left with the unpleasant conclusion that people who could greatly benefit from modern technology will find the road toward national development filled with almost insurmountable difficulties?

Objections to the suggestion of such a discouraging conclusion may be raised on the grounds that we have been too greatly influenced by the particular choice of country and of informants for our study. Had we selected some country other than Burma—Nigeria, India, or the Philippines, for example—perhaps the mood of our conclusion would have been more optimistic, and perhaps even in Burma we should have been able to find informants who were less troubled by the psychic dimension of social change. In order to capture the subtleties of sentiments, and to introduce a note of realism, we had to focus intensely upon particular, concrete experiences; perhaps we should now accept the inevitably confining nature of the particular and the concrete, and not try to draw broad implications from our findings.

We certainly have no intention of claiming universal applicability for our particular study. The great variety represented by the transitional societies cannot be denied. Some are plagued more by certain problems than others, and some are likely to progress more rapidly than others. Nevertheless, to deny or overlook the general implications of specific research findings can be quite as dangerous and intellectually misleading as to generalize recklessly about the unique. Political analysis often tends to reject the general implications of behavior which can in any way be definitely associated with a particular time and setting. This is especially true if the generalization conflicts with our preconceptions or threatens our self-esteem. That is to say, insistence on the uniqueness of events can be merely another way of saying that only others have limitations and are restricted by irrationalities. The historian who presses for the importance of the unique and the limits of the particular may be unwittingly striving only to place himself, as a historian and as an individual, outside the confining limitations of history.

With these considerations in mind let us recall that among the reasons why Burma was selected for detailed examination was the fact that it is not strikingly unique among the newly developing societies. In terms of its history and culture it has much in common with the vast majority of new countries; there is, in fact, a considerable literature on Burma holding that its prospects are quite as hopeful as those of most transitional countries. The fact that we have taken an intensive look at the experiences of some Burmese leaders is still no reason to conclude that they may have had more than normal difficulties adjusting to the demands of the contemporary world. One should indeed be careful not to attribute undue distinctiveness to what we have been describing as "Burmese" behavior. All people going through a profound process of social change must cope with some variation of the same fundamental psychological problems. There may be differences as to the degree and the form of reactions, depending upon the circumstances of acculturation and the nature of the traditional culture. These differences, however, can only occur within the limits imposed by the inherent and universal character of the human personality.

The disturbing prospect which we must face is that not only Burma but most transitional societies are likely to be faced in the years to come with increasingly pressing problems. As their populations expand, their need for efficient utilization of more advanced forms of technology will increase, and they will require the maximum advantages which come from rationality and efficient administration, but their politics are not likely to permit them to realize such standards of efficiency. As transitional peoples they are peculiarly prone to intensely human but essentially self-defeating political practices; and, as we have noted, they lack the stable and more impersonal institutional forms which can harness man's more irrational compulsions and aggressions and turn them to the furtherance of public purposes. Transitional people are likely to be caught in an intimate and closed form of politics which seems to magnify the disruptive consequences of all expressions of aggressive and irrational emotions.

Two Approaches to Finding New Identities

Fundamentally, the hope for transitional peoples resides in their quests for new collective as well as individual identities. Their development hinges on their capacity to find meaning in a fusion of what we have called traditional and modern modes of action, a fusion of the world culture and their own historic cultures.

As we have observed, the demands of acculturation can produce a wide range of very deep and disturbing reactions which in various ways reduce political effectiveness. Threats to the individual's sense of identity can impede his competence in human and political relationships, and the resulting fears of inadequacy produce anxieties which further paralyze action. If the pace of national development is to be accelerated, this vicious circle of psychological inhibitions must be broken so that new sets of sentiments and attitudes can replace those blocking decisive and purposeful action at the level of individual choice and impeding the creation of effective organizations at the collective level.

Since the crisis of identity in transitional societies grips both the individual and the society as a whole, the prospects for national development must depend upon realizing a greater sense of order at the levels of both personal psychology and political sentiments, and in the relationships between the two. This suggests two general ways in which the latent obstacles to development may be overcome and the path opened to more effective diffusion of the world culture. If any particular transitional society is to advance in nation building it will have to realize a satisfactory combination of these two approaches.

The first approach is that of the grand ideological solution in which some leader, out of the depths of his own personal experience, is able to give his people an understanding of the new sentiments and values necessary for national development. This would be a solution according to the Eriksonian model of the relationship between ideology and personality which suggests that the struggle of the ideological innovator to find his own personal sense of identity may provide a vehicle for an entire people to find their collective sense of identity.[1] Fundamentally this is the quest of the charismatic leader. If such a leader can fully and honestly face the problems of his times as they emerge in his own personality, he can give powerful and meaningful expression to new attitudes and values which can in turn inculcate in a people the feeling of a new order of legitimacy and redirect their feelings of trust and distrust, of aggression and anxiety, of repudiation and commitment.

In transitional societies the scene is set for the prophet, for the ideological reformer. Those who are facile with words may have great appeal, for the people are in search of the word which can open a new way. In this fundamental sense words are more important than actions in transitional societies. But these are also societies in which words are cheap and actions become impossible. The setting is right for the politically anxious to experiment—possibly with enthusiasm, but certainly without profound commitment—with all manner of ideological formulas. Before a nation can develop, leaders must emerge who have found integrity in their own quests for identity and who can hence speak in terms that can bring meaning to other people's search for personal identity. The need is for that set of shared orientations that will force a people to face reality steadfastly. Pronouncements that seek to shield people from reality cannot meet the test of being an ideology that helps to create a sense of collective identity.

Historically, the grand ideological solution to the problems of transitional societies has proved to be powerfully effective—witness for example, the abiding consequences of Luther's words and of the Reformation in producing modern industrialized Europe—but this has only rarely occurred. Unfortunately in recent years charismatic leaders in the new countries have generally failed to realize a grand ideological breakthrough for their peoples. The almost universal pattern has been one of leaders communicating uncertainty and confusion as they have failed to resolve the crises of identity in their own persons; artificial protestation and distasteful compromises cannot provide the basis of new world views for people who are plagued with ambivalence and unsure of the nature of

1. Erikson, *Young Man Luther.*

political action. It has been all too easy for charismatic leaders to emphasize the negative dimensions of the issue of identity, to stress what is foreign and to point to possible enemies. The full realization of identity calls for an appreciation not only of how the self is differentiated from others but also of how the self can and must be related to others.

There has been no shortage of attempts to realize new national self-images through ideological experimentation in the new countries. Certainly in Burma the political leaders have ceaselessly though with discouraging results sought to strike true notes in their search for some ideological resolution of the problems of nation building. Unfortunately, however, failures by this approach tend to reconfirm rather than weaken the vicious circle of psychological uncertainty. When ideological pronouncements seem to ring more false than true, people tend to withdraw from the search for a collective identity, and politics is likely to become an arena for opportunism.

The second broad approach by which the latent psychological restraints to effective development may be broken lies in assisting individuals as individuals to find their sense of identity through the mastery of demanding skills. By this approach national development would be furthered as ever-increasing numbers of competent people meet in their daily lives the exacting but also psychologically reassuring standards of professional performance basic to the modern world. The emergence and interaction of such people as they fulfill their professional activities would provide transitional societies with communities of modernizers who would constitute islands of stability in an otherwise erratically changing world. The establishment of such communities would provide the necessary environment in which the more ambitious transitional people could escape the paralyzing effects of feeling isolated and alone in the search for new identities.

What we are suggesting is that the test of profession may prove to be a means of overcoming many of the psychological ambivalences produced by the acculturation process. The concepts and standards of the modern professions can uniquely serve the dual functions of assisting the individual in realizing his potentialities while also providing the community with the skills and abilities necessary for national development. In nation building it is not just the society that needs modern skills; the people must also feel skilled in modern terms. As individuals, the intelligent and ambitious peoples of transitional societies can acquire the skills and competences appropriate to membership in the modern world and readily become the equals of citizens of industrial societies as teachers, lawyers, scientists, soldiers, and, yes, as administrators and politicians. They can achieve essentially modern standards even though their countries may still have inadequate school systems, undermanned legal professions, and militarily weak armies. If the test of individual identity is tied more to personal roles and less to national indices, the problem of becoming a citizen of the modern world is greatly reduced. It will be a long time before Burma becomes an industrialized society, but it need take far less time for numbers of modernizing Burmese to prove to themselves and to others that they are the equals of any people in specific roles or professions.

The historical irony of this age of nation building is that the overpowering thrust of nationalism forces people to rivet their attention on the nation as the unit of self-expression and to discount the worth of the individual, and yet the task of nation building calls for precisely the opposite orientation of stressing the individual in his social role. Expressions of nationalism that seek to conquer deep feelings of collective inferiority can produce the opposite effect and raise anxieties about an individual's worth. The inescapable realities of relative national power can impress upon people the incorrect conclusion that they as individuals may be inferior to others. Only by meeting honest standards of competence can such people convince themselves that they are the equals of all others.

On the other hand, if people can experience in their professional lives the sense of accomplishment which comes from meeting meaningful and demanding standards, they are likely to realize the self-confidence necessary to become competent citizens of the modern world. Once different communities of modern people begin to assert themselves in transitional societies, the islands of stability which they represent may steadily expand; in time they can be joined together and, reinforcing each other, they will become the infrastructure of more modern and stable nation-states. In the past the West has often unintentionally impeded the development of these islands of stability by not expecting transitional people to meet the rigorous standards of performance of which they are capable. To demand less of such people is to suggest to them that they are probably unequal to the demands of the modern world.

In each transitional society a mixture of these two approaches is needed to provide the basis for the nation building effort. In recent years the urgency of the problems of the underdeveloped countries has dramatized the attempts of quasi-charismatic leaders to find grand ideological solutions to their people's problems. Consequently people have tended not only to expect too much but to attribute too much to the nation-building powers of charismatic leaders. The significance of the other aspect of nation building should not be discounted, for in the last analysis the power of a charismatic leader can never replace the need for a wide distribution of competent people. Nothing is detracted from the historic contribution of Nehru to India's development by noting the existence of sizable and relatively advanced communities of modernizers in India who feel that they have a culture and a destiny of their own. In such a social atmosphere people can feel that in joining the thrust for progress they are behaving in a normal, acceptable fashion and not according to foreign ways.

Although the relative emphasis upon ideological identification and growth of competent personnel may differ from society to society, successful national development seems to require that the two approaches complement and not conflict with each other. The search for individual and collective identity is greatly accelerated when people are confident that in finding themselves they are also contributing to the collective search for fulfillment. Unfortunately, however, in Burma as in most of the new countries, the quest for ideological solutions to national crises is easily perverted into attacks upon the search for individual competence in modern skills. In seeking to give meaning and form to the spirit of a new nation, the politicians have tended to attack the administrators not just because they seemed to flaunt a foreign technology but also because they seemed to be too close to finding competence and effectiveness as individuals. Even when the political leaders accept the need for new skills, they may reject the legitimacy of conspicuous communities of modernizers, thereby preventing the emergence of the colonies of new men which are essential for maintaining and continually raising the levels of new skills in the nation. It is all too easy for those who are trying to express the national identity to promote anxieties in the minds of those who are experimenting with new and manifestly foreign ways.

The Need for Predictability and the Fear of Order

The search for both personal and collective identities in transitional societies can be successful only with the achievement of a psychologically satisfying and organizationally effective fusion of traditional and rational attitudes. Such a fusion is essential to provide a basic element of coherence for the developing political culture. In endeavoring to foresee the possibilities of such a fusion in a particular society, it is necessary to appraise not only the substance of the traditional but also the crucial aspects of the modern world culture which must in some degree be integrated. In this study we have observed how the basic socialization process of a people places powerful restraints upon the ways in which they perceive and react emotionally to the challenge of the modern world. We have also noted the way in which the acculturation process can leave a people confused as to what is basic and what is superficial in the world culture to which they aspire, and from which they may also wish to withdraw. In their search for new identities transitional peoples are likely to find it peculiarly difficult to uncover the secret of the specific elements of the modern world that must be accepted if the other wonders of a modern economy and society are to be realized. Often, in fact, the dynamics of the acculturation process seem to operate so as to make most attractive the merely superficial qualities of the world culture. Consequently people can miss the essential measures that must be adopted if they are to become effective citizens of the modern world. Such people, deeply conscious of the psychic costs of giving up some of the old to take on a part of the new, can be left puzzled and disappointed when, having paid what they felt should be the price of admission to the modern world, they seem to get none of its benefits.

Unfortunately, as our initial survey of the theories of nation building suggested, there are no easy guides to the specific sets of attitudes and practices that constitute the essential prerequisites of what we have called the contemporary world culture. The experiences of transitional peoples suggest that it is impossible to achieve national development by selecting in a random fashion elements of the world of science and technology, of impersonal law and democratic practices, and of industrialized and innovating economic performance. The pieces must fit together to constitute interrelated systems of social, political, and economic action.

The capacity of a people to sense the existence of ordered systems of human relationships is a crucial achievement in the nation-building process. It is this sense for an elaboration of systematic relationships that makes it possible for people to accept the concept that an economy can be developed, a polity strengthened, and a society opened to constant innovation. Without it economic activity becomes the enrichment of some at the expense of others, political action becomes little more than personal aggrandizement of power, and social relations become essentially matters of relative status. Only as people are able to realize the full implications of such concepts as an "economy," a "polity," a "society" can they find a rational basis for relating their own actions to the building of a modern nation.

As we observed repeatedly, our Burmese informants found it difficult to conceive of themselves in any way associated with objective and regulated systems of human relationships. Their concern was almost entirely with the immediate, the concrete, and the particular; and since they had very little feeling for more abstractly perceived relationships, they lacked a basis for judging and evaluating the broader social significance of their actions.

It is not strange that people in erratically changing transitional societies have little sense for ordered and systematically related human ties. The very process of acculturation challenges individual expectations about orderly arrangements. Yet at the same time economic, political, and social development require that people believe that they can to a limited degree foresee the consequences of alternative choices of action. The more social relations are seen as systematically related, the more rational choice can become a significant part of human behavior. Indeed, the infusion of rationality into social relationships depends upon a minimum sense of predictability in the social aspects of behavior. For a people to accept the importance of intelligent policy as a basis of politics, their political culture must inform them that there is enough predictability in affairs to make meaningful the weighing of consequences of alternative public actions.

Nation building thus requires the emergence of a feeling for predictability in human relationships. We observed this earlier when we stressed the importance of trust in building modern organizational forms. The sense of predictability can widen a people's belief in the range of possible eventualities; it can provide them with a greater sense of command over their fate; and it can encourage them to raise their levels of collective ambitions.

At the same time this sense of predictability can be a reminder that social systems require a degree of social control and self-discipline which place restraints on all participants. Nation building calls for submission to newly imposed controls; and in the context of contemporary history this requirement may appear to the individual who is unsure of his identity as "foreign" demands that the self be placed under new and alien "controls." The inherent requirements of the modern world—in all the realms of economics, education, urban life, and politics—may seem to transitional people provocative, threatening, and frustrating. This is particularly true of people who are unsure of where they should want to belong socially, and do not know what they can rightfully expect of life. To people who have just emerged from the controls of colonialism it may seem that to accept the requirements of modernization is only to fall back under a new form of "foreign" control.

The problem transcends the issues of politics and power, for it springs from changing concepts of man's relation to his environment and of the ability of the individual to control his destiny. People who have just learned that they should be able to push aside the concept of fate as the work of malevolent spirits may find it peculiarly difficult to accept as just and right a new sense of fate as the work of scientific laws defined by statistics and probabilities. It seems to take a special courage to leave a world filled with unpredictable but realistic spirits and enter a probabilistic world based upon new laws of chance. More specifically, people who have finally come to accept the hope that science and technology can make their lives easier may also be precisely the people who will feel most acutely a sense of resentment on learning that science and technology are also exact and demanding taskmasters.

Along with the sense of being liberated, the need to accept new disciplines lies at the heart of both the acculturative process for the individual and the nation-building process for the society. A fundamental conclusion arising from our examination of the Burmese political class is that the dynamics of social change generate profound anxieties over precisely this issue of being controlled and manipulated. Our need in the West to reassure ourselves that our motives are altruistic seems to deaden our sensitivity to the fact that people we are helping to become more modernized can be intensely uneasy about being subtly controlled by outside forces, and that until the new sense of freedom and the new social controls of modern life have been psychologically internalized, they may be peculiarly sensitive to the "dangers" of "foreign control."

As against these concerns and anxieties over being controlled, our exploration of Burmese reactions also revealed the apparently contradictory anxieties of people in the acculturative process over the dangers of being abandoned and ignored by those who represent to them the culture to which they aspire. In part the declining effectiveness of the Burmese administrator stemmed from his feeling that the British had first wooed him, trained him, and won him over to a new set of values and then had suddenly deserted him at the crucial moment by unexpectedly accepting the Burmese politician as the truer and hence more honorable representative of Burmese society. The willingness of people who are just emerging from the confusing world of tradition to accept new forms of dependency is dramatically present in most transitional societies. Such people frequently have powerful urges to seek out new patrons, sponsors, or masters who, they hope, will in a diffuse and all-embracing way take care of all their concerns. Many will, for example, restlessly seek in political parties, administrative services, and other new groupings replacements for the old web of relationships which they knew in the extended family of the traditional order. This form of the "escape from freedom" is a common hallmark of transitional people.

Thus at the base of the acculturative process are the conflicting fears of being controlled and of being abandoned or ignored. The need to resist controls and the desire to be accepted seem to contend for domination and to produce erratic and unpredictable reactions.

Assisting the Nation-building Process

It is against this background that American foreign aid as a major instrument in the diffusion of the world culture must be appraised and appreciated. Our analysis has indirectly suggested in numerous ways both the potentialities and the limitations of foreign aid as a mechanism for facilitating social change. Our purpose here is not to evaluate American foreign aid doctrines, though we must observe that much of the debate in America over the appropriate levels of foreign aid has been beside the point. In some situations massive amounts of external assistance might produce precisely the opposite effects of those intended, for if the pace of acculturation is forced in psychologically disturbing ways, anxieties and ambivalences may be provoked which will paralyze the nation-building process. On the other hand, the hesitation of those who appear to be powerful and affluent to provide expected assistance on an adequate scale can encourage equally disturbing concerns over the possibility of abandonment by the modern world. There is no simple relationship between objective need for aid and subjective capacity to utilize it.

A combination of impatience for action, a sense of competition with communism, and a deeply felt confidence in the universal virtues of its own body of knowledge seems to compel the West often to place excessive demands upon the organizational abilities of the new states. Although in public discussions it is currently still conventional for Americans to proclaim that we are as yet nationally unaware of the problems of the underdeveloped areas, a strong case could be made that Americans have frequently displayed a greater sense of urgency over the problems of nation building than have some of the leaders of new countries themselves. In striving to find ways of coming to grips with the problems of the new countries, we have responded largely by relying on the checkbook and by establishing novel agencies for our relations with the underdeveloped countries. We have not been creative in exploring the prerequisites of successful assistance programs, and we have tended to vacillate between a narrow-minded economic approach and a diffuse desire for uncritical and "friendly" relations with the underdeveloped countries. Our urge to be hardheaded, to employ stiff criteria for our aid, and to avoid being black-mailed by weak countries conflicts with our general desire to be under-standing and sympathetic toward those we feel to be less fortunate than ourselves.

American foreign aid has emphasized the training of increased num-bers of peoples in modern skills. In thus influencing the development of techniques and skills our aid programs have been involved in the socializa-tion process, but not at the most fundamental level. In the light of the analysis used in this study our assistance can also be seen as primarily de-signed to help create expanding numbers of competent individuals who have been able to resolve their identity crises by the realization and mastery of new skills. In the past the focus of our efforts has been largely on the individual and not on the collective community of modernizers. We have established many successful programs for training individuals but we have not done as much toward building environments in which these individuals can associate with each other and thus create the communities of modernizers that can serve as islands of stability in the nation-building process.

Our field investigations in Burma uncovered large numbers of people trained either under colonialism or since independence in a wide range of modern skills who are now merely isolated individuals, withdrawn from the main political process. Unless something can be done to establish a sense of community among these people, their skills will be lost to the nation-building process. The tragedy is that although the manifest short-age of skills in the country calls for the repeated introduction of new train-ing programs, the hopes behind these programs are rarely realized; the most recently trained people, like their predecessors, slip back into the general society when they are unable to find a community of modernizers with whom to associate. If ways could be discovered to recapture the effectiveness of people already trained there would result a dramatic in-crease in the supply of modern skills in most of the transitional Asian societies.

In those countries where the training of individuals has not been ac-companied by the development of a community of modernizers there is a strong likelihood that those who have experienced the stress of accultura-tion will be especially plagued with fears of abandonment. This was the pattern of reaction observed among the Burmese administrative class; they came to feel that the British had in the end displayed more respect and even trust toward the politicians than toward those whom they had trained. American assistance programs often have the same effect, for we too tend to communicate the feeling that we hold in greater respect those who seek grand ideological solutions than those who possess "mere" technical skills. We are prepared to train the competent modernizers but not necessarily commit ourselves to their collective support, while at the same time we would like to support the ideologically articulate political leader but we do not know how to train him. The resulting irony and frustration is that American aid administrators often find themselves in precisely the same compromised position as the former colonial authorities, that of being able to assist substantially only in creating administrators despite a professed wish to further the development of politicians.

For these and many other reasons we have had considerable difficulty in gaining a mature sense of perspective toward our aid program. In alternating between the false ideal of allowing our aid to be allocated by rigid economic criteria and the equally false ideal of relating it to specific political considerations, we have tended to miss the prime objective: that of facilitating both the acculturative and the nation-building processés in ways that will contribute to the development of a stable international community of states. The urge to allow technical economic considerations to shape our programs is understandable; such considerations seem to provide us with objective and neutral standards that protect us from appearing to be unduly arbitrary. Economic criteria are not unimportant and certainly should not be casually disregarded, but they are not adequate for policy in one of the most important matters of our time. The fundamental framework for our policy toward the underdeveloped areas must be defined by the entire range of our associations and our interactions with them, and it would be a gross if not insulting reversal of priorities to place at the heart of our relations with other societies such limited matters as our technical and economic assistance programs. To assist the process of nation building in transitional societies we must be able to provide in addition to material support the human reassurance necessary to smooth over some of the profound difficulties in the acculturation process.

The fact that questions can be raised concerning the appropriate criteria for our aid programs is testimony that our policy is in search of purpose. At times we seem ready to allow technical considerations to become the masters of our actions, and to forget that economic theories should be the servants of human purpose. Our confusion of purpose toward the underdeveloped countries stems in large measure from the host of different, but apparently equally legitimate, ways in which we can perceive and interpret the significance of these societies and of our relations with them.

We have tended to lose sight of the fundamental fact that behind all the competing considerations that might influence our policy actions there is one fundamental, overriding constitutional issue: this is the question of what kind of a world order we hope to create to replace the classical international system of the colonial era. The clear and present dangers of the Cold War tend to obscure the fact that in addition to our political struggle with communism we also have the fundamental responsibility to help shape a satisfying new world order in which people at different levels of technology and with differing systems of values can realize satisfying relationships. In our concern with "winning the game" we often forget that we must also help establish the agreed "rules of the game."

Unquestionably the new international order will eventually emerge out of a host of contemporary political issues and processes, ranging from the struggle between democracy and communism to ways in which the world culture is spread throughout the transitional countries. It would also, however, be helpful if we had a clearer vision of the structure and dynamics of the international order we are seeking. The energy expended in striving to make more explicit our feelings about a satisfying democratic world order may not greatly accelerate the realization of that order, but it might give more coherence to our day-to-day policy actions. The effort would assist us and others to separate more clearly in our minds those policies that reflect our partisan political commitments as a nation from those that reflect our commitment to a larger international community. We could then make it unmistakably clear to the people involved in the nation-building process that we at least do not confuse "modernization" with "Americanization." By learning to distinguish more sharply between policies advanced in support of a viable international order and those in support of our particular interests as a nation within that order, we should also be able to clarify the distinction that we feel exists between those "neutralists" who seek to avoid deep involvement in the Cold War and those who are opposed to the creation of a system of responsible international relations. We would likewise be able to distinguish between forms of "anti-Americanism" which are annoying to our national pride and those which are veiled attacks upon the very concept of an orderly and cooperative international system.

Beyond all these considerations is the prospect of achieving a far more secure and viable basis for our relations with the new countries if we can offer them the vision of a new international system that will enable them to realize their national honor and dignity. If we can give substance to the fundamental idea that we are joined with them in a constitutional endeavor to create a world order in which all peoples can find their separate identities, it should be possible for us to achieve that degree of integrity in our relations which will make it possible for us to avoid hypocrisy and to disagree at times without malice. Acculturation need no longer appear as a process in which some people take on the ways of others but as one in which everyone is seeking to change and develop in order to build a better world community.

In this very fundamental sense the individual's search for order in his life, the quest of a people to build a national order, and the groping of free peoples for a stable international system are directly connected. The politics of nation building brings out most sharply the link Harold Lasswell saw between *World Politics and Personal Insecurity*.[2] As we observed at the beginning of this study, the diffusion of the world culture and the very concept of the nation-state have had meaning historically in the context of the development of a world system of national political communities. Thus, just as the individual's quest for personal identity is conditioned by the national political environment, so the quest for collective identity behind the nation-building process is conditioned by the international environment. Since the basic threat inherent in the acculturative process, which implanted psychic ambivalences in the individual and discontinuities in political cultures, was associated with "foreign" sources and the challenge of other states, it is peculiarly important to hold out the hope for a more benign international system. American policy can perhaps make no greater contribution to the nation-building process than to give transitional people confidence that there is now emerging a strong international community in which they can find their national destinies and achieve self-respect and genuine acceptance for what they are as human beings.

Possibly we can also assist people in purely political matters to a far greater extent than we appreciate. For different reasons, both Westerners and the leaders of the new countries have tended to shy away from the fundamental issues in nation building, preferring to talk about supposedly innocuous technical and administrative matters than about politics. Nation building is above all else a political matter, which means that at the heart of the problem lie questions of values, of human trust, and of the

2. New York, Whittlesey House, 1935.

proper sharing of power. In destroying the world of traditional societies, the West forced the emerging countries to confront profound issues about fundamental values; the West should not now try to retreat into innocent discussions about impersonal technical and economic matters. We should rather be projecting through all of our actions the vision of a just world order composed of new political societies.

To overcome our uneasiness about speaking across the gap in culture and technology between our society and the underdeveloped countries we need to remind ourselves that a primary thrust behind the quest of transitional people is their vision of more just and more democratic ways of life. It is the democratic element within the world culture that continues to have the greatest potency in moving men to act. To an extraordinary degree, and in the face of all the anxieties produced by the acculturation process, the transitional peoples have continually committed themselves to realizing democratic values and forms. It would not only be inaccurate but most unjust to be in any way cynical about the Burmese respect for law and the desire to develop representative institutions. The degree to which legitimacy has already been related to some formulation of the democratic spirit in most of the newly emergent countries is truly impressive.

If American policy is to be turned to the furtherance of democratic political development, the stage must be set for frank and candid discussions about fundamental political values. Given all the anxieties and insecurities produced by the acculturation process, this can be done only if we demonstrate a full commitment to associate ourselves for better or worse in assisting and strengthening those transitional peoples who would build democratic societies. By communicating our genuine concern and real respect for them and for their problems, we can produce a quality of relationship which will make it possible for us to confront together fundamental issues. If we are prepared to commit ourselves truly to assisting in the task of nation building, we can provide sufficient reassurance to a transitional people to enable us both to break out of the falsely sentimental and unduly hypocritical moods that have surrounded so many of our associations in the past. In such a spirit of association it should also be possible for us to assist the acculturation process by sympathetically but rigorously pushing for exacting standards of performance. Without a basic sense of commitment in our relationship with the underdeveloped countries we shall either continue to find it impossible to apply hard and meaningful standards in granting our aid or we shall discover that our insistence upon standards will be seen as insulting and degrading.

The outcome of the acculturation process should mean that more and more people have been able to overcome illusions and fantasy and to dominate reality. The logic of competitive politics is possibly the most effective mechanism yet known for forcing people on a community-wide basis to discover their real values and to realize a fundamental coherence between ends and means in their social life. It is not just an idle democratic sentiment which holds that there is virtue in widening political participation. As people are continually exposed to the babble of conflicting and fantastically unrealistic promises that arise from the open political market place, they are likely to develop the healthy skepticism necessary to check illusion and false ambitions. Only after people have observed enough false political prophets can they appreciate the real ones. This is as true for the domestic political scene as it is for the building of a democratic world order.

The logic of competitive politics also forces people to measure their own interests against those of others, and thus to discover both their real individual interests and their shared interests. In traditional societies and in authoritarian systems people are constantly being enticed into believing that their identities will be served if they are willing to sacrifice themselves to the will of leaders. In democratic politics leaders must induce people to indicate their real interests and thus to find their identities according to a calculus of sacrifice. The same basic political dynamics apply on the international scene, for nations too must find their shared as well as their separate interests. Without this basically democratic sense of how the self can be related to others without losing its integrity the idea of an evolving world culture becomes the repugnant vision of the mass society.

It is thus the democratic ideal, both in domestic and world politics which illuminates the links between politics, personality, and nation building.

Index

Abegglen, James C., 41
Acculturation, 211 passim, 255–56; case studies in, 231–43, 267–82; to modern world, 11–13; and motivation, 49–51. *See also* Burmese political culture; Socialization
Administration: introduction of British system, 82–84; Indian Civil Service, 101–02; Provincial Civil Service, 102; Subordinate Civil Service, 102
Administrative politics: 103–08; career considerations, 107; corruption, 107–08; legalistic approach, 105–06
Administrators, 97–109, 159–60, 211–30; apprenticeship of, 220, 222–23; attitude toward politicians, 164–65; backgrounds of, 217–18; British, association with, 99, 224–25; community of, 101–03; fear of innovation, 228–29; formalism of, 216; peasants, association with, 221; opposition to change, 220; politics of, 103–08; profiles of, 231–43; recruitment of, 102–03, 227; role introduced, 98–101; training of, 102–03
AFPFL. *See* Anti-Fascist Peoples' Freedom League
Aggression: and associational sentiments, 51–52; and Burmese national character, 136–43; and fear of provocation, 146–55; and transitional politics, 54–55
Agriculture, in Burma, 85–90
Ahmudan, 73
Ah-nah-deh, 148-49, 252-53; in male and female, 149
Alaungpaya, 66
Almond, Gabriel A., 16, 22, 25, 26, 37, 45, 122
Ambivalence: toward British, 265; toward independence, 156; toward religion, 191
Amity-enmity, 205 passim
Andrus, J. Russell, 60, 99, 103
Anglicized Burmese, 235

Anti-Fascist Peoples' Freedom League (AFPFL), 62, 94, 115–17, 129–30, 135, 144, 151–52, 163, 206, 226, 230, 235, 239, 251, 267–69, 271, 276–77, 279; split in, 116-17
Anxiety. *See* Aggression; Acculturation; Socialization
Anawratha, 65
Anthropologists' view of Burmese culture, 179 passim
Apter, David, 82
Arakan, 65, 180
Arnold, Matthew, 178
Asian Socialist Conference, 155
Associational sentiments, 51–52, 54–55
Astrologers, 151
Asu, 73
Athin, 73
Aung San, 154
Ava, 66
Awza, 147–48, 155, 252–53

Ba Maw, 112
Ba U, 70, 105, 110, 150, 196, 232
Banfield, Edward C., 51
Barnard, Chester I., 39, 90
Bellah, Robert, 36
Bendix, Reinhard, 35
Berelson, Bernard, 37
Blackmer, Donald L. M., 10
British rule in Burma: economic changes under, 85–92; establishment of, 81 · 84; image of colonial officials, 144
Brown, D. Mackenzie, 67
Buddhism: and Burmese kings, 66–67; as central in Burmese culture, 189 passim; division between sacred and secular, 190 passim; introduction into Burma, 65; in traditional Burmese society, 74–77; Mahayana, 189; monastery training, 190; and quest for power, 146, 152; and search for identity, 266; Therevada, 189; time perspective, 203
Burdick, Eugene, 37

303

THE YALE PAPERBOUNDS